A History of Wales

1906–2000

WELSH HISTORY TEXT BOOKS

WELSH HISTORY TEXT BOOKS – VOLUME 4

A History of Wales

1906–2000

D. GARETH EVANS

UNIVERSITY OF WALES PRESS
CARDIFF
2000

British Library Cataloguing-in-Publication Data.
A catalogue record for this book is available from the British Library.

ISBN 0–7083–1594–1 paperback
   0–7083–1553–4 hardback

Typeset at University of Wales Press
Printed in Great Britain by Creative Print and Design Wales, Ebbw Vale

TO JANET, RACHEL, CARYS

AND HELEDD

Contents

Preface

This is the final volume in a series on the history of Wales which began in 1972 with the publication of Hugh Thomas's work on Tudor and Stuart Wales. This was followed by E. D. Evans's book on Wales 1660–1815 in 1976, and a third volume on the period 1815–1906 published in 1989. In this present study, I have endeavoured to follow the broad pattern established in those previous works, and I hope very much that it will appeal to the general reader as well as to undergraduates and students pursuing advanced studies in Welsh history.

I have tried to describe the main economic, social, religious, political, educational and cultural features of the history of Wales from 1906 to the present day. The survey of material that is offered cannot be complete, for the volume of writing on twentieth-century Welsh history is too great for any individual to cover in its entirety. Statistical output, government publications, theses, historical and literary works are extensive and it would be impossible to produce a detailed description of all these. It has often been difficult to order the mass of wide-ranging and complex material, and the synthesis that follows must inevitably be somewhat arbitrary. The period has been divided into two chronological sections, 1906–1945 and 1945 to the present time. Each section contains four chapters on the main features of the period. The chapters are sub-divided to provide the reader with signposts as they journey through the terrain.

Inevitably, much of the analysis will depend on the published work of many earlier writers. The magisterial history of Wales from 1880 to 1980 by Professor Kenneth O. Morgan stands as a beacon for this and other surveys of Wales in the present century. Pioneering studies by Professor Gareth Elwyn Jones in the history of education, Dr R. Pope on religion, and the late Professor D. J. V. Jones on crime in twentieth-century Wales, and by a host of other scholars and research students have formed the backbone of this present tome. My debt to them is immeasurable, and I sincerely hope that my borrowings from them have been accurately and adequately represented. The surge of interest in Welsh history in recent decades has produced a range of academic journals, periodicals, and monumental histories of various Welsh counties. I owe so much to the scholarly output advanced in these publications.

Acknowledgements

In researching and writing this book I have benefited enormously from the advice and support of many friends, colleagues and advisers. The original stimulus came from Professor Kenneth O. Morgan who, with customary generosity, suggested that I should trace the odyssey of the Welsh in this turbulent and exciting century. I should like to acknowledge the help of Professor C.C. Harris, who provided me with much material and guidance on religion in contemporary Wales. I am also greatly indebted to Mr Paul Chambers, research student at the University of Wales, Swansea, for allowing me to consult chapters from his unpublished PhD thesis on religion in Swansea and district. The staff of the Miners' Library, Hendrefoelan, and Dr Ian Glen, of the University Library, Swansea, were models of patience, courtesy and support.

I am especially grateful to Susan Jenkins, Director, and to Ceinwen Jones of the University of Wales Press for their kindness and encouragement during the periods of research and publication. It is a great pleasure to thank Mrs Iona Squire, a loyal family friend, for typing the manuscript at such short notice. I am also deeply grateful to Iona for producing the final version in such a meticulous form. Diolch o galon.

Over a period of thirty years I have enjoyed the friendship and support of my mentor and former postgraduate tutor, Professor Sir Glanmor Williams. His generosity to generations of students and research workers is legendary. I am enormously grateful to him for his advice and encouragement at all stages of my career.

My wife Janet has been a constant source of encouragement, inspiration and reassurance. Without her steadfast support, there is little doubt that this book would not have been completed. Our energetic and vivacious daughters, Rachel, Carys and Heledd, provided fun, laughter and playful diversions in parks, playrooms and pools. I hope that they will read a little of the history of

Wales when they grow up. I dedicate this volume to Janet and our girls. Gyda diolch a llawer o gariad.

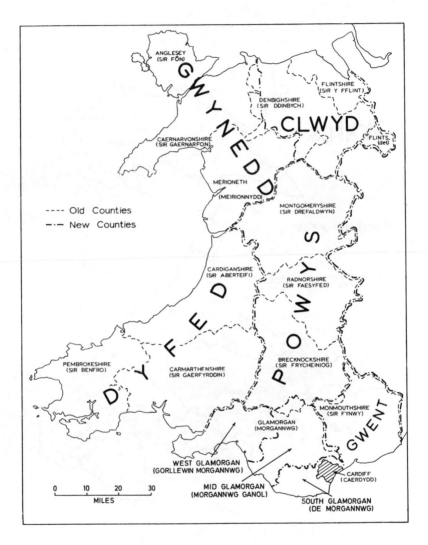

The main administrative units of Wales before and after local
government reorganization in 1974.

Wales

Local Authorities

Local Authority Boundary
(April 1999) ——— Powys

Isle of
Anglesey

Conwy

Flintshire

Denbighshire

Wrexham

Gwynedd

Ceredigion

Powys

Pembrokeshire

Carmarthenshire

Neath
Port
Talbot

Swansea

Bridgend

Rhondda
Cynon
Taff

Merthyr
Tydfil

Blaenau
Gwent

Caerphilly

Torfaen

Monmouthshire

Newport

Cardiff

The Vale
of Glamorgan

The local authorities of Wales after 1996.

Introduction

MODERN Wales emerged during the nineteenth century with the transition from a predominantly agricultural society at the outset to a vastly increased number of industrial and urbanized communities towards the beginning of the twentieth century. Nineteenth-century Welsh society was shaped by a number of important developments: the increase in population and the general tendency for that population to be redistributed; secondly, industrialization, and especially the rapid expansion of mining and manufacturing throughout the later eighteenth and nineteenth centuries, transformed the economic life of Wales; thirdly, the growth of Nonconformity, and the spread of a pervading Nonconformist ethos, radically altered Welsh society; and fourthly, the gradual disappearance of the old social and political dominance of the landed classes and the period of Liberal ascendancy in Wales from 1868 to the close of the First World War witnessed the democratization of politics in the Principality.

In 1801 the population of Wales was 587,245; by 1851, it had climbed to 1,163,000; in 1901, it stood at 2,013,000. The nineteenth-century pattern throughout Europe was one of an unprecedented acceleration in population growth, and Wales was not immune from this broad trend. The population of Wales had doubled during the first half of the century, and almost doubled again in its second half. The most dramatic increase occurred during the decade from 1901 to 1911, when the population increased by over 400,000 people. Wales also experienced a general redistribution of its population, with the balance tilting towards the southern half of the country. Whereas less than 20 per cent of the population of Wales had been found in the two counties of Glamorgan and Monmouthshire in 1801, by 1911 almost 63 per cent of the people of Wales inhabited these two industrial counties.

Although there had occurred a rapid rise in the population of all Welsh counties down to 1841, the rate of increase in the agricultural counties was falling. Montgomeryshire and Radnorshire reached their peak levels at the 1841 census, and thereafter Welsh rural counties began to experience decreases in their total numbers. These falls were due to people leaving the countryside, most of them gravitating to the industrial areas of south and north Wales. In the half-century before 1914, five Welsh counties – Brecon, Cardigan, Montgomery, Pembroke and Radnor – suffered a net loss by migration in every single decade; and, in four other counties – Anglesey, Carmarthen, Flint and Merioneth – there was a net loss in every decade except one. There are strong indications that this migration represented an outflow from agriculture itself. The total number of persons engaged in agriculture, despite a doubling of the total Welsh population, declined between 1851 and 1911; and most of that reduction occurred in the number of farm workers. The rate of decline was usually steeper in the more agricultural counties: in 1911 the number of males occupied in agriculture in the five counties of Brecon, Cardigan, Merioneth, Monmouth and Montgomery was less than three-fifths of the number in 1851. People moved out of the countryside in search of employment, rarely as a result of the impact of technical change in agriculture, and largely in response to the effects of foreign competition, which increasingly pushed Welsh agriculture towards a heavier concentration on pastoral as opposed to arable farming.

Whereas 35 per cent of all occupied males were engaged in agriculture at the time of the 1851 census, by 1911 only 12 per cent were employed in the industry. Many of those who left the rural areas were absorbed into industrial south Wales. Professor Brinley Thomas has shown that, in the 1880s and 1890s, almost all the total rural exodus was being absorbed into the expanding coalfield of the south. In the 1900s the number being absorbed was actually far greater than the numbers being released from the rural districts. Between 1881 and 1911 in five of the most industrialized counties – Carmarthenshire, Denbighshire, Flintshire, Glamorgan and Monmouthshire – the population increased by well over a million. The two counties of Glamorgan and Monmouthshire accounted for nearly 800,000 of this increase. The transition of Wales from an agricultural to an industrial nation was accomplished during these years.

The transformation of Wales into a modern and democratic society was largely effected by industrialization. The first phase of that process, which lasted up to about the middle of the nineteenth century, was characterized by metal smelting. By 1800 Swansea was firmly established as Britain's major copper-smelting centre, with twenty-one works responsible for producing nearly 85 per cent of national output in 1830. The other industrial concentration along the north-east rim of the south Wales coalfield emerged as Britain's foremost iron-smelting region. Between 1760 and 1830 some twenty ironworks were established along an eighteen-mile strip from Hirwaun to Blaenavon. A second phase of industrial growth, beginning around the middle of the nineteenth century, saw the expansion of the south Wales coal industry. Output of coal increased from 4.5 million tons in 1854 to 18 million tons in 1879, 39 million tons in 1900, and 56 million tons in 1913. Although the expansion was witnessed in most parts of the coalfield after 1840, it was the eastern half, and especially the steam coals of the Rhondda Valleys, which saw the most dramatic growth. By 1913 the Rhondda had fifty-three pits, producing a total output of over 9.5 million tons of coal. When war broke out in 1914, the south Wales coal industry employed around 210,000 men.

In the western parts of the south Wales coalfield sheet-steel manufacture expanded as the basis of a tinplate industry, which replaced the area's declining copper smelters. By 1911 there were about eighty works in south-west Wales, mainly located in Swansea and Llanelli, producing over 800,000 tons of tinplate and providing employment for over 22,000 men. In 1913 the economy of south Wales was thriving, with production and exports of coal, steel and tinplate all reaching record levels. Coal mining, though on a far lesser scale, also promoted the industrial advancement of north Wales and ensured the development of various metal-smelting and metal-working activities, including brass, lead, copper and silver. The major industrial development, the erection of John Summer's steelworks at Hawarden in 1896, established an industrial nucleus for north Wales.

A third factor of considerable importance in the shaping of nineteenth-century Welsh society was Nonconformity. Despite the fact that only a third of the Welsh population attended a place of worship, the vast majority of them were Nonconformist. The contributions of Nonconformity to nineteenth-century Welsh society were immense: religious communities provided familiar and friendly surroundings in an often hostile 'frontier' society; the democratic organization of the chapels and Sunday schools provided outlets for many talented working-class people; the Sunday schools themselves tutored many generations of industrial and rural workers and ensured the survival of the Welsh language; the chapels were centres of cultural and educational activities, promoting competitive meetings, eisteddfodau, literary societies, musical events, singing festivals, and penny readings; Nonconformity also encouraged higher standards of behaviour and fostered the virtues of thrift, sobriety, cleanliness and honesty in impoverished, wretched, unhealthy and often violent communities. Contemporaries, as well as more recent scholars, have commented on a fundamental social distinction (*buchedd*) in Welsh communities between those who belonged to the 'church' and those of the 'world', with many of the latter attending chapels only as 'listeners', enjoying secular pastimes, frequenting public houses and possibly undervaluing Nonconformist teachings. The chapel's influence on Welsh identity, society and politics was, however, pervasive until the early years of the twentieth century; and, although it weakened in the years following the Great War, religion continued to play an important part in the lives of people down to the 1940s.

On the threshold of the twentieth century, Welsh politics reflected the self-confidence emanating from a prosperous economy and the overwhelming influence of Nonconformity. Since the 1830s religious groups had become increasingly vociferous about the civil disabilities of their sects. Their grievances were felt to be those of the Welsh people in general, and they were intensified by the adverse comments of the Blue Books on Education and Nonconformity in 1847. In spite of the protests of earlier decades, it was the half-century from the 1860s to the end of the First World War which proved to be a decisive watershed in the politicization of the Welsh people. A number of factors accounted for the steady growth of democracy and freedom during these years: the 1867 franchise extension, and the fact that the 1868 election was fought over Irish disestablishment, dealt the first blows to political landlordism in Wales; the Ballot Act of 1872, the achievement of household suffrage in 1884, which had enfranchised significant numbers of the working classes, and the Local Government Act of 1888 gave Liberals control of both national and local government; with the inauguration of urban and district councils in 1894, the landed gentry's control of the government of Wales, which had predominated since Tudor times, was finally destroyed. In every parliamentary election from 1885 to 1918 Liberals gained the overwhelming majority of both urban and rural seats in Wales, and gentry candidates were rejected *en masse* at the polls in favour of the Nonconformist middle classes. The alliance between Liberalism and Nonconformity was firmly cemented, and the leadership of a largely professional and commercial middle class – farmers, shop-keepers, ministers of religion and solicitors – was endorsed by the working classes.

A new Liberal ascendancy dominated Welsh parliamentary politics in the years between 1868 and 1918, and there arose a generation of young Nonconformist radical politicians, such as David Lloyd George and Tom Ellis, who ardently pressed the claims of Wales as a Nonconformist nation. A variety of well-organized national campaigns emerged as a result of this new Liberal–Nonconformist hegemony: there was a long campaign for disestablishment of the Church in Wales; a campaign to reform the system of landed tenure; and movements to establish a new educational structure and the national federal University of Wales. Temperance legislation and reform of the magistracy were also seen as requiring special treatment to accommodate the distinctive needs of Wales.

The Welsh radical programme secured some notable victories, and not least was the establishment of a distinctive system of university colleges (Aberystwyth, Bangor and Cardiff) and inter-mediate schools. The 1881 Sunday Closing Act was the first legislative enactment to apply to Wales a different set of prin-ciples from those obtaining in England. The founding in 1907 of the National Library of Wales and the National Museum of Wales created additional badges of nationhood in this exhilar-ating period of Welsh politics. Although national awareness remained a predominant feature of Welsh politics during the 1880s and 1890s, and permeated other walks of Welsh life, especially in sport and Welsh literature, there was no vigorous public clamour from the ordinary people of Wales for self-government. Unlike the Irish who demanded home rule, the Welsh sought, by peaceful and constitutional methods, to achieve equality within the United Kingdom, and not separation from it. The campaign to disestablish the Church in Wales was not a precursor of separation, but an alternative to it.

Economic expansion, political achievements, educational successes, religious enthusiasm, cultural accomplishments and sporting victories seemed to be the hallmarks of Welsh life in the late Victorian and Edwardian period. But there were clear signs of intellectual and cultural uncertainty, industrial unrest and political unease as the new century dawned. Confrontation in labour relations at the turn of the century was paralleled by the growth of a new politics and the rising challenge of the Labour movement. The revival of religion in 1904 was short-lived, and Nonconformity's hold on the Principality was loosening. If Nonconformity was a crucial badge of Welsh ethnic identity, of even greater importance in this respect was the Welsh language. The decade 1901–11 attracted such large numbers of immigrants from England that they could not be successfully absorbed into the Welsh-speaking heartlands, and the Welsh language proceeded along its downward path. Many of the major developments of the post-1918 period were casting their shadows before them.

Part I
1906–1945

1. Economic Activity and Change

The Edwardian Era

THE Edwardian period from around 1906 to the outbreak of war in 1914 was an era of economic expansion, of political achievements and of burgeoning national awareness in Wales. In the last quarter of the nineteenth century industrial wealth had catapulted Wales from the periphery of Britain to a position of world economic importance. At least 90 per cent of the copper smelted in Britain came from south Wales. In 1898, 70 per cent of the UK slate production was quarried in north Wales. In 1901, the largest nickel works in the world was established at Clydach, in the Swansea Valley. From 1914 to 1918 the Swansea area produced 75 per cent of Britain's zinc. The tinplate industry of west Wales was producing 823,000 tons of tinplate in the years before the First World War, of which 544,000 tons were exported.

The most dramatic growth had occurred in the coal industry. In 1911, 14,500 men were engaged in the north Wales coal industry, but it was in south Wales that the most pronounced expansion occurred. In 1913, of the 485 collieries in Wales, 323 were located in Glamorgan. By 1913 the combined Rhondda pits produced 9,500,000 tons of coal and employed 41,000 miners. South Wales was producing about one-third of world coal exports, and in 1901 the region accounted for 46 per cent of Britain's coal exports to Europe, South America and the Middle East.

The occupational pattern of Wales in the period 1851–1914 had been dominated by mining and agriculture. In 1851, agriculture had accounted for 35 per cent and mining for 17 per cent of the occupied male population of Wales. By 1914 agriculture had slumped to 12 per cent, and mining now accounted for 32 per cent of the occupied male population. The dominant sector in the Welsh economy by 1911 was 'Mines and Quarries'. Few industrial nations could display such a marked concentration in their occupational structures. By 1911 'Mines and Quarries' were increasingly becoming identified with one industry – King Coal. In that year alone, 30 per cent of the occupied males were in the one industry of coal mining. This was an astonishing figure when one recalls that most of the Welsh counties contained no coal deposits. The numbers engaged in coal mining had escalated from 80,000 in 1880 to 242,000 in 1914; and the south Wales coalfield accounted for most of that increase. Other mining sectors, such as lead, iron, copper and slate, which had accounted for over two-fifths of this employment group in 1851, had become relatively insignificant by 1911. There were only 167 iron miners in the whole of Wales in 1911.

The year 1913 was the peak year for coal output in south Wales, with a total production of 56.8 million tons. The First World War soon imposed further demands upon the industry, but wartime capital neglect and the post-war profit incentive brought into production thinner seams and pits which had previously been abandoned. Employment peaked in 1920 at 271,516, but output was 11.5 million tons less than in 1913.

Changes in the industrial pattern were matched by improvements to the transport infrastructure. By 1890 south Wales already possessed one of the most densely developed railway networks in the world. In the Edwardian era there were impressive extensions, with an additional 32 miles for the Barry Railway, 23 miles for the Cardiff Railway, 17 miles for the Rhondda and Swansea Bay lines, and 21 miles for the Port Talbot Railway. One of the most significant manifestations of economic expansion was the provision of additional port facilities: Barry No.2 Dock opened in 1898, the Queen Alexandra Dock at Cardiff in 1907, and a dock extension of 20 acres at Newport in 1893, a new dock at Port Talbot in 1898, a 28-acre extension to the Prince of Wales Dock at Swansea in 1898, and in 1909 the King's Dock was also opened at Swansea.

This economic prosperity was not, however, shared by the whole of Wales. After 1903 there was a continuing depression in the slate industry, and population declined in the prominent centres of production. From 1889 to 1918, the quantity of slates exported fell from 79,912 tons to 1,592 tons. The decline in the

German demand which, in 1876, had accounted for 72 per cent of the quantity exported, was the main reason for the contraction in the export trade. In 1910, only 54 per cent of slates were sent to Germany. One important reason for the decline of the export trade was the imposition of duties on imported slate which began to operate in Germany in the 1890s. By 1910 France and Switzerland were also imposing duties on the importation of slates. Other contributory factors were: first, unemployment in the building industry in 1901–5, and in 1906–10; secondly, a number of countries exported slate to the United Kingdom, and imported slates from Holland, Turkey, Italy, Canada, Norway, Portugal, Belgium, the USA and France contributed to the decline of the Welsh slate industry; thirdly, the increasing use of the tile helped reduce the demand for slate; fourthly, traditional uses for slate declined, e.g. earthenware had replaced slate slabs for sanitary purposes; fifthly, the Board of Education discouraged the use of writing slates in schools; finally, the onset of war and the consequent loss of German trade had a devastating effect upon the industry.

In 1906, wages in the Ffestiniog district alone fell by 10 per cent. Several hundred men were reported to have lost their jobs at Llechwedd Quarry in March 1906. At Port Penrhyn and Port Dinorwic stocks were piled up at the quarries in 1908. In 1917, slate-quarrying was declared a non-essential industry and a large number of quarries were closed for the remainder of the war.

Agriculture's role in the Welsh economy declined over the course of the nineteenth century and increasingly so from the 1850s onwards. The population of Wales increased from 587,245 in 1800 to 1,163,000 in 1851, and 2,013,000 in 1901. In a single decade, from 1901 to 1911, the population of Wales increased by over 400,000. There was also a general redistribution of this population. In 1801, less than 20 per cent of the population was located in the counties of Glamorgan and Monmouthshire. By 1911 almost 63 per cent of the population of Wales were to be found in these two counties. The movement of people from the land was especially important in the period 1880–1914. Starting with the 1851 census it is possible to chart a net loss by migration in every single decade in the five Welsh counties of Brecon, Cardigan, Montgomery, Pembroke and Radnor. In four other counties there was a net loss in every decade except one. The counties where the net migration was most marked were those which were predominantly agricultural. At the beginning of the nineteenth century over 80 per cent of Welsh people inhabited rural areas; by 1911 fewer than 20 per cent lived in the countryside. The numbers engaged in Welsh farming decreased by 31.4 per cent from 1851 to 1911. While 33.1 per cent of the total Welsh labour force was occupied in farming in 1851, by 1911 some 11.3 per cent was so engaged. In Brecon, Cardigan, Merioneth, Monmouth and Montgomery, the number of men occupied in agriculture was less than three-fifths of the number for 1851. It would seem, therefore, that a substantial number of those who had formerly been engaged in agriculture were driving the process of out-migration.

What had caused this significant shift of people away from the countryside? Wage differentials were an important factor. There is sufficient evidence to show that agricultural wages in nineteenth-century Wales were relatively low and that the expectation of higher remuneration in industrial centres was a real incentive. This was magnified in the late nineteenth century when agriculture was generally depressed and industrial south Wales displayed all the signs of vigorous economic growth. Technical change in agriculture was also reducing the need for labour and, in particular, the number of agricultural labourers. A more important reason for the reduction in labour was the impact of foreign competition. This pushed Welsh agriculture towards heavier concentration on pastoral as opposed to arable farming. The total acreage under permanent pasture in Wales increased from 1,500,000 to 2,300,000, whilst arable cultivation fell from 1,100,000 to 700,000 acres in the years between 1867 and 1914. As a result of this process there was less demand for agricultural labourers in pastoral-farming areas.

Professor Brinley Thomas has shown that most of those who moved from Welsh rural areas from the 1800s stayed mainly within Wales. More precisely, in the period from 1880 to the First World War most of the Welsh rural exodus remained within the Principality. The number being absorbed into industrial south Wales was almost sufficient to account for the total rural exodus. In 1901–11, a net rural exodus of 38,000 was matched by a net absorption of 129,000 into the Glamorgan–Monmouthshire coalfield. Wales had become an immigration country.

One of the features usually associated with this rural exodus is that of rural depopulation. It is important, however, to be clear as to the nature of this trend: it was highly concentrated; it was limited; and it was a relative phenomenon. Five counties (Breconshire, Cardiganshire, Merioneth, Montgomeryshire and Radnorshire) experienced some fall in the absolute level of their population in the period 1851–1911, and these were the counties in which agriculture was predominant. From 1881 to 1911 the decline in population was concentrated in only three counties: Cardigan, Merioneth and Montgomery: but the fall was not shattering. The total of the five counties (Breconshire, Cardiganshire, Merioneth, Montgomeryshire and Radnorshire) fell from 269,300 in 1881 to 240,500 in 1911. Nevertheless, this did set in motion a long-term and extended trend of rural depopulation. Secondly, the population decline in these rural counties should be viewed alongside the population increases registered by five of the industrializing counties between 1881 and 1911. The two counties of Glamorgan and Monmouthshire alone accounted for nearly 800,000 of this population increase. Thirdly, the rural exodus affected a larger proportion of the counties of Wales than of England. Between 1881 and 1891 eight of the Welsh counties suffered a population fall, compared with only twelve of the English counties.

Despite these rather gloomy facts the overarching impression during the Edwardian epoch is one of economic vitality and industrial prosperity. In the period 1901–11 Wales was unique in having an annual rate of immigration of 45 per 10,000 population, with population being absorbed at a rate not much less than that of the USA. The economic success of industry and commerce in south Wales brought employment and wealth to the whole of the Principality. By 1913 the south Wales coal industry was at its apogee. The tinplate industry of west Wales shared in this feast of optimism and buoyancy.

Rural Society 1914–1945

Physical factors dictated that, for much of Wales, farming was mixed, with an emphasis on store animals and dairy produce. There were some exceptional lowland areas, such as the Vales of Glamorgan and Clwyd, and south Pembrokeshire. During the war years of 1914–18 the prices of agricultural products soared and Welsh arable farming underwent a brief revival. The demand for Welsh milk, livestock and corn spiralled upwards. The spread of the Agricultural Organization Society encouraged farmers to enter trading societies on a co-operative basis. By 1917 there were seventy societies in south Wales with nearly 12,000 members, and sixty in the north with 6,000 members. Another wartime development was the creation of Allotment Societies in rural areas. The Corn Production Act of 1917 guaranteed high prices for the production of oats and wheat. It gave agricultural labourers a guaranteed minimum wage and a reasonable standard of living.

The repeal of the Corn Production Act in 1921 resulted in a sharp fall in cereal production in the years down to 1939, and in the depressed years of the 1920s and 1930s the proportion of arable land fell by almost a half. Although Welsh pastoral farmers did not suffer as much as their corn-producing counterparts in eastern England in the early 1920s, prices fell after 1920 in other farm produce and the reduction lasted in some products down to the early 1930s. Most Welsh farmers seem to have scraped a living at least until the mid-1920s.

The First World War added to the problems of the landlords, who were already fighting a rearguard action against the twin encroachments of political democracy and stifling taxation. In 1887, only 10.2 per cent of the total cultivated land surface of Wales had been owned by the men who farmed it. By 1970, 61.7 per cent of the land of Wales was owned by its cultivators. In 1887, the remaining 89.8 per cent of the land was held by landowners. Around 1870 land sales had begun to create fragmentation in the countryside. After 1910, and especially between 1910 and 1914, every major landowner in Wales, with the exception of the great estates in the south Wales coalfield, sold some land. Almost without exception, the tenants bought most of the holdings. In 1915, the Duke of Beaufort disposed of his estates in Breconshire, as did the Marquess of Abergavenny in Monmouthshire. Even the landowners who had profited from the establishment of the south Wales coalfield began to sell. Lord Tredegar marketed much of his urban land in the Monmouthshire Valleys. After 1918, and especially from 1918 to 1922, there was a great surge of land for sale. In Wales the proportion of land owned by the occupier rose from 10.2 per cent in 1909 to 39 per cent in 1941–3. Most of the sales occurred during the boom years of 1918–22, and few of the major landowners of Wales sold their entire estates. Of the twenty great estates of Wales, which, in 1883, had exceeded 20,000 acres, not one had ceased to exist by 1922, so that the final eclipse of the great estates was a protracted affair.

Why exactly did the landlords sell portions or even the whole of their estates? The essential trigger was the emergence of an industrial and democratic society in Britain. This placed enormous burdens upon landowners, who were increasingly reluctant to incur the wrath which inevitably followed from substantial rent rises. During the war, agricultural prices rose steeply, by almost as much as 300 per cent. On the other hand, net rents fell, and on most estates income fell by up to a half, even though the value of the land itself might increase steadily. Most of the greater Welsh landowners who sold between 1918 and 1922 had financial and commercial interests outside agriculture. They considered that any kind of investment seemed preferable to land. Most of the landowners who sold in the pre- and post-war boom, did so, not because of crippling financial difficulties, but rather in order to diversify their investments. Death duties had little effect before the First World War. High wartime mortality and increased levels of death duty by 1919 created a drain on resources. The Gladstones of Hawarden paid in 1918 six times what they had paid in 1891.

Many major estates usually sold to their land-hungry tenants. The land-sale boom created a deep-seated feeling of insecurity among farmers and a craving for security of tenure. Most tenants were terrified of sacrificing their homes and livelihood to unknown purchasers, which led many to pay inflated prices for their farms. In the years 1910–18 most farmers had to raise at least 80 per cent of the purchase price of their holdings. During the depression years the repayment of these mortgages became intolerable, and some farmers sold out to their neighbours. As a result, the number of holdings in Wales fell from 63,594 in 1918 to 58,024 in 1939.

The First World War completed the process whereby the social ascendancy of the landlord over the rural community was undermined. The combined impact of the advent of democratically elected county councils, the damaging effects of wartime taxation, falling rent returns and the loss of so many heirs of landed families during military action effectively shattered the control of the landowner over the social and political life of the countryside.

Throughout most of this period, although the typical Welsh holding was a family farm, its organization changed significantly between 1851 and 1931. Whereas in 1851 there had been on average more than two male farm labourers to each male farmer, by 1931 there was less than one. Increasingly, the Welsh farm was becoming a one-man concern, with the farmer depending upon the assistance of his wife and family. Until 1920 the production of almost every type of commodity on the small, largely self-sufficient, family-run holdings protected the Welsh farmer from the ravages of price fluctuations. Welsh farmers were generally poor, able to scrape a living only by dint of hard work and frugal lifestyle. Farming was characterized by a low level of mechanization and a lack of technical organization in the industry. By the early 1930s farmers in most parts of Wales were struggling to survive.

During the depression of the 1920s and 1930s the one source of hope for the hard-pressed farmers was the establishment of the Milk Marketing Board in 1933. The number of registered milk producers in Wales grew by 92.4 per cent from 1934 to 1939, and by a further 47 per cent in the years to 1947. One implication of this was that traditional livestock rearing and butter production declined.

In the 1930s sales of crops were negligible compared with those of livestock and its products, which accounted for around 95 per cent of the total income of the Welsh farmer. During the Second World War a ploughing-up campaign and soaring prices produced a doubling in the proportion of arable land between 1939 and 1946 from 11.9 per cent to 26.4 per cent of the total agricultural land. By 1959 the extent of arable land had diminished to 21.8 per cent.

For all the improvement in money wages that occurred during the railway age up to 1918, farm labourers in those areas which were distant from industry remained very impoverished. Most farm servants in Cardiganshire in 1918 handed over the bulk of their cash earnings for the use of their families back home. The long working day was still a grievance in 1918. Although improvements were introduced by the late 1930s, farm labourers still worked on average fifty-two hours a week. Rural accommodation remained atrocious down to the Second World War. The cottages of married labourers were disgraceful abodes, with particularly high levels of overcrowding in Anglesey and Caernarfonshire.

The Industrial Scene 1914–1945

The First World War had brought a massive extension of governmental control. The state impinged upon the daily life of people in Wales as never before. There were control boards for agriculture, shipping and engineering. The mines and the railways were also put under public control for the duration of the war. The Welsh economy pulsated with prosperity and success. The mines and docks were revitalized as they struggled to cope with the insatiable demand for Welsh coal. Welsh steel-making revived as new blast furnaces were opened at the long-stagnant works at Blaenavon and Ebbw Vale. The John Summer works in Shotton on Deeside opened more blast furnaces, while the rayon factory at Flint began a new era of textile manufacture. Overall, Wales basked in the sunshine of affluence and economic growth on the home front.

For a brief period after 1918 the prosperity and economic vigour of the wartime years continued. There were new pits opened up near Wrexham in 1923. Collieries were booming in 1919 with coal exports from Welsh ports rising from 2,092,289 tons in December 1918 to 2,993,850 tons a year later. At the beginning of 1920 a record number of 272,000 men were employed in the collieries of Wales.

Soon, there appeared flickering indications of unsteadiness on the economic front. In April 1920 the government pushed up the bank rate to 7 per cent to counter the post-war inflationary trend. In May, domestic prices collapsed suddenly and, by the end of the year, coal mining and many other industries were experiencing the onset of depression.

I Economic Stagnation and its Effects
Many parts of Britain displayed signs of recovery in the later 1920s, as domestic demand for consumer goods and the products

of new light industries began to revive. In parts of Wales, especially in the coastal resorts of north Wales, there was some expansion in the 1930s as small industries were set up. Tourism regenerated the seaside resorts, while steel-smelting, building and rayon manufacture restored relative prosperity to Flintshire. In the south, however, the picture was bleak and forbidding. Many of the inland Valleys of south Wales were plunged into a deep and extensive ocean of depression and unemployment. These were the industrial communities which had a uniquely high proportion of the working population engaged in extractive industries, such as mining and quarrying.

The coal industry: The 1921 Occupational Census showed that 43 per cent of the occupied male population were engaged in two (out of twenty-six) occupational groups – Mining and Quarrying, and Metal Manufacturing and Engineering. If others engaged in Transportation and Agriculture (who were largely dependent upon these two dominant occupational groups) are added to the overall figure, then over a half of the occupied male population would be accounted for. The precariousness of such a narrowly based economic structure was greatly compounded by the fact that these sectors were heavily reliant on the ability to export.

Coal mining determined the economic scene in Glamorgan, with approximately 60 per cent of the insured labour force employed in the industry in 1924. The collapse of markets for south Wales coal by the end of the 1920s reduced average annual sales by about 25 per cent. This largely explains the economic plight of Glamorgan during the inter-war years. The crucial market for coal, which was lost from the early part of the century, was that of shipping. In the years from 1870 to 1910, as the steam fleet rapidly expanded, south Wales benefited enormously from the increased demand for coal. In the peak export year of 1913 the Admiralty took 1.75 million tons of coal from the mines in south Wales. By 1925 this had fallen to 350,000 tons. From 1913, when about 90 per cent of shipping generally was coal-fuelled, the figure had fallen by 1930 to barely one half of that level.

Other markets also began to disappear: the demand for electricity as a source of power reduced the market for coal; the amount of coal needed to produce a ton of pig iron was cut by a quarter from 1920 to 1940; that needed to produce a specified quantity of steel fell by a half; gas works in 1940 took almost the same amount of coal as they had done at the end of the First World War.

Competition from American, German and other overseas mining industries imposed further restraints on the struggling Welsh coal industry. Exports from south Wales fell sharply by 23 per cent in the period 1913–27/30, and by a further 25 per cent between 1927/30 and 1933/8. Over 80 per cent of the coal exports from south Wales had been to three major regions: north-west Europe, the western Mediterranean area and South America. It was the loss of these markets which largely explains the enfeebled position. The return to the gold standard in 1925, with the resulting overvaluation of sterling, exacerbated an already critical condition in the mining industry. The outcome was a disaster for British coal exports which were now seriously overvalued in relation to foreign currency.

A basic reason for the weak position of the coal industry in south Wales was its poorer productive capacity. Although the general level of productive efficiency in British coal mining in 1913 compared favourably with all the other competitors, apart from the USA, productivity in south Wales was lower and it continued to deteriorate as the period progressed. In 1913, whereas output per man-shift in the British coal-mining industry (21.6 cwt.) was almost the same as in most of the major European countries, in the south Wales coalfield it was 17.6 cwt. In 1935, the south Wales figure of 21.3 cwt. was still below the British average of 23.5 cwt., when the figures for Poland, Holland and Germany averaged 36.2 cwt., 35.9 cwt. and 33.7 cwt. respectively.

A central cause of this divergence was the extent to which mechanization was applied to productive methods. In 1913, whereas the proportion of total output cut mechanically in British coalfields was 8 per cent, the figures for 1937 in Germany, Holland and Poland were 83 per cent, 75 per cent and 67 per cent respectively. The geological conditions in south Wales were largely unsuitable for the cutting machines which were then available. The overriding geological characteristic of the coalfield was that it was much more disturbed and much less stable than other coalfields. In 1922, only 4 per cent of south Wales coal was cut mechanically, but the 1930s saw a more intensive application of mechanization to coal mining. In 1930, 94 mines in south

Wales used a total of 460 coal-cutting machines, and were responsible for 10 per cent of the total output of the coalfield. By 1938, 535 machines were used in a total of 118 mines. The Second World War witnessed a significant acceleration in the adoption of mechanized methods of coal cutting in south Wales and, in 1944, 117 mines were using 608 machines to cut 32 per cent of total output. A major influence upon the productive capacity was the average age of coal mines. In 1946, the vast majority of mines in Glamorgan had been in production for forty years or more, and some for as long as a hundred years. In many of these older collieries the richer seams had been exhausted and there was little prospect of high returns on investment.

Depression in the coal industry was not uniformly intense in all places and at similar times. The industry was able to produce a tolerable level of output until the end of 1924. In 1923, output at 54.3 million tons had almost reached its 1913 zenith, and coal exports from south Wales were slightly higher (35 million tons) than in 1913 (29.8 million tons). Unemployment in south Wales in 1923 and 1924 was well below the UK average. Thereafter, the coal industry declined up to the end of the decade. The contraction in markets and production was intensified by the 1926 General Strike. The collapse of Wall Street in 1929 further accelerated the shrinking process, so that from 1929 to 1933 there occurred a fall of 9 million tons in the output of non-anthracite coal in south Wales. Although 1937 witnessed a recovery in the international market, the industry diminished once more in the years immediately preceding the Second World War.

Between the wars, the coal industry underwent substantial changes in structure of ownership and organization. Although the south Wales coalfield comprised too many small and poorly planned mines, the industry was dominated by large enterprises. The 1914–18 war had stimulated the process of consolidation in ownership. Two types of consolidation occurred: first, there was the natural market connection between coal mining and iron and steel production. The Guest, Keen and Nettlefold Company had emerged in the pre-1914 period as a significant metal and engineering enterprise. As a result of the war the company extended its control of coal mining in Glamorgan. The firm of Baldwins Ltd achieved a similar influence by the end of the 1920s. The second form of consolidation occurred independently of the growing iron and steel interests. By the end of the 1930s, a number of companies had succeeded in achieving a substantial degree of horizontal integration. The Powell Duffryn Colliery Company Ltd was the largest coal firm in Britain by the middle of the 1930s, with over a hundred mines, most of which were located in Glamorgan. In 1935, the Powell Duffryn and the Welsh Associated Collieries Co. were consolidated, when Powell Duffryn Associated Collieries Ltd was established with a productive capacity of 21 million tons of coal per annum. In the anthracite mining area the Amalgamated Anthracite Group, which in 1940 was responsible for the production of 4 million tons, or 80 per cent of total output, had progressively enhanced its market share since 1923.

The structure and organization of the British coal industry were a primary source of weakness in the period. The Sankey Commission of 1919, the Samuel Commission of 1930, and the Coal Mines Act of 1930 and the Coal Act of 1938 tried unsuccessfully to resolve the inherent problems of the industry. Consolidation of ownership did little to improve productivity or to reduce waste in the industry. Throughout the Second World War Glamorgan's coal producers seemed to suffer most, as the export trade almost ceased after the fall of France. The level of activity in south Wales fell, and output declined in every war year from 35.3 million tons in 1939 to 26.7 million tons in 1942, and eventually to 21.6 million tons in 1945.

The iron, steel and tinplate industries: In 1914, the iron and steel industry in south Wales was in the throes of transition and redevelopment, but the war was to delay many necessary changes. Every steel producer strove to expand capacity and output, so that in 1920 productive capacity in Britain was around 50 per cent greater than it had been in 1914. Expansion in steel capacity had occurred in other parts of the globe, so that oversupply became an endemic feature of the inter-war years. In Glamorgan, during the worst years, such as 1931–2, the industry was running at only 50 per cent of existing capacity. What exacerbated the crisis for it in south Wales was its undue reliance on export markets.

There were two subdivisions within the industry. The first was the heavy iron and steel-producing sector, which was largely located in the eastern and central parts of Glamorgan. This had grown out of the traditional iron and steel-producing activities along the northern rim of the coalfield. Long before the First World War the advantages of a northern location had been eroded. There had been a movement to the coast in order to minimize the costs of transporting the imported iron ore to the works and the finished steel for export. The Dowlais Company had moved part of its works to Cardiff in 1891; Cyfarthfa (Merthyr Tydfil) was finally closed in 1921; and steel-making at Dowlais ceased in 1930. As the inland centres of heavy steel production declined, two major steel-making locations emerged rapidly on the coast – at Port Talbot and Cardiff. The growth of the two centres was largely the result of the emergence of a single firm, the British Iron and Steel Company. By the end of the 1930s, Port Talbot emerged as the main centre of steel-making in Glamorgan.

The second subdivision was located in the south-western part of Glamorgan. It relied on Siemens open-hearth steel, with scrap rapidly replacing pig iron after 1918 as the major ingredient of the steel-making process. This sector was fragmented, with a relatively large number of small firms and a lack of cohesion. Virtually the entire output of the thirteen steelworks in this south-western region was supplied to the local sheet and tinplate works for further processing. The bulk of the tinplate bar was produced by the specialist steelworks in the Swansea, Briton Ferry and Llanelli districts.

The inter-war years had checked the upward trend in the south Wales steel industry. Demand was weak, and iron output fell by two-thirds and steel production by two-fifths in the years 1929–31. Producers were generally slower to innovate than were their main foreign competitors and, with so many comparatively small units of production, the sheet-steel and tinplate industry failed to benefit from the advantages of the closer degree of productive integration which was giving a commercial edge to the major competitors. The three massive integrated works which were created at Cardiff, Ebbw Vale and Port Talbot eventually accounted for three-quarters of south Wales steel output. At Cardiff, the East Moors Works was started on a coastal strip in 1936. From 1935–8 Richard Thomas and Company built a modern integrated strip-mill plant on the site of the old Ebbw Vale Steel Company.

The 1920s had exposed the state of the Welsh steel and tinplate industry. As the 1920s progressed, so the foreign supplies of tinplate bar increased. In 1928, they comprised almost one-third of all the steel used in sheet and tinplate manufacture in west Wales. Competition from Germany, France and Belgium was severe. Although south Wales increased its output of tinplate from 822,000 tons in 1913 to 879,844 tons in 1928, and augmented its exports from 495,192 tons to 604,726 tons, in the same period French, German and US production all recorded a much greater proportionate increase. From being the world's major producer and exporter of tinplate in 1913, south Wales had lost its pre-eminence to the USA by the end of the 1920s. Consistent overcapacity meant that firms were generally forced to work to only 75–80 per cent of their potential and, during the poorer years of 1925 or 1927, to as low as 55–60 per cent.

The slate industry of north Wales: The demand for slates spiralled upwards at the end of the First World War as the demand for houses intensified. Between March 1919 and March 1933, 2,062,000 new houses were erected in England and Wales, as unemployment in the building industry plummeted from 16.8 per cent in 1922 to 9.8 per cent in 1925. Fluctuations in the building trade affected the fortunes of the slate industry. In the immediate post-war period the demand for slates surged ahead, output increased and firms profited once more.

Table 1.1 Employment and output figures in the slate industry

Years	Number employed	Total output (tons)
1919	6604	164098
1920	8304	215269
1921	9520	237350
1922	9523	231410

Wages fluctuated in response to economic oscillations within the industry. From 1920 to 1922 wages fell from 12s. 6d. per day to 9s. 4d., whereas from 1922 to 1930 they were reasonably stable. In 1930, however, when the selling price of slate was reduced, the pressure on wages mounted, and in 1932 the proprietors of Nantlle and Dorothea quarries requested their men to accept a 10 per cent reduction in wages. By November 1932 a new scale of wages was implemented which reflected the plight of the industry. Quarrymen were now paid a maximum of 8s. 1d. and labourers a maximum of 7s. 4d. per day.

Employers complained that the reduction in working hours from 1919 to 1933 had decreased output per head. The problem of falling output resulted in the introduction of more labour-saving devices, such as excavators and cranes. Output per man at Dorothea Quarry did rise slightly between 1933 and 1938, and average daily earnings there returned slowly to their 1920 level. Costs of production in the industry rose steadily during the years 1939–45. Most of the accessible and productive rock had already been mined, with the result that quarries became deeper and the transportation costs progressively increased. At Llechwedd Quarry, the total costs of production for four weeks ending on 16 February 1935 were £5,194 for 730 tons of slates. Since the wages were not high, economies could only be achieved by a costly process of further mechanization. Very few quarries made profits in the period before the First World War, but dividends were forthcoming in some instances after 1918, as with the Dorothea Company, which paid dividends from 1919 to 1926. Thereafter, dividends became smaller and, from 1930 onwards, the quarry worked only three days a week.

Before the First World War the building industry usually declined at a faster rate than the slate industry. When the building industry expanded in the period 1922–38, there was no comparable expansion in slate production, and in these years the average annual output of slates in Great Britain was only 281,000 tons, yet in 1913, when the number of new houses being built was small, the average annual output had been 353,000 tons. The main reasons for the contraction in demand were the substitution of roofing tiles for slate in the building industry, and the importation of cheaper foreign slates in preference to Welsh ones. In the 1930s there was a higher rate of building than in the 1920s, but the production of slate did not rise correspondingly.

The production of tiles expanded swiftly: in 1935, it was estimated at 1,200,000 tons, which was six times that of 1912. In 1935, the output of slates from north Wales was 271,000 tons, as opposed to 364,000 tons in 1912. Mass-produced tiles were

Table 1.2

Years	Average number of houses built per annum	Average tonnage of slates produced per annum
1922–9	163650	286002
1930–9	274691	278239

usually so much cheaper than slates, and during the depressed 1930s local authorities scrambled for the least costly building materials. In the eastern parts of London new slum legislation produced plans for tenements, often up to ten storeys high, most of which were flat-roofed or roofed with tiles. In 1882, north Wales had produced 85 per cent of the United Kingdom's total share of slates, but by 1933 this proportion had contracted to 75 per cent.

The chemical disadvantages of foreign slates did not prevent builders from importing large quantities of French, Belgian, Norwegian, Italian and German slates in the inter-war period. The low prices of Portuguese slates were made possible by the low wages paid to quarrymen in Portugal. In 1889, 17.5 per cent of British slates had been exported, but in 1932 the figure had fallen to 5 per cent, the export trade having been adversely affected by the high tariffs on imported slates imposed after 1918 by Germany, Australia and Ireland.

The outbreak of war in 1939 led to further contractions in the demand for slates as new controls were introduced on building programmes. By 1940 about 4,600 workers had been forced to leave the industry in search of new avenues of employment, and, during the war, about 2,000 quarrymen enlisted in the armed forces. The bombing of urban settlements after 1940 created an urgent demand for slates, but the new shortage of labour resulted in the neglect of development work, and reserves of slate were quickly exhausted. A number of quarries in Merioneth and Caernarfonshire were forced to close down; some of these did later reopen.

Transport and communications: The transport and communications network in Wales reflected the impact of the development of heavy industry. The need was for more efficient road transport, and the construction of a road bridge across the Severn estuary. In south Wales during this period a considerable expansion occurred in road transportation, at the expense of the railways. The first developments were in passenger traffic, with buses providing a more flexible service than the railways. The most rapid explosion in public road transport services occurred during the 1920s, when road passenger traffic gradually whittled away the isolation of the mining villages as travel became more of a daily occurrence. The 1930s were to see a consolidation of services, an improvement in facilities and an increase in the number of private cars, with 55,000 private cars licensed in south Wales by 1938, and 21,000 in north Wales. Cardiff, with 8,300 private cars, had the largest concentration, followed by Swansea with 5,000. The number of people using public trams in Wales reached 100,000 in 1919, and remained at that level throughout the 1920s.

Improvements in the south Wales railway network were facilitated by the amalgamation in the early 1920s of several smaller companies with the Great Western Railway. But the railways soon encountered new problems, as the traffic of coal exports declined and the import of iron ore or semi-finished steel to Merthyr Tydfil and Tredegar virtually evaporated. This diminution in the basic trade of the railways was aggravated by competition from road transport.

Although there was an increase in the number of long-distance carriers and in local haulage companies, the development of road transportation was hampered by the traditional communications network of the south Wales region. The physical and economic structure of the coalfield had determined that the road system was largely oriented in the same direction as the railways. The economies of the straggling south Wales Valleys had largely obviated the need for inter-valley links, and the movement of traffic was in a north–south direction between the Valleys and the ports. In the south the main road routes followed the same general direction as the railway lines. A number of improvements were undertaken during the inter-war period with the building of new roads, the widening of surfaces and the replacement of bridges. But the overriding need for improved road communications with other regions remained paramount, and the impact of road transport was restricted. In the mid-1930s about a dozen firms operated daily goods services between south Wales and

London, and regular services existed to Birmingham, Liverpool and Manchester. The essential challenge for road transport to provide long-distance hauls into England was severely restrained by the absence of a road bridge across the Severn, the case for which was actually rejected by a Select Committee of the House of Commons in May 1936. This confirmed the semi-monopoly of the railways in long-distance traffic, and proved to be unsatisfactory for the new light industries.

The peak of activity at the south Wales ports had been reached in 1913, when the total volume of traffic amounted to just over 47 million tons, of which the outward traffic, mainly of coal, accounted for 90 per cent. After the war was over, the ports of south Wales experienced substantial changes. In January 1922, the docks at Cardiff, Penarth, Barry, Port Talbot and Newport were amalgamated with the Great Western Railway Company, and in July, the Swansea Docks were also absorbed into the same company. Vast sums of money were spent on renewing railway tracks and on a thorough modernization of the whole docks system, which allowed larger ships to be accommodated and serviced. However, with the decline in the mining industry after 1923, there was considerable contraction at the south Wales ports. The peak of Cardiff's prosperity had been reached when the steam-coal industry was at its apogee, but, when unemployment ravaged the mining areas, Cardiff's economy haemorrhaged. Whereas exports of coal and coke at Cardiff in 1913 had totalled 10.5 million tons, by 1930 they were down to 6.3 million tons, and in 1938, coal and coke shipments amounted to only 4.9 million tons. A similar pattern emerged at the Penarth and Barry docks. Ports further west, at Port Talbot and Swansea, were spared the worst effects of depression because of the relative prosperity of the anthracite coalfield and the slightly more diversified industrial hinterland. The nickel works at Clydach benefited from the demand for nickel steel from the growing car industry. Additionally, the import of oil for the new oil refinery at Skewen meant that the Queen's Dock at Swansea was busy handling ocean-going tankers, and Swansea as a port never underwent the full rigours of depression experienced elsewhere in south Wales. As late as 1935 nearly 25 per cent of the working male population of the Cardiff and Barry district was registered as wholly unemployed.

The major reason for the decline of the ports was the slump in the coal trade, but the problem was compounded by the paucity of other export and import activities. Even in 1929 imports amounted to only 14 per cent of total traffic, and still consisted mostly of the raw materials for the heavy industries. As the coal trade declined, there was little compensation in the form of the export of a greater variety of manufactured goods, or in the import of more food and raw materials. Seaborne trade continued to follow its long-established patterns, and many products manufactured in south Wales were still exported from other ports outside the region, while a great amount of food and other commodities consumed in south Wales were also imported through other ports and brought by railway across England.

II Government Responses to the Depression

Since early 1920 governments had responded to the economic and industrial stagnation with a miscellany of ineffective and vacuous measures. Successive Conservative governments, and the first Labour governments of 1924 and 1929–31, applied the standard deflationary instruments of a high bank rate, controls of the money supply, a rigid control of government expenditure and orthodox methods of budget balancing in largely negative and unsuccessful attempts to control the economy. Churchill's policy of a return to the gold standard in 1925 was particularly disastrous for the older industrial regions, such as south Wales and the north-east. Trenchant critics of this deflationary and positively harmful policy were John Maynard Keynes and David Lloyd George, who produced a series of schemes for revitalizing the economy and for public-works programmes. Notable among them were the 'yellow book', *Britain's Industrial Future*, in 1928 and the 'orange book', *We Can Conquer Unemployment*, in 1929.

Contemporary governments, however, felt that soaring unemployment and industrial stagnation were transitory features, which would soon disappear when the economy returned to normality. Both Conservative and Labour administrations took a stern Treasury view of public-works schemes, which were deemed to be inherently inflationary. In January 1928 the Ministry of Labour set up an Industrial Transference Board, which was to form the basis of government policy towards unemployment until the passing of the Special Areas legislation in 1934. It reflected the official view that the solution to the problems of south Wales lay in the transference of population out of the areas. In March 1928 Neville Chamberlain decided that up to 200,000 miners in south Wales were unlikely to find permanent employment in the mining industry ever again, and the only solution was a mass transfer of population to other parts of Britain. Areas of high unemployment were targeted and resources made available to them in the form of financial assistance for moving people to a new location. In 1928, 41 per cent of all the offices scheduled under the IT scheme were located in south Wales, and even as late as 1938, south Wales still had the lion's share of such offices. But the IT scheme was never seen as a cure for unemployment in the south Wales Valleys, when large numbers of people, especially those over thirty-five years of age and married men, were considered unsuitable for it. The scheme presupposed the existence of suitable sources of employment at a time when there was widespread unemployment; in 1936–7 it was estimated that 37 per cent of those involved in the total directed and undirected transfers returned to their depressed places of origin.

In 1931, an industrial survey of south Wales was carried out, which included an analysis of the existing industrial position. The report considered the transfer of labour to other parts of the country and the introduction of new industries. Unfortunately, by the time it was completed, national and international pressures had ensured that the problems of south Wales and other depressed areas were temporarily obscured. After 1933, when general economic improvement had begun in the country as a whole, the government could no longer afford to ignore the continuing plight of the depressed areas, and it was decided to send investigators to four depressed regions, one of which was south Wales. The reporter for this region, Sir Wyndham Portal, concluded that vigorous efforts should be made to transfer surplus men and boys between the ages of eighteen and forty-five out of the area, and that a preparatory training centre should be established at Merthyr Tydfil or Tonypandy. In November 1934, the report was presented to Parliament, along with those of the three other regional investigations. The problem of the depressed areas was now highlighted, and the Special Areas Act, which became law in December 1934, was drafted to designate the four areas investigated as 'Special Areas'.

By 1936 the limitations of the Act were all too obvious. In south Wales the boundaries of the Act excluded the anthracite coalfield, the County Borough of Swansea, the County Boroughs of Newport and Cardiff, the Borough of Neath and the Urban Districts of Penarth, Barry and Porthcawl. Even commissioners themselves reacted against the bureaucratic restrictions imposed on their work, and as late as 1936 progress in the Special Areas was negligible. In November 1934, there had been 157,174 persons unemployed in the south Wales area, and, as late as September 1936, the figure had dropped to only 141,771, or to 34.2 per cent of the insured labour force.

The Special Areas commissioners were able to give no financial assistance towards the establishment of industries, and the results of the legislation were modest. During the period 1932–8, 42 new factories, employing twenty-five or more people, were opened in south Wales, only 24 of which were located within the Special Area boundaries, including 13 at the recently established trading estate at Treforest, the one real contribution made by the Special Areas legislation. In June 1936 the Commissioner set up a new company called the South Wales and Monmouthshire Trading Estates Ltd. By July 1936 it had decided that Treforest was the most suitable location for the site of the first industrial estate in Wales, and, within three years, it employed over 2,500 persons in 66 firms.

Apart from this and related ventures there still existed a paucity of new industrial developments in the area. The reconstituted Special Areas legislation of 1936–7 proved to be largely ineffective in attracting new industries to the chronically depressed pockets of south Wales. The majority of local Welsh industrialists were reluctant to venture into new fields, while English firms balked at the thought of establishing bases in the bleak Valleys of south Wales. Even at Treforest, the one successful centre of industrial development, the nature and quantity of employment did little to reduce the endless suffering of the unemployed inhabitants of the area. In June 1939, of the 2,196 people employed on the estate, only 914 were men over the age of eighteen. The Special Areas policy was clearly failing to encourage new industries to the depressed zones, and the employment opportunities it provided were usually inadequate to deal with the towering economic and social problems of the area.

The one lasting contribution of the trading estates was that they had demonstrated the possibility of establishing light industries in communities with a long tradition of heavy metal and mining industry.

Economic Recovery and the Second World War

Throughout the 1930s governments did very little for the people of Wales. Tariffs and imperial preference policies, which benefited the Midlands and the south of England, rendered little assistance to the exporting industries of Wales. Unemployment began to fall in south Wales from 1936 onwards, largely as a result of the fillip given to the British economy by international recovery and the rearmament process. In general, 1937 proved to be one of the best years since the depression had engulfed Wales: in the twelve months up to September of that year, the largest proportionate reduction in unemployment of all the Special Areas in England and Wales was experienced by the South Wales Area. The figure for total registered unemployed fell from 141,771 to 98,580, or from 34.2 per cent to 24.4 per cent. But the general improvement needs to be viewed cautiously: about 55 per cent of the decrease in the number of unemployed men in the South Wales Special Area in 1936–7 took place in the eighteen–thirty-four age group, largely as a result of transference; and the percentage of the older unemployed men also increased more rapidly in south Wales than in other areas. A worsening trend was noticeable for those in the long-term unemployed category – of the men wholly unemployed in July 1937, 17.3 per cent had been on the register for five years or more, compared with 12.4 per cent in the previous July. At Merthyr Tydfil, which had experienced a decrease of 22.2 points, unemployment still stood at 35.7 per cent; while Ferndale and Pontypridd still recorded levels of over 40 per cent in September 1937.

The impact of the Second World War was certainly foreshadowed during the period of war preparation. There was some expansion of iron and steel output to meet the needs of armament manufacture, and an increased number of military establishments were sited in the presumed safety of south Wales. Ordnance and Shadow factories, engineering shops, aircraft stations and storage depots began to be located in the area. Six

Royal Ordnance Factories (ROFs) were established in south Wales, the biggest located at Bridgend. The latter soon became the largest ammunition-filling factory in Britain, and at its wartime peak 37,000 workers, mainly women and girls, converged daily on the factory from a wide radius. Another ROF was built at Hirwaun, where 14,000 were engaged in the manufacture of small arms, while in Carmarthenshire, the ROF at Pembrey, near Llanelli, was the major supplier of TNT.

Although these preparations generated a higher level of economic activity, the employment picture on the eve of the war was still one of deep distress. In August 1939 nearly 55,000 people were unemployed in south Wales, and over 4,000 of these were inhabitants of Merthyr Tydfil. It was the outbreak of war in September 1939 which eventually solved the problems of the depressed regions of Wales, although no one could have foreseen in 1939 the profound effects which war would have on the Welsh economy. By July 1941 the number unemployed in Wales had plummeted to 35,000. The redistribution of industrial plants, which had been desperately sought in the locust years, was now implemented on the grounds of strategic necessity. The unemployment scene in Glamorgan improved dramatically: by July 1944, at the Cardiff, Swansea and Port Talbot labour exchanges the percentage of workers registered as unemployed stood at 0.2, 0.8 and 0.9 respectively, while at Merthyr Tydfil the figure had fallen to 3.5 from 47.7 per cent in July 1939. The corresponding figures for the Rhondda Valleys were 1.3 at Pontypridd, 1.0 at Treorchy, 1.7 at Porth and 3.7 at Tonypandy. The virtual elimination of unemployment was the result of the need to expand production during the war years, and the diversification of industries in south Wales had melted away the massive unemployment queues. The Barlow Report of 1942, on the geographical distribution of industry, was of special interest to Wales with its espousal of new policies to provide for the redistribution and relocation of industry in Britain.

New government-built establishments were accompanied by an inflow of new enterprises. In Glamorgan a range of productive activities were undertaken in response to wartime demands. At Aberdare, the cable works added shells and torpedoes to its output, while in the Rhondda Valley the recently established clothing and textiles factories clothed and equipped the civil defence and military forces. Cardiff became a vast armoury, as new factories produced cartridges, shells, armoured vehicles, heavy guns, parachutes and naval photographic equipment. Although wartime industrial expansion was dispersed widely, in south Wales the Treforest Trading Estate remained the cynosure. By the end of the war, the estate had grown to around 1,500,000 square feet of industrial space, where total employment had reached a peak of 16,300.

Despite the influx of new enterprises, the basic industries of coal, steel and tinplate still dominated the industrial scene. During the war years the coalfield slowly deteriorated, as, after the end of the 'phoney' war, the coal export trade collapsed swiftly, and the number of workers diminished, especially in 1940 as young coalface workers joined the colours, while others simply transferred to other industries or new regions. The run-down ceased temporarily in 1941, as some mines reopened in response to the demand for coal as a source of power. By 1944, however, the number employed in coal mining had fallen to around 112,000, and output stood at 22.4 million tons, compared with 39.3 million tons in 1938.

Nevertheless, there were some favourable developments in the coal industry during these years. Opencast mining appeared as a new feature on the landscape, and the south Wales coalfield steadily increased its share of the inland market as inland orders were diverted from other areas. This meant that, in the post-war period, the priority was one of maintaining supplies to home markets rather than scrambling for the export markets. Overall, the post-war outlook seemed bleak: output had declined during the war years; coal stocks were low; exports had become negligible; the workforce was severely reduced; many mines were obsolete and most of the easily worked seams had been exhausted; mechanization was relatively slow in developing; and productivity levels were generally low.

The tinplate industry was no better placed. As its export trade was completely abandoned during the war years, production was concentrated and the number of tinplate mills contracted sharply, between 1940 and 1943, with the loss of 14,000 jobs. After 1943 few of the former employees wanted to return to an uncertain future in the industry, although the end of the war saw some tinplate mills restored to use and remanned to meet a revived domestic and export demand. The labour force in 1946 was still only 60 per cent of its 1939 level, and the shortage of experienced workers was the crucial factor retarding the industry's resurgence.

The steel industry suffered much less than its partner, with the major areas of production enjoying a period of great prosperity. The large integrated works at Cardiff and Port Talbot responded well to the wartime challenges. The incidence of closures and the scale of redundancies were not as marked in the steel industry and, in 1946, the scale of production and the size of the labour force were not much below their pre-war levels.

Finally, the ports flourished during the war years, as vast quantities of military traffic, foodstuffs and raw materials were imported through Wales. The increase in the range and amount of activity saw the ports handle a huge volume of tonnage. For the last complete year before the war the total of the cargoes imported and exported at the principal south Wales ports was only 592,000 tons, while for 1943 it was 2,935,000 tons. Of the 250 million tons of import and export traffic which passed through the UK ports during the war, over 83 million tons were handled by the south Wales ports.

The war of 1939–45 left an indelible impression upon the Welsh economy. First, it eliminated the mass unemployment of the 1930s, which became only minimal throughout most of the 1940s. Secondly, there was a sharp growth of collectivism and of intervention by the state in the lives of ordinary people; the Essential Work Order of 1941 directed workers to industries working on war contracts, and the Barlow Report of 1942 advocated policies for the redistribution and relocation of industry. The wartime administration secured operational control over the coal mines and various strategic private industries. These, and a myriad other instances, demonstrate the intervention of government during these critical years.

A third important feature of the war years was the development of manufacturing industries. At its height, the war had pulled the Welsh economy into a largely unfamiliar mould. From 1939 to 1944 there was an increase in the labour supply in chemicals, paints and oils from 4,000 to 69,000; in engineering from 11,000 to 48,000; and in vehicle construction from 7,000 to 30,000. Before the war 40 per cent of the insured population of

Wales had been employed in the traditional heavy industries of coal mining, iron and steel, but by 1946 that proportion had receded to 32 per cent. There was an increase of 80 per cent in the number employed in general manufacturing from 69,800 to 125,400 in the period between 1939 and 1946. General manufacturing accounted for one-fifth of total employment in 1946 as against one-ninth before the war. Another new feature was that one out of ten persons employed in Wales was either a national or a local civil servant. This was an absolute increase of 129 per cent, which had occurred during the war years, and which reflected the strengthening of collectivism.

Fourthly, and perhaps the most significant effect of the Second World War, was the growth in the number of working women, who, from 1939 to 1946, had poured into the factories in unprecedented numbers. In 1946, female employment in Wales totalled 158,000, or 83 per cent more than in 1939, so that four out of every ten people employed in manufacturing were women. In the middle of 1944 there were 219,000 insured women workers in Wales, compared with only 94,000 in 1939; an increase of 134 per cent, compared with a figure of only 30 per cent for Great Britain as a whole.

By vastly increasing the number of women in employment, the war considerably added to the potential labour force for the post-war period. An increase in semi-skilled and female labour created new industrial legions well equipped for the needs of the new industries. Gradually, deep-seated prejudices and misconceptions concerning Welsh labour and industrial practices were eroded during the war years. The Second World War produced a transformation in the economy of Wales with the introduction of light manufacturing industries and with a revival of some of the traditional stalwarts.

SUGGESTED READING

Colin Baber and L. J. Williams (eds.), *Modern South Wales: Essays in Economic History* (Cardiff, 1986).

K. D. George and Lynn Mainwaring (eds.), *The Welsh Economy* (Cardiff, 1988).

Trevor Herbert and Gareth Elwyn Jones (eds.), *Wales Between the Wars* (Cardiff, 1988).

Philip Jenkins, *A History of Modern Wales 1536–1990* (London, 1992).

A. H. John and G. Williams (eds.), *Glamorgan County History*, vol.V (Cardiff, 1980).
Kenneth O. Morgan, *Rebirth of a Nation: Wales 1880–1980* (Oxford, 1981).
Brinley Thomas (ed.), *The Welsh Economy* (Cardiff, 1962).
Gwyn A. Williams, *When Was Wales?* (London, 1985).

2. Organized Religion and Social History

Religion

Early Revivalism

THE decline in the numerical strength and social influence of organized religion and the ascendancy of the Labour Party in national and local politics are two of the most dominating features of modern Welsh social and political history. Yet in 1900 the scene was set for an entirely different drama. Religion, and especially the Nonconformist churches, and the Liberal Party appeared to be comfortably in control of the social and cultural life of Wales. Nonconformity's influence in political circles had also burgeoned by the end of the nineteenth century. Churches and ministers actively supported the Liberal Party and there had emerged a common ideology based on the importance of individual choice and personal freedom. The relationship between the Nonconformists and the Liberals was often complex, but usually intimate.

By 1904 there were increasing indications that ministers were addressing large and expanding congregations once more. The revivalist movement associated with Evan Roberts attracted thousands of new members to the denominations. As early as 1903 the Calvinistic Methodists of south Cardiganshire, under the direction of two local ministers, Joseph Jenkins and John Thickens, had appealed for a new awakening, similar to that of 1859. By 1904 the revival was under way, and Evan Roberts, a ministerial student, had become the instrument by which this religious impulse spread to the occasional adherents and to those who had completely forsaken their religious affiliations. In the last three months of 1904 the dissemination of the revival seemed unparalleled as Roberts took the revival to his home town of Loughor, and thence into the eastern valleys and coastal towns of south Wales, before moving north in 1905. By the end of 1904 it was estimated that 34,000 conversions had taken place, and a final figure of over 100,000 conversions was often quoted in religious circles. Chapel membership of the big four denominations rose from 463,000 in 1903 to 549,000 at the end of 1905. Evan Roberts had become a national figure of some standing, whose influence resounded throughout the Principality.

Between 1906 and 1910 a royal commission inquired into the condition of the various religious bodies in Wales, as a preliminary step towards possible disestablishment of the Church. It concluded that 'the people of Wales show a marked tendency to avail themselves of the provision made by the churches of all denominations for their spiritual welfare'. Its reports seemed to offer further evidence of the profound strength of the churches in Wales. Attendance at communion services for all the Nonconformist denominations amounted to 550,280 persons, and if Church communicants are added to this figure, then the grand total of attendance reached 743,361. Taking the population of Wales (deducting children of three and under) to be 1,864,696, we find that two out of every five persons in Wales were communicants; or 40 per cent of the total population. This figure becomes even more impressive when we consider that a salient feature of Welsh Nonconformity was the popularity of the Sunday school, whose primary function was to serve as a training ground for the creation of full members; attached to the chapels also were large numbers of adherents or *gwrandawyr* who were not full members, but people who came to hear the sermons and to enjoy the congregational singing. Membership figures represent one aspect of the strength and vitality of organized religion during the early years of the century.

Although the Nonconformist chapels had reached the apogee of their success in 1906, as early as 1908 newspapers were reporting that revivalism was depleted. Evan Roberts announced that he was exhausted, and from 1907 he devoted himself to a ministry of intercessionary prayer. During later years he lived as a recluse in Cardiff until his death in 1951. In 1908, a Caernarfon newspaper attempted two surveys of attendance at places of worship: the first was held on a cold Sunday in January; and the second on a warm, sunny day in July. Each exhibited the same pattern: only about one in eight of the population attended church or chapel on Sunday, and even the attendance of children at Sunday schools was disappointing. By 1914 all the main denominations were again recording annual decreases in membership, with at least 26,000 members having disappeared since the revival had peaked.

Many ministers had complained about the emotional excesses of the revival and bewailed the fact that young people were ignoring their guidance. Evan Roberts's own chapel, Moriah, Loughor, was the scene of disturbances and £60 worth of damage was caused to the building. Later religious commentators added their voices to the chorus of complaints about certain lamentable features of the revival, yet the sudden burst of religious excitement was, in many ways, a reaction to the oppressive social and industrial conditions of the period, bringing hope, comfort and spiritual release for countless numbers of people who lived in harsh and often appalling material conditions.

The New Theology

The revival produced an infectious social enthusiasm and inspired theologians and secular thinkers alike to consider its social implications. The revival was followed by the intrusion into Wales of a short-lived, but influential, social philosophy, the New Theology. Christian leaders had become increasingly concerned at the estrangement of certain groups from the Church. The cultivated or educated classes no longer found orthodox and Calvinistic interpretations of the faith convincing, while the working classes had been frozen out by a largely middle-class aura of respectability within the churches. The New Theology attempted to appeal to both groups. Its leading interpreters in Wales were the Bradford-based Congregationalist minister, the Revd Thomas Rhondda Williams, and the Revd R. J. Campbell of the City Temple, London. Campbell's book, *The New Theology*, which appeared in 1907, claimed that the Christian religion was primarily a gospel for this life. He condemned contemporary society, with its slums and antisocial ideals of selfishness, cruelty and injustice, and offered a vocal and enthusiastic support for socialism. Campbell was a close friend of Keir Hardie and in 1907–8 he toured south Wales lecturing and preaching, often to ILP branches, in towns as far west as Carmarthen. It would be misleading, however, to view the New Theology as a socialist message in religious garments; rather it was a fusion of modern liberal theology with a heightened social conscience. It emphasized the immanence of God in the creation, the moral value of Jesus' example and teachings, and the evolutionary process of history culminating in the perfecting and ultimate uniting of the whole creation. The stress on morality and unity led naturally into a discussion of society and a condemnation of the existing economic and industrial system. However, Campbell, in fact, won very few supporters for his ideas in Wales and most of his meetings were poorly attended.

It was David Thomas of Talysarn, Gwynedd, who probably came closest to achieving an early synthesis between socialism and Welsh religious enthusiasm. Although socialism had not gained much ground in north Wales, nine of the ILP branches that existed in 1910 had been founded by Thomas. In that year he published *Y Werin a'i Theyrnas*, an appraisal of socialism in Welsh. Believing that socialism and religion were compatible, at the 1911 National Eisteddfod in Carmarthen he called a meeting to consider the possibility of establishing a Welsh Labour Party. Delegates at the conference included the Revd Silyn Roberts of Tanygrisiau, the colourful and ebullient Revd T. E. Nicholas y Glais, and the academic, T. Hudson Williams. The meeting was largely abortive, and socialism now seemed destined to be associated increasingly with an English-language and progressive future, while the Welsh language would be inextricably identified with Nonconformity and a Liberal past.

Churches, Socialism and Society
Contemporary evidence suggests that the churches were initially confused in their discussions about the nature, role and implications of the new political creed, and uncertain of the appropriate Christian response to its apparent claims. Most of the churches recognized the need for social reform, but they disagreed over the methods to achieve improvements. Nonconformists had spent the best part of two centuries trying to win liberties for the individual believer in the face of hostile state oppression. It was hardly surprising that they were deeply suspicious of the socialist creed with its apparent emphasis on nationalization and state action. The traditional Nonconformist message of individual responsibility and individual moral

regeneration made the acceptance of a collectivist creed extremely difficult, if not impossible. The main opposition to socialism arose from its emphasis on material improvement and its faith in the redemptive effect of environmental change. For so many Christian leaders it was the existence of sin, deeply embedded in the human heart, which rendered futile any attempt at social reform without first seeking individual regeneration. The majority of Nonconformist ministers, even those who were manifestly sympathetic towards socialism and the Labour movement, endeavoured to demonstrate the unique and indispensable mission of Christianity. A fundamental difference was that Welsh Nonconformist ministers believed that Christianity involved the making of Christians, while Labour supporters and socialist agitators argued that it involved the creation of a perfect state.

There was, however, a group of ministers who actively supported the Labour movement. The Revd R. Silyn Roberts established the ILP branch in Blaenau Ffestiniog in 1908; John Gwili Jenkins, a tutor at the Gwynfryn Academy and later professor of New Testament Studies at the North Wales Baptist College, advocated the social basis of Christianity and claimed that all Christians should be socialists, and all socialists should be Christians. The Revd T. E. Nicholas (Niclas y Glais), who exhibited a unique blend of Christianity and socialism, in 1906 helped to establish a branch of the ILP in Glais and became a prominent figure in the Ystalyfera branch of the Gower Labour Party. At Keir Hardie's request, he became editor of the Welsh column of Hardie's ILP newspaper, *The Merthyr Pioneer*. For T. E. Nicholas Christianity and socialism were inextricably linked; and socialism did not represent a new religion, but a purifying force within Christianity.

Some church ministers suffered on account of their political allegiances. The Revd Daniel Hughes, Pontypool, was locked out of his chapel by the deacons. The pulpit was used as an effective propaganda weapon against socialist sympathizers, while Nonconformist luminaries often published articles in denominational journals attacking presumed anti-religious and atheistic elements in the Labour movement. The turning-point for the social conscience of organized religion came with the industrial unrest of 1910–11. The Nonconformists, with their tradition of Liberal affiliation, became increasingly concerned that the estrangement of the working classes from the chapels often accompanied their adoption of socialism. It was this politicization of Labour on the one hand, and the reaction of organized religion to it on the other, which proved to be decisive for the future of the churches. Nonconformists began to withdraw from overt political activity during this first decade of the twentieth century as they feared that chapel congregations would become increasingly divided between Liberal Party supporters and Labour activists.

The unrest of 1910–11 also highlighted the need for the churches to formulate an effective Christian response to the social questions of the day. From 1910 onwards, social problems were catapulted to the forefront of denominational discussions. The Union of Welsh Independents discussed social issues at Lampeter in 1910, when Daniel Lleufer Thomas urged the formation of a Welsh Union of Social Service. Eventually, the Welsh School of Social Service was established as a joint venture between Independents and Baptists, its purpose being to discuss social problems from a Christian standpoint. The Baptist Union of Wales formed a Social Service League during its annual assembly at Mountain Ash in September 1911. In April 1912, a 'Religion and Labour' week was held at Cardiff to discuss the importance of the Labour movement, socialism and religion. Nonconformists realized that many of their former political aims had been achieved by the beginning of the century, but, although awakened to the plight of the working classes, they were reluctant to endorse political activity in response to the social problems of the day. Ironically, as the Labour movement was becoming more politically orientated, organized religion became less overtly political and sought to construct a distinctively Christian answer to social issues. Welsh Nonconformity concentrated on presenting the unique and eternal significance of the gospel while contributing to the social question and attempting to recover Labour supporters for the chapels.

During the First World War Welsh people concentrated on the conflict, and a moratorium descended on the discussion of social issues. Although from 1918 onwards the churches sensed that their days of political influence had been eclipsed, the 1920s brought fresh opportunities for the religious groups to demonstrate their sympathy with the working classes. A succession of labour disputes, the General Strike of 1926 and widespread depression required practical and sympathetic responses from the churches. The Revd J. Derlwyn Evans, of Ynysymeudwy in the Swansea Valley, called on those involved in lockouts to attend church, and he offered to take a cut in wages to suffer with them. The Maerdy churches sent a delegation to the Board of Guardians in Pontypridd in 1927 calling for increased relief. Churches passed numerous resolutions during periods of industrial dispute, but many within the Labour movement perceived the churches' Christianity as an irrelevance. The newly disestablished Church in Wales was rarely involved in the national life of Wales in the first few decades of its existence, seeing its immediate task to be the establishing of a machinery for its own governance. During the locust years of mass unemployment and widespread poverty, the Church in Wales was preoccupied with its own constitutional, legal and financial problems. An appeal to raise £1 million, to compensate for the losses of disendowment, had produced the sum of £661,730 by 1923, and £722,552 by 1935. There were some isolated instances of its involvement with suffering communities, such as the Governing Body's contribution to the national fund for the relief of distress in the coalfield in 1928, or Bishop Timothy Rees's work in the diocese of Llandaff, where he initiated direct relief and served as chairman of the Llandaff Industrial Committee.

Ironically, the Welsh Nonconformist denominations expended more verbal energy on social issues during the 1920s than in any other period. The Calvinistic Methodists led the way after 1918 with the establishment of their Reconstruction Commission. According to their reports, social questions were issues of morality, and their prescriptions for reform concentrated less on specific economic and social problems than on the moral condition of individual citizens. Ethical and religious considerations, rather than a concern for the suffering of the working classes, fuelled their campaign. The Calvinistic Methodists' Campaign for Morals and Religion, launched in 1921, advocated better personal relationships between the representatives of capital and labour as a solution to the economic and social problems of the day. The Union of Welsh Independents in September 1921 appointed a committee of three to advance the Church's social mission. The report also stressed the moral responsibility of every individual and urged the Church to develop into a society of people free from the clutches of political parties.

By the early 1920s organized religion was at the stage of identifying principles for a fairer society, but it seemed incapable of progressing further along the path of political and social reform, since Welsh Nonconformity had singularly failed to translate social issues into practical measures. There were only individual, localized and isolated attempts at some form of social mission. R. J. Barker, as the minister of Tonypandy Wesleyan Methodists, ensured that his church was involved in various social activities during the 1920s. The Revd Leon Atkin opened the Methodist Central Hall in Bargoed for seven days a week so that the unemployed could have free haircuts, shaves and meals, and boots repaired at minimal cost. Denominational pressures forced him out of Bargoed, and he moved to Swansea to become minister of St Paul's Congregational Church, where, during the 1930s, he became the champion of the unemployed and preached stirring sermons in favour of poor and redundant workers. In the Rhondda, the Revd T. Alban Davies, the Congregationalist minister at Tonpentre, spearheaded relief work in the years after the General Strike. He collected money, shoes and clothing for the distressed inhabitants of the Valleys, and urged the Congregational Union of England and Wales to distribute clothing and food in the areas most affected by unemployment.

For the first three decades of the century organized religion had been beset by confusion over its theology and social role. The adoption of liberal theology and a genuine social concern had neither reformed society nor regenerated the Church, and membership of the Welsh Nonconformist denominations plunged steadily after the General Strike of 1926:

Table 2.1 Membership figures for the three principal Nonconformist denominations in Wales, 1926–1939

Year	Baptists	Independents	Calvinistic Methodists
1927	129758	134971	189132
1930	125704	125806	185827
1935	122375	117961	182221
1939	116813	105576	177448

The attitudes of religious denominations to the social problems of the day had become solidified. There were at least five main strands discernible within the social philosophy of the churches: first, an overriding concern that the churches should avoid involvement in party political activities; secondly, a conviction that social problems were so great as to require an inter-denominational approach; thirdly, an emphasis on education and understanding as the pillars of social concern; fourthly, the churches approached social amelioration through individual regeneration – society could only be reformed through the moral reformation of individuals; and finally, there was a growing conviction that social evils pointed to far wider issues than justice for the working classes. The Welsh churches argued that unjust and impure principles lay at the heart of civilization and that values of brotherly love, justice and service were needed as the basis of a new Christian society.

Throughout the early decades of the century religious leaders were increasingly concerned about dwindling congregations and studiously eschewed political affiliation in a determined effort to prevent division and rancour from infiltrating their ranks. Despite this policy of political detachment, or perhaps because of it, the denominations maintained an influential position in society until the 1950s. Welsh society was never structured along simple lines. It was a complex web of faiths, in which the chapel was still a potent force. Neither the Labour movement nor the chapel could claim a monopoly of allegiance in Wales as long as there were many who felt comfortable in both the religious temples and the political citadels.

Social History

As we saw in the first chapter on the economy, industrial Wales in the early years of the century was prosperous, expanding and confident. The entrepôts of the mining industry, Cardiff, Newport, Barry and Swansea, were booming towns. Commercial centres were thriving, shops were well stocked, expenditure on drink, sport and other recreational activities manifested the opulence and optimism of the industrial population. In the years before 1914, Welsh economic and social life was relatively prosperous, and the advent of war brought further affluence and economic growth on the home front. Even as late as the end of 1920 Welsh industry still basked in the warm prosperity of the pre-war and wartime years. The confidence of the south Wales miners' claim for a 30 per cent wage increase in March 1919 had illustrated the pervading feeling of optimism.

Unemployment and the Migration of Labour
By the end of 1920, however, the staple industries of coal, steel and tinplate manufacture were beginning to feel the first effects of the onset of depression. South Wales, with an incredibly high proportion of its working population engaged in extractive industry, mining and metal manufacturing, suffered unremitting depression, unemployment and misery in the years that followed. Coal mining, steel and tinplate manufacture were highly labour-intensive activities, accounting for over 70 per cent of total employment in south Wales in 1913. Throughout the 1920s and 1930s the major social consequence of economic decline was chronic and long-term unemployment.

Unemployment in Wales increased from 8.6 per cent in 1924 to 16.5 per cent in 1925, and 19.5 per cent in 1927. In the coal-mining valleys of Glamorgan unemployment soared to 24.1 per cent in 1927 and, despite a fall to 21.3 per cent by 1929, it accelerated to 37.9 per cent in 1933. Although the scourge of unemployment touched all parts of industrial south Wales, the incidence was highest in those areas which were normally dependent upon steam coal mining and the iron and steel industries. In south-western Wales, where anthracite mining and tinplate manufacture dominated the industrial scene, the unemployment rate was comparatively low, at 3.4 and 8.3 per cent in 1922 and 1930 respectively. Along the north-eastern boundary of Glamorgan, and mainly in the County Borough of Merthyr Tydfil, the rate of unemployment reached 50.1 per cent in June 1930

After the financial crisis of 1931 the position worsened, and the 1930s witnessed even higher levels of unemployment. In 1932, Merthyr Tydfil, a major urban centre in south Wales, recorded 62.3 per cent unemployed. In 1937, when economic recovery was slowly reaching most of the depressed areas, Merthyr Tydfil still experienced an unemployment rate of 45.6 per cent, Ferndale 55.9 per cent, and Pontypridd 40.1 per cent. The scale and intensity of unemployment were matched by the length of time that individuals were without work. A survey on long-term unemployment which took the Rhondda as one sample area, showed that between 1932 and 1936 the proportion of the total unemployed there who could be classed as long-term increased from 33 per cent to 63 per cent. The age-composition of the unemployed also attracted attention during the 1930s. A vicious circle of limited opportunities, poor training facilities and the movement of large numbers of young persons out of south Wales, further exacerbated the economic plight of the industrial regions.

For many the only alternative to long-term unemployment was to leave Wales to find work elsewhere. At least 430,000 Welsh people left between 1921 and 1940, most of them emanating from the Valleys. The population of the Rhondda fell by 13 per cent in the 1920s, while that of Merthyr Tydfil dropped from 80,000 to 63,000 between 1921 and 1937. Throughout the mining Valleys of Glamorgan and Monmouthshire, thousands of young people left Wales every year.

In the coalfields of north Wales the 1930s were generally far worse than the 1920s. Total population showed a comparatively small decline from 83,306 in 1931 to just over 82,000 by 1935, but from 1931 to 1939 over 3,000 people emigrated from the area. Unemployment in the Greater Wrexham area was only 12.2 per cent in 1927, but in the 1930s structural unemployment hit the area as the coal industry went into sharp decline. In north Wales, unemployment rates of 50 per cent and over were recorded, for short periods only, in both Brymbo and Rhos. The closure of the Brymbo steelworks, partially in October 1930 and entirely from June 1931, resulted in unemployment rates exceeding 80 per cent. The Gresford colliery disaster of September 1934 left 2,000 men unemployed until 1936. In the period 1927–33 unemployment in Greater Wrexham rose at approximately the same rate as employment in the coal industry declined. Coal production fell by 28 per cent from 1929 to 1935, and the number employed in the north Wales coal industry dropped from 19,100 in 1924 to 8,741 in 1935.

Health, Housing and Welfare

In 1935, government ministerial statements and official reports argued that the social services were effectively supporting the poorer sections of society against the worst effects of the depression. Recent writers have often invoked welfare benefits as a factor capable of dispelling the 'myth' of the hungry thirties, asserting that Britain had a more comprehensive system of welfare services by 1939 than any other country. Overgenerous scales and the liberal administration of benefits have been cited as the primary cause of high unemployment, yet for substantial sections of the population, the 'myth' of depression and deprivation represented a grim and painful reality. Academic revisionism, in this context, merely identified the rather obvious fact that conditions in depressed regions did not hold good for the whole of society.

The unemployed and lower-paid workers often found it impossible to meet their financial obligations without sliding into debt. There is very little contemporary evidence to suggest that benefit rates were adequate for subsistence. According to the prevailing rates for 1931–4, barely 6s. would be left for all the family needs after food had been paid for. The whole of the residue would have been absorbed by rent, allowing nothing for clothing, heating and medical care. Besides, many of the forward-looking welfare services were not available until the economic recovery preceding the Second World War; for most of the inter-war period the emphasis was on retrenchment.

The prolonged depression imposed an enormous burden on local authorities in the industrial regions, which were confronted with the problem of increasing welfare expenditure on a reduced earning capacity. On the one hand, rate increases which were needed to counteract the losses arising from the closure of collieries and works imposed an additional charge on existing industries, a deterrent to new ones and an additional burden on the ordinary householder. The position worsened with the decline in the purchasing power of the depressed regions, where the rateable values of shops, public houses and the like had to be reduced, as did those of houses and weakened industrial enterprises. In the Rhondda Urban District the rateable value of collieries fell from £241,000 to £24,000 in the period 1925–35. Many people found themselves unable to pay their rates or rents at a time when deteriorating economic and social conditions required public funds in excess of expenditures which would normally be undertaken. In the circumstances rates spiralled upwards, becoming some of the highest in the country.

Many local authorities faced severe financial restrictions, and public services were adversely affected. In 1928 school meals were being given to only 32 out of 23,500 children in the Rhondda, while Pontypridd, Mountain Ash and Aberdare were providing no school meals at all. Only Abertillery maintained school meals without a break after the 1926 strike, and Monmouth recommenced its meals service in 1927. In 1936, about one-third of children in the Welsh mining districts who were assessed as being malnourished were receiving neither milk nor meals at school. One problem was that there were wide disparities in income scales adopted for means testing in depressed areas. When the scale was relaxed in the Rhondda in November 1935 there was an immediate increase from 19.5 per cent to 33.8 per cent in the number of children receiving free milk or solid meals, but this still left 41 per cent of the children assessed as malnourished without free meals or milk at school.

Table 2.2 Supplementary feeding of schoolchildren in south Wales, July–August 1936

District	% receiving milk or meals	% malnourished without supplementation
Glamorgan CC	11.0	34.8
Monmouth CC	9.7	43.3
Merthyr Tydfil County Borough	36.0	25.4
Rhondda Urban District	34.4	41.0
Abertillery Urban District	29.7	32.4

It is well known that major welfare services varied enormously from one district to another. Lack of uniformity partly reflected a chaotic system of local administration, and partly the local political situation. The widespread malnutrition and suffering in the Rhondda Valleys in the 1930s illustrated the low standard of general health. The general death rate there increased in the 1930s from 12.9 per 1,000 persons in 1931–4 to 13.4 in 1937, as compared with an overall death rate for England and Wales of 9.3 per 1,000 persons. A sample of miners in south Wales showed that 8 per cent in the 15–24 age group had lost all their teeth, while the comparable figure for the 25–34 age group was 23 per cent. Welfare provision aimed at pregnant women and nursing mothers was not effectively counteracting the adverse consequences of the depression. The inter-war period also witnessed a spectacular rise in maternal mortality. The Rhondda was quite exceptional in providing milk for 50 per cent of children under three, and 32 per cent of 3–5-year-olds. Most authorities only gave milk to young children up to the age of one.

By the mid-1930s it was apparent that Wales was not sharing in the British decline of tuberculosis, and deaths from the disease in the Rhondda actually increased from 790 in 1932 to 1,030 in 1937.

Table 2.3 Death rates per 100,000 population from TB

Period	Wales	England	Scotland
1916–20	144	144	147
1921–5	116	108	116
1926–30	103	93	94
1931–5	97	79	80
1935	92	70	74

The regional differences are accentuated if the depressed areas of Wales are analysed. The decline in the death rate from TB from 1921–3 to 1931–3 was 22.7 per cent for England and Wales as a whole, 12 per cent for Wales, 2 per cent for Glamorgan and 2.3 per cent for Merthyr Tydfil. Breconshire and Monmouthshire registered actual increases of 2.5 per cent and 0.6 per cent respectively. The high TB rates in parts of Wales were an embarrassment for the Ministry of Health, which attributed the figures to the racial susceptibility of the Celtic race and the intense social conservatism of the Welsh people. In 1910 David Davies, Llandinam, Thomas Jones and other prominent Welshmen, had established the Welsh National Memorial Association in an attempt to tackle the disease in certain localities. The first sanatorium was founded in 1900, and there were eighteen in existence by 1938. At the end of 1933 the *Welsh Outlook* rejoiced that the death rate from TB in Wales had fallen from 1,468 per million in 1911 to 896 in 1932. Yet, by 1933 the seven counties in Britain with the highest mortality rates from TB were all in Wales. In 1937, 1 per cent of the Welsh population was on the TB register, and the mortality rate in Wales was 20 per cent higher than in England or Scotland.

A Committee of Inquiry into the anti-tuberculosis service in Wales and Monmouthshire published its report in 1939, painting an appalling picture of social conditions in all parts of Wales. Clement Davies, the committee's chairman, asserted that the report reflected the performance of local authorities in Wales over a twenty-year period. Authorities fell into two broad categories: those in the industrial north-east and south-east had sought to respond to government measures; and those in the north and south-west had been dilatory and ineffective. The incidence of TB was higher in Anglesey, Caernarfon, Merioneth, Cardigan and Pembrokeshire than in any other county in southern Britain. In 1914, the death rate was twice as high in these rural counties as in Merthyr Tydfil, with Cardigan heading the list in successive decades for the incidence of TB, deaths in childbirth and other illnesses. The evidence supplied to the committee of inquiry furnished many damning instances of neglect and indifference by the rural authorities. One glaring manifestation was the failure to create a network of full-time medical officials. By 1938 only one such appointment had been made in rural Wales, despite the fact that the Local Government Act of 1929 had made this compulsory. In 1921 the medical officer of health condemned the condition of the water supply in many parts of Carmarthenshire. He particularly deplored methods employed for the disposal of excreta in the urban districts of Newcastle Emlyn, Kidwelly, Burry Port and Cwmaman, and in the rural districts of Carmarthen, Llanelli, Llandeilo, Llandovery and Whitland. In the years 1935–6, 10–12 per cent of the total expenditure of Glamorgan, Denbighshire and Flintshire had been earmarked for public health, while in Anglesey and Montgomeryshire the corresponding figures were 6 per cent and 4 per cent.

Working-class housing had also deteriorated during the depression years. Wales had taken less advantage of the Public Housing Acts of 1919, 1923 and 1924 than had other parts of Britain, and only 55,750 houses had been completed to the end of the 1920s. Clement Davies's report of 1939 underlined the extent of insanitary and slum housing in many parts of Wales. Merthyr Tydfil was sharply condemned for its failure to embark upon a radical programme of slum clearance. There were 118 basement or cellar dwellings of extreme squalor in the town, and no fewer than 400 basement tenements in the Rhondda. The county councils of Cardiganshire, Pembrokeshire and Carmarthenshire were designated as having failed in their duty, while the county councils of north-west Wales were singled out for the severest criticisms. Housing conditions in Anglesey remained indescribably bad, while the local authorities in Caernarfonshire and Merioneth were castigated for their housing records. As a result of the contraction of funds and mounting unemployment in the building industry, the number of new houses built in Wales either by local authorities or private bodies fell steadily from 10,851 completed in 1926 to only 1,410 in 1931. Only after 1933 was there any appreciable improvement, with 8,257 houses built in 1935. Even in the 1930s the pattern of building council houses varied from twenty-one for every 1,000 of the population in Swansea and Flintshire to fewer than ten per 1,000 in the rural counties.

The depression years saw a decline in so many areas. The fall in community income meant that hospitals, public libraries and the retail trade were seriously affected. In 1935, for example, there were no fewer than 318 empty shops in the Rhondda Urban District. Poverty was accompanied by social and psychological despondency in the Valley communities. Social institutions were undermined by the lack of financial support, and individuals were often prevented from participating in a full range of cultural and communal activities.

Despite the manifold and widespread social despondency, the human misery did not go completely unrelieved. Assistance often came from outside the Principality, and a number of 'settlements' were established in various depressed districts by philanthropic agencies. The Maes-yr-Haf Settlement at Trealaw in the Rhondda provided the model social community in a Christian context, and experiments begun there soon spread to other parts of the country. Unemployed Men's Clubs, allotment schemes, small-scale factory production of various consumer goods, the revival of weaving, embroidery and quilting were only a few of the schemes devised to counteract the worst effects of industrial and social dejection. Meanwhile, Labour local authorities in south Wales endeavoured to maintain a high level of expenditure on health, housing, education and other social necessities. The local authority in Merthyr ensured that over 90 per cent of the town's secondary-school pupils had free places, while those at Newport and Swansea battled against the Board of Education's means test. Communities such as Brynmawr, Llanelli and Bargoed demanded better facilities for their impoverished inhabitants and encouraged various forms of recreation and public works.

In other parts of Wales, and especially for middle-class groups and communities, the inter-war years brought affluence and new forms of consumption. Although the average earnings of coal miners had slumped from 16*s.* a shift between 1914 and 1920 to 8*s.* in 1921, and remained at that level throughout the rest of the period, the real wages of public servants, such as teachers and administrators, actually rose. The 1937 Marketing Survey of the United Kingdom revealed that the purchasing power of the leading south Wales towns actually compared favourably with most towns in Britain. Cardiff was regarded as an above-average market, only slightly behind Greater London, while Swansea and Newport were comparable to cities such as Manchester and Coventry.

Consumption patterns in the relatively wealthy districts revealed a process of increasing demand for the new range of consumer goods on offer. There were 56,970 wireless licences issued at Cardiff in 1937, or approximately one per household. At Bangor, where unemployment was below 10 per cent, virtually all the houses were wired, and there was one telephone per nine households. Similar patterns could be found at Wrexham, Deeside and in the coastal resorts of Llandudno and Rhyl. The spread of the motor car and motor bike improved opportunities for travel. By 1938, there were 55,000 private cars licensed in south Wales, and 21,000 in north Wales. Cardiff had the largest concentration, with 8,300 private cars, followed by Swansea, with 5,000. Elsewhere, the picture was less sanguine and more familiar: there were only 932 telephone subscribers in the Rhondda, or one for every fifty households.

Women's Lives
The First World War created an unprecedented demand for female labour in all areas of Britain. Women were needed to fill

the civilian jobs vacated by men who had joined the military forces. They were employed in manufacturing industries, in munitions factories, in the manufacture of shells, bullets, planes and tanks. Women swept chimneys and roads, they dug graves, ploughed the fields, drove trams and buses, and laboured in shipyards. The Great War revolutionized women's work in Wales. The Cardiff Tramways Corporation first proposed engaging female conductors in the spring of 1915, but it met with considerable opposition from the male-dominated union, the Cardiff Tramways Association. In munitions factories, however, women usually formed the majority of workers. At Queensferry in north Wales, which produced TNT, over 70 per cent of the production workers were female. At Newport Shell factory women constituted 83 per cent of the workforce by 1918. Many took up nursing posts and joined the Army Auxiliary Corps or the Voluntary Aid Detachments. Others became clerks, shop assistants, library assistants and post office workers. All sections of contemporary society lavished praise on women for their sterling contributions to the war effort.

The end of war in 1918 augured well for the future. It was felt that women had successfully challenged numerous traditions during the military conflict, and that equality and freedom would be the eventual prize. The winning of the vote for qualified women over thirty had established the principle of women's suffrage in 1918, and the Sex Disqualification Removal Act of 1919 had, in theory, opened the door for the entry of women to the professions. Other measures had granted women divorce on the same terms as men, introduced widows' pensions and granted sex equality with regard to the guardianship of infants. But, once the war ended, women were expected to return meekly to their erstwhile position of inferiority. If women wished to remain in paid employment, the only avenue deemed to be suitable for the vast majority was that of domestic service. For the three-quarters of a million in Britain who were compelled to leave their posts after November 1918, the immediate problem facing the legions of female workers was unemployment. Unemployed women war workers were entitled to collect 25*s.* for thirteen weeks, but, in order to qualify for this benefit, they had to attend the labour exchange daily. Most labour exchanges offered women work as domestic servants, but young Welsh women, like their English counterparts, were determined not to return to the arduous hours, low remuneration and personal indignities of service. A powerful concentration of forces was mobilized to force women back into the domestic sphere: first, media propaganda projected the image of housewife and mother as the only desirable role for women; there were loud protestations from the press against women who ostensibly usurped men's jobs; national insurance legislation attempted to coerce women into domestic service by making it virtually impossible for them to claim unemployment benefit; and marriage bars were introduced into the professions to eject women from well-paid employment.

Throughout the inter-war period economic activity rates among women in Wales continued to be lower than in England. In 1921, the Welsh rate was 23 per cent, and only 21.5 per cent in 1931, as compared with 32 per cent and 34 per cent for England and Wales as a whole. Although domestic service did not retain its commanding pre-war position, it remained the largest single employer of women in England and Wales until 1939. In 1921, 33 per cent of all working women were occupied in some form of personal service, and by 1931 that figure had increased to 35 per cent. Only 13.6 per cent of females over fourteen were employed in the County Borough of Merthyr Tydfil in 1931, 10.3 per cent in the Rhondda Urban District, and 14.3 per cent and 14.2 per cent respectively in Glamorgan and Monmouthshire. It was generally accepted that women would not work outside the home after marriage. Most paid work for women was transitional and undertaken at particular points in the life-cycle – before marriage, during early widowhood, or after children had left home. Economic necessity, rather than career aspirations, usually determined the participation of women in the employment market. Few women took paid work outside the home, although unofficial activities such as child-minding, cleaning, washing other people's clothes and sewing were common means of supplementing the family income during exigent times. Government support, or training, for unemployed women was concentrated exclusively upon domestic service. The Ministry of Labour would only provide funding for courses which would increase the supply of servants. In the period 1924–39 it established Home Training Centres and, after 1931, non-residential courses were launched in south Wales at Aberdare,

Cardiff, Hengoed, Maesteg, Merthyr Tydfil, Neath, Pontypool, Pontypridd, Swansea and Ystrad Rhondda. Welsh women were trained to provide a vast army of migrant cheap labour for the well-to-do districts of south-east England.

For the great majority of women who remained at home, all aspects of domestic organization, including financial management and child care, rested firmly within the arena of their responsibility. Men would occasionally undertake such chores as blackleading the grate, or cutting coal and sticks. Women were expected to keep the homes, outside pavements and the backyards in pristine condition. While the miners worked a seven-hour (lengthened to eight hours in 1926) day, their wives usually toiled for seventeen hours, depending on the requirements of the shift system. In order to ensure that domestic organization ran smoothly, women had to operate a rigorous timetable: washing on Mondays; ironing and bread-making on Tuesdays; cleaning upstairs rooms on Wednesdays; beating the mats on Thursdays; cleaning the downstairs rooms on Fridays; shopping and baking on Saturdays.

Women's lives were enacted against the industrial and economic background of the period. While the war years had brought misery and hardship, there had been economic growth and comparatively high wages for most workers. The General Strike of 1926 and the onset of depression soon transformed the lives of ordinary people into a nightmare of despair and deprivation. Women now had to balance exiguous family incomes and devise new remedies to supplement earnings. Lodgers were often accommodated in the family home. Young children's skills were utilized to support family earnings: they would perform piecework at home; assist with the shopping; care for siblings; and even search for scraps of food. The operation of the means test from 1931 meant that the earnings of children living at home were also taken into account before benefits could be paid. To compound the difficulties, housing in the period was characterized by chronic shortages, appalling living conditions and soaring rents. A government survey published in 1936 showed that 1,066 working-class families in Merthyr and 1,453 in Cardiff lived in homes which were officially designated as overcrowded. In homes which lacked the basic amenities of hot-water supplies, indoor toilets and bathrooms, housework was an intolerable and endless toil.

In 1920, only 5 per cent of houses in the Rhondda had baths, and 2.5 per cent in the south Wales coalfield. The interminable task of preparing these baths for two- or three-shift systems imposed enormous additional burdens on the doughty womenfolk of the coalfields. No pithead baths had been provided under the 1911 Coal Mines Act, and progress depended on voluntary provision by the coalowners. Ocean Coal's colliery at Treharris was one of the first two in Britain whose modern pithead baths were operational by 1916. Women like Mrs Vernon Hartshorn were prominent in the movement before the First World War to mount a public campaign in support of pithead baths. After 1918, agitations recommenced and the Women's Labour League came to the forefront. In 1938 there were thirty-two baths in operation, and, by 1946, baths were provided at forty-one of the 200 collieries which employed more than fifty men. Yet, as late as 1951, four-fifths of households in the Rhondda, double the figure for England and Wales as a whole, lacked the exclusive use of a fixed bath.

During the depression years women were active in various social and political campaigns. In 1935, thousands of women took part in protests to demand an end to the means test. They were at the forefront of crusades to fight for social welfare reforms, such as family allowances, improved maternity and child welfare, nursery education and the increased availability of birth-control information. It was the women of south Wales who ensured that the issue of maternal and child mortality was brought to the attention of the public. They participated in the peace movements of these years, and organized fund-raising social events. Women's clubs also emerged, and 260 were recorded in south Wales alone by 1939. Women were no longer the traditional passive observers of earlier times: the Great War of 1914–18 had awakened their expectations; the industrial struggles of the inter-war years had sharpened their organizational skills; and the Second World War was to consolidate and heighten their determination to be active citizens in the post-war world.

Recreation in Wales
The impact of the cinema: In the years after 1896 the commercial exhibition of motion pictures spread rapidly outside Paris, London and New York. The earliest picture shows were held in

music halls and converted shops. Itinerant showmen often exhibited films in temporary booths. One of the most successful and distinguished film-makers was Walter Hagger, of Aberdare, who opened his first Kinema there in 1910. He shot scenes in south Wales and then displayed them at various fairgrounds throughout the area. By 1914 there were twenty-one 'picture theatres' in Cardiff and nineteen in Swansea.

The First World War had effectively scuppered any hopes of a recovery for the British film industry, and the silent cinema of the 1920s was almost entirely a product of Hollywood. Only about 5 per cent of the films seen by British audiences were of home origin. There were glimpses of the miners' disputes in 1921 and 1926 and of the accompanying poverty in newsreels, but the newsreel companies were soon advised to jettison contentious issues and concentrate on future events. It was in the 1930s that Wales made its film debut. Although an unofficial but very effective code of film censorship prevented film and newsreel companies from recording the political activities of working-class communities, creative film-makers began to focus on Welsh miners as the epitome of the long-suffering working-classes. Sponsored documentaries were made in south Wales, but they made no reference to the politics of the area nor to the miners' unions. They depicted many of the problems associated with unemployment and permitted the unemployed to address the cameras. One of the best-known Welsh documentaries was *Today We Live*, produced in 1937. By the end of the 1930s American companies established studios in London and began to produce films with a social realism theme. In 1938, MGM made *The Citadel*, which depicted an ambitious young doctor valiantly combating the evils of private medicine. *Proud Valley* was another film set entirely in a Welsh pit village, in which Paul Robeson was recruited to sing the solo bass part in a local choir's performance of *Elijah*. He also joined in a protest to save the pit from closure and helped save lives in a pit disaster.

Cinema attendance was a vital source of entertainment and recreation for the generations who strove to forget the horrors of the Great War and the gloomy shadows of industrial depression. The cinema was a focal point in the relatively flourishing town of Swansea, where the Plaza cinema was opened in February 1931 with 3,000 seats, a lounge, two cafés, six shops, an organ and lavish interior designs. Two months after opening, 100,000 had been admitted and prices ranged from 2*s*. 4*d*. to 6*d*. By the end of the 1930s, three new cinemas had opened in Swansea, bringing the total to eighteen. Many people seemed to have developed the habit of visiting the cinema two or three times a week, and the youthful Dylan Thomas was reputed to have been an inveterate film-goer. On occasions, influential figures like the vicar of Swansea and its chief constable would protest that the cinema was dominating the lives of ordinary people.

There were more miners' cinemas in south Wales in the 1930s than in all the other mining regions of Britain combined. In Glamorgan alone there were twenty-five listed in 1940, of which twenty-one were controlled by workmen's committees. 'Cinema-ization' occurred on a significant scale after the establishment in 1920 of the Miners' Welfare Fund, which provided cash for the purchase of projection equipment, seating and various materials. The main reason for the spread of 'cinemaization' was the need to provide financial sources for the emergent miners' institutes. Cwmllynfell Miners' Hall and Institute, which began to operate a cinema in 1935, screened the world heavyweight fight between Tommy Farr and Joe Louis in 1937. Maerdy and Tredegar halls and institutes showed films on Spain in an effort to promote their Spanish Aid initiatives. For a while, the miners' institutes seemed to offer an independent cinema throughout the coalfield. But it proved impossible to challenge the might of the commercial sector, and the miners' cinemas were compelled to base their programmes on American output in the 1930s.

Local communities often reacted forcefully against the perceived cultural and social threat of the American screen. Nonconformist and Welsh-speaking groups protested loudly that Wales was importing foreign and inferior cultures. Many Labour politicians, such as James Griffiths, argued that the miners' halls and institutes should fulfil cultural functions in their community. At Ystradgynlais, the miners' cinema was largely a failure for this reason, and in its first year of business it had sustained a loss of £300. The religious denominations were still able to flex their muscles and influence local communities. The chapels led the campaign against the infiltration of 'alien' culture in their successful battle against the Sunday opening of cinemas. So pervasive was their influence that, as late as 1952, only 8 per cent of cinemas in Wales ran regular Sunday performances, as compared with 97 per cent in London and south-east England. Nonconformity was still a social reality in the 1950s.

Sporting Life

The development of sport acted as an opportunity for self-expression and entertainment, as well as a focus for local and community identity in the early decades of the century. For most Welshmen sporting achievements were a far more meaningful and vigorous representation of identity than the arid arguments of intellectuals. Rugby football soon became the game of the masses and the classes, and a focus for national pride and expression. Rugby's arrival in Wales in the 1870s had pre-dated that of soccer by twenty years. In the Edwardian era, the Welsh reputation for unique skill at rugby was firmly established. Wales had not been beaten at home by any of the home countries since 1899; and England had not won in Wales since 1895. In the golden years between 1900 and 1912 Wales had won the 'Triple Crown' six times. Perhaps no event better symbolized the growing national confidence of the Welsh than their defeat of the All Blacks in December 1905. Before arriving in Wales the All Blacks had destroyed all opposition in England, Scotland and Ireland at club, county and national levels, amassing over 800 points to a mere 27 against. The Welsh victory of December 1905 was viewed as a national achievement.

Throughout the First World War clubs were encouraged to stop playing, and international fixtures were discontinued. At least eleven Welsh rugby international players were slain on the fields of conflict. Rugby slowly re-emerged in the 1918–19 season, but the 1920s were to be the least distinguished in the history of Welsh rugby. From 1920 to 1929 only seventeen of the forty-two games played were won, and twenty-two were lost. From 1923 to 1930 England won every game against Wales, except for a draw in 1926. From 1920 to 1927 Scotland won every game against Wales, except for a draw in 1922. In 1924, Wales played thirty-five different players, including fourteen three-quarters. The Welsh Rugby Union's takings were halved during the despondent 1920s as international crowds dwindled and clubs defaulted. Cross Keys, Ebbw Vale, Pontypool, Blaenavon and Pontypridd sought financial assistance in 1926–7 in the aftermath of the crippling coal strike of 1926. Since joining the constabulary was one route out of the bottomless pool of unemployment, there were more policemen than miners in the Welsh sides of the inter-war years. In 1926, six of the eight Welsh forwards were policemen. Cardiff had, on average, ten policemen in its First XV every year from 1923 to 1939. Tensions spilled on to the field and old scores were often settled in violent matches. In a game in the Swansea Valley one constable was crippled for life; while in the Afan Valley a referee strapped a revolver to his waist.

Throughout the years of depression many rugby clubs were in danger of extinction. By the end of the 1920s Pontypool was on the verge of bankruptcy with an overdraft of £2,000. Penarth Rugby Football Club fell into a £1,000 debt, while rugby at Barry had ceased in 1923. In the inter-war period English clubs actively sought to attract Welsh players with various inducements. Torquay Corporation found employment for a number of Monmouthshire players in the late 1920s. In the 1930s Oxford took in a legion of Welshmen as college servants or car workers. In the 1939 Rugby League Cup Final, half of the players on the field were Welshmen. Professional rugby clubs were bursting at the seams with Welshmen who had moved north in the 1920s and 1930s, among whom were sixty-nine capped Welsh international players.

In south-west Wales, where the industrial picture was not quite as bleak, rugby clubs were more stable. The West Wales League was founded in Swansea in 1929; and Llanelli RFC recorded a profit of £300 in the 1930–1 season. There were signs of some improvement in the early 1930s: in 1931 Wales won the international championship for the first time since 1922; in 1935 Wales defeated the All Blacks; and in 1937 the Welsh team captured the championship. Some historians have seen the revival in rugby fortunes as a symbol of resurgence in Welsh morale during the mid-1930s. Yet, unemployment stood at astronomic levels in many industrial centres, and clubs were still forced to disband: Abercynon closed in 1934 and Taibach in 1937.

Soccer also made rapid progress throughout Wales in the final decades of the nineteenth century. A South Wales Soccer League had been in existence since 1890, and a Mid-Wales League was formed in 1901. Twenty clubs had entered the Welsh cup in

1900, and by 1903–4 there were 63 clubs affiliated to the South Wales and Monmouthshire Football Association. In 1906 there were 74 affiliated clubs, and 262 in 1910. Wales soon had its first professional soccer team in Cardiff City. In the 1920s Welsh soccer enjoyed innumerable successes: Welsh teams won the championship three times; Cardiff City was promoted to Division One in 1921 and reached the cup final in 1925; in 1924 a Welsh XI won the soccer Triple Crown and the championship; and in 1927 Cardiff City won the FA (Football Association) cup. The depression years soon cast long shadows over the soccer field, however, and, following their early triumphs, Cardiff dropped to the Second Division in 1929 and slipped further down in 1931. Most Rhondda soccer clubs were forced to withdraw from southern and Welsh leagues in the 1920s. With two-thirds of Merthyr's workforce unemployed, the club was in the poignant position of having thousands of spectators watching its soccer team train, but with empty terraces on Saturdays because the admission charges were beyond the resources of the unemployed workers.

The inter-war years were promising ones for cricketers. Glamorgan entered the first-class county championship in 1921, and in the 1930s Maurice Turnbull's teams contained players of the calibre of Dai Davies and the legendary opening partners Emrys Davies and Arnold Dyson. In 1937 Emrys Davies reached a personal landmark with 2,000 runs and a hundred wickets in one season. Organized sport had become an important outlet for the depressed regions of Wales, acting as a focus for national sentiment and a safety valve in turbulent times.

Reflections on Crime in Society
In the first two decades of the century the legal profession and police authorities frequently commented on the good conduct of the population. Although there was serious industrial unrest and a high level of non-indictable offences, inhabitants of the city and country were described as increasingly 'well behaved' by 1918. This apparent improvement in public behaviour was attributed to a variety of factors: war conditions encouraged a fall in heavy drinking; higher rates of pay and economic buoyancy reduced the propensity to engage in criminal activity; better education was seen to improve people's conduct; and finally, the churches

were seeking to promote higher levels of moral behaviour and respectability.

From 1921 to the outbreak of war in 1939 the rate of indictable crimes moved on to a higher plateau, with significant increases in 1921, 1926 and 1931–2. Throughout the mid-1920s there were loud protests in Merthyr Tydfil over the looting of coal trucks, burglaries in stores and offices, the theft of goods from shops and the vandalizing of chapels and churches. The theft of coal amounted to a half of recorded indictable crime in the town. Police inspectors met in 1930 to express their concern at the increase in crime. In May 1931, an editorial in the *Western Mail* complained of an 'Epidemic of Juvenile Crime' prevailing in south Wales. Discussions about the causes of the crimes usually reflected the periods in which they were conducted. In the early part of the century commentators saw delinquency as the prerogative of a criminal class. Alcohol was usually blamed as the agent which drew people into a life of misery, deprivation and crime. The initial emphasis was placed on the deleterious effects of alcohol on working-class people, but by the 1920s and 1930s, the focus had moved to the damage inflicted on the young.

After the Great War, as proceedings against drunkards, prostitutes and vagrants fell sharply, it became less fashionable to attribute the evils of society to a criminal class. A novel, though transient theory, was that post-war delinquency could be explained by the psychological problems and social disillusionment of that generation. With the advent of industrial stagnation it was realized that economic circumstances could affect people ordinarily of good character and influence crime rates. There seemed to be no alternative explanation for the exceptionally high crime rates of 1921, 1926 and 1931. As personal consumption fell, so the number of recorded property crimes increased. Although the precise connection between unemployment and crime has not been firmly established, there is little doubt that a large number of those who were arrested in the peak years of 1921 and 1931 were temporarily unemployed. It is important to observe, however, that a preponderance of unemployed people during the 1920s and 1930s never indulged in criminal activity: migration represented an escape route for many; there was a genuine community feeling which abhorred participation in crime; educational and political interests diverted people from wrongdoing; and religion and the chapels were still influential forces in people's lives.

It would seem that the character of the criminal has changed little during the century. Most convicted offenders were young, male and of working-class origin. In the early years of the century, three-quarters of those charged with crimes, and seven-tenths of the inmates of Cardiff and Swansea gaols were male. By 1936, only 5 per cent of those proceeded against for indictable and non-indictable offences in the county of Glamorgan were female. The overwhelming impression is that most of those people taken into custody in the early years of the century were from the working classes. Yet, it is also important to remember that convicted criminals have always been a minority of the population, and most have appeared before the courts only once. Well over half the defendants at all the Welsh courts in 1900 had no criminal record.

Statistical evidence suggests that recorded offences were much higher in 1900 than is usually thought, and fell sharply until 1939.

Table 2.4 Reported indictable offences against the person, and persons proceeded against for non-indictable assaults, 1900–1938

Year	Ratio of population to one case
1910	281
1913	524
1923	580
1938	1269

The experience of crime depended on a number of factors: geographical location; the character of housing; and social class. In 1901, it was said that settled rural communities were the most peaceful areas of Glamorgan. In industrial and urban society conflict could often erupt in public houses, in the workplace and in streets. The seafront at Aberavon was described in 1907 as an 'exceedingly rough place'. There were regular instances of public disorder in the years prior to 1914. During the Greenhill riots of 1905 in Swansea, windows were smashed, homes destroyed and people treated in hospital for wounds. In Cardiff there was almost incessant fighting in the dockland communities between resident Greeks and Arabs, and between Scandinavian, Chinese and British seamen. As we shall see in later sections (see pp.72–7), south Wales experienced some of the worst industrial troubles in Britain between 1910 and 1926. There was a succession of small, bitter strikes in Glamorgan during the first decade of the century, involving such industries as the nickel works at Clydach and collieries at Ynystawe. During the Cambrian strike of 1910–11 miners and their families closed virtually every pit in the Rhondda. In 1920, there were further clashes at Tonypandy, but the General Strike of 1926 proved to be more peaceful than the Home Office or the redoubtable chief constable, Lionel Lindsay, had predicted.

There were coalfield strikes in the mid-1930s, but serious industrial disturbances were rare. From 1929 to 1936 Chief Constable Lindsay was convinced that 'communists and trouble-makers' were responsible for a wave of demonstrations, and the alleged leaders were arrested in large numbers. In the spring of 1935, there were disturbances across south Wales, sparked by police interference with marches and changes in the payment of relief. There followed protests against the British Union of Fascists and the proposed visit of Sir Oswald Mosley to the Rhondda. The government was alarmed by these manifestations of unrest and extended the powers of the police through the Public Order Act of 1936.

In conclusion, it does seem that the amount of serious violence and disorder has declined over the century. The challenge of industrial and political disturbances was greatest in the first decades, when protest had a distinctly political character. Despite the claims of the increase in violence since the Second World War, there has been little to compare with that of the Edwardian era.

SUGGESTED READING

D. Beddoe, *Women in Britain Between the Wars* (London, 1988).

D. Berry, *Wales and Cinema* (Cardiff, 1994).

Trevor Herbert and Gareth Elwyn Jones (eds.), *Wales Between the Wars* (Cardiff, 1988).

Philip Jenkins, *A History of Modern Wales 1536 –1990* (London, 1992).

D. J. V. Jones, *Crime and Policing in the Twentieth Century* (Cardiff, 1996).

Gareth Elwyn Jones, *Modern Wales: A Concise History* (Cambridge, 1994).

Kenneth O. Morgan, *Rebirth of a Nation: Wales, 1880–1980* (Oxford, 1981).

R. Pope, *Building Jerusalem* (Cardiff, 1998).

D. Smith and Gareth Williams, *Fields of Praise* (Cardiff, 1980).

Carol White and Sian Rhiannon Williams (eds.), *Struggle or Starve: Women's Lives in the South Wales Valleys between the Two World Wars* (Cardiff, 1998).

3. Political Transformation

The Edwardian Years

Liberal Wales

AT THE general election of January 1906 the Liberals, under Campbell-Bannerman, presented the electorate with a traditional, and almost sacred, amalgam of themes. Free trade, church schools, temperance and the rights of labour were debated on Liberal platforms throughout the land. The election produced a landslide Liberal victory, and the Conservatives were decimated in the four corners of the Principality. The Liberals captured all thirty-four seats, except for the second seat in Merthyr Tydfil, which was gained by Keir Hardie for the Labour Representation Committee. By-elections at East Denbighshire in 1906 and at Pembrokeshire in 1908 merely confirmed the strength of Liberal domination during these halcyon years. In the two general elections of January and December 1910, when the Liberal Party nationally was deprived of much of its vitality, the Liberal strength in Wales remained largely undiminished. In January 1910, two marginal border seats, Denbigh District and Radnorshire, were lost to the Unionists. In December 1910, Radnorshire was regained, but Denbigh District and Montgomery District, another marginal border seat, were won by the Unionists. The port of Cardiff also fell into the hands of the younger son of the Marquess of Bute. Apart from these interruptions, the pattern of Liberal domination remained largely undisturbed.

The Welsh Liberal scene was dominated by coteries of small, locally based, and self-perpetuating middle-class élites who linked the world of municipal government, local politics, the chapels and social leadership in an intimate, democratic community. The personnel of local Liberal associations in places such as Cardiganshire and Merthyr Tydfil was basically similar.

Shopkeepers, merchants, solicitors, doctors, journalists, Nonconformist ministers and industrial owners formed the backbone of
the ruling élite. In the southern constituencies, there were
working men active in some local associations. The new county
councils, which had been created in 1888, provided opportunities
for the new Nonconformist middle classes to express their views
and exercise their burgeoning powers. In the local government
elections of 1889, 175 Liberal councillors were returned in north
Wales out of a total of 260, while in south Wales, there were 215
out of 330. The landed gentry lost their control of local politics
and virtually disappeared in a gigantic social revolution.

In the years after 1906 it was the social, municipal and religious
issues which predominated in Liberal discussions. It seemed
inevitable that the new Liberal government of 1906 would attempt
to settle the education question, which had simmered since
Balfour's Act of 1902. Birrell introduced a new Education Bill into
the House of Commons in April 1906, the aim of which was to
satisfy Nonconformist expectations and ensure that all public
elementary schools were controlled by the local authority. The Bill
also proposed a national council for Wales, with representatives
from all of the new councils. Although the Bill did proceed through
the Commons, it was savaged by the Lords and returned to the
Lower House in a much distorted form. It was eventually
withdrawn and the government introduced a new scheme for a
Welsh department in the Board of Education in February 1907.
Even this modest proposal ignited party hostilities and, after 1906,
the education question gradually receded from the forefront of
Welsh politics. Most local authorities administered Balfour's Act by
1914, and their control of the management and financing of
Church schools was far greater than expected.

Temperance was losing its ability to engender passionate
debate. The failure of the government's licensing bill in the Lords
aroused a measure of protest, while the failure to extend the
Welsh Sunday Closing Act to Monmouthshire met with little
opposition. The land question no longer aroused heated
discussion in Welsh Liberal circles. There had been some
improvement in the countryside since 1900, and the farming
community now concentrated on land as a productive enterprise.

The cause of Church disestablishment, which had tended to
crystallize traditional aspects of the national movement, now

presented a challenge to the Edwardian Liberals. Although the King's Speech made no mention of disestablishment, the incoming government could hardly fail to grasp the nettle. The prime minister, Campbell-Bannerman, proposed a royal commission to inquire into the position of the Church and other religious bodies in Wales. Its ostensible aim was to gather sufficient information to enable the government to prepare a considered measure. Instead, it created the impression that the government was conveniently shelving a controversial issue in favour of more urgent matters. The royal commission, which began its work in October 1906, confirmed the worst suspicions of Nonconformists. Its chairman, Lord Justice Vaughan Williams, excluded evidence brought by Nonconformists, and treated fellow commissioners and Nonconformist witnesses in a peremptory fashion. The Nonconformists criticized the government, with its majority of over 300, for the delay in introducing a disestablishment measure. Throughout 1907, there were mild protests against the government, which Lloyd George could easily quell. In 1909, the new prime minister, Asquith, eventually introduced a Welsh disestablishment bill, clearly designed to placate Welsh Liberal members, but it was not expected to proceed beyond a second reading.

From 1909 to 1912, the People's Budget, the Parliament bill and National Insurance dominated public debate. The subsequent passage of the Parliament Act meant that, within two years, the Lords' veto could be surmounted. The disestablishment controversy was given a fillip with the eventual publication of the report of the royal commission on the Church and other religious bodies. Only two members signed the report without reservation, and five Liberal members appended notes and memoranda casting doubt on the accuracy of the Church figures. The government produced the first version of its disestablishment measure in April 1912. Twice passed by the House of Commons, and twice rejected by the Lords, finally on 19 May 1914, the Welsh Church bill received its third reading in the Commons. There were no constitutional barriers remaining and, in September 1914, the bill was finally passed and given the Royal Assent. As Welsh MPs sang their national anthem in the lobby of the House of Commons, it appeared that Welsh Liberalism had secured a historic victory.

The denouement of Welsh Nonconformist radicalism was acted out in an empty House of Commons and in an atmosphere of anticlimax. The report of the royal commission had shown that Nonconformity was already losing its fervour and that it was weakened by wasteful denominational rivalry. In 1912 Lloyd George had organized great disestablishment meetings at Caernarfon and Swansea, but the popular rallies of the past were now sadly absent. The old enthusiasm for religious equality had waned, and the memory of 1868 conveyed little to a generation brought up in the era of Nonconformist county councils.

A final issue which failed to grasp the political imagination was the Home Rule movement for Wales. Its resurgence was the work of a middle-aged iron manufacturer from Middlesbrough, E. T. John, who had returned to his native county to become Liberal MP for East Denbighshire in December 1910. He joined forces with the experienced journalist, Beriah Gwynfe Evans, and in a series of letters to the press they expounded the need for Welsh self-government as part of a wider framework of imperial devolution. John founded his own Welsh National League, and in March 1914 he introduced a Welsh Home Rule bill in the Commons. It envisaged that a single-chamber Welsh legislature would be established, with ninety members, to govern Welsh domestic affairs. The bill received a formal first reading, but interest soon evaporated as the demands of war took precedence.

During this period of ascendancy, the main ideological concerns of the Liberals, at both national and local levels, were those of social and religious equality and civil libertarianism. For the most part, Welsh Liberals were noticeably silent on industrial and economic issues. Despite the occurrence of industrial conflicts, such as the south Wales miners' stoppage of 1898 and the strikes of Penrhyn quarrymen in north Wales from 1896 to 1903, Welsh politicians adhered to the old themes and 'New Liberalism' hardly penetrated the hallowed portals of Welsh Liberal associations. There was virtually no discussion of new liberal ideas and few references to social or economic issues in leading periodicals such as *Y Traethodydd*.

This failure to engage with social and economic matters was an important factor in the eventual collapse of Welsh Liberalism. In the years before 1914, however, Liberalism continued to espouse the old causes and seemed secure enough to withstand the twin challenges of new social thought and the Labour movement. With the outbreak of war the overwhelming majority of Welsh people initially embraced the common cause and eschewed political disagreements. By the end of 1914, *Welsh Outlook* announced that the task of training 50,000 men for the Welsh Army Corps was making great progress. Over 280,000 Welshmen eventually served in the armed forces, and the proportion of the male population enlisting outstripped that for either England or Scotland. A new Welsh Division was created in the army in November 1914, and a new brigade of Welsh Guards in 1915. The appointment of Lloyd George as Minister of Munitions in May 1915, and as Secretary of War in July 1916, intensified the patriotic fervour which seemed to pervade the land. In north Wales, the most spontaneous and unquestioning support for government policies in Gwynedd emanated from the leading members of its English-speaking community. The contributions of the Welsh-speaking members of the pro-war coalition were just as significant. The latter represented the cohesive Liberal–Nonconformist élite whose influence permeated most spheres of Gwynedd life. Nonconformist luminaries made eloquent contributions to the war effort in recruitment meetings. The local press also played an immeasurable role in supporting British intervention. The English-medium press in Gwynedd wholeheartedly endorsed the war effort, while the Welsh-language newspapers reflected subtle divisions of opinion. All the important newspapers, such as *Yr Herald Cymraeg*, *Y Genedl Gymreig*, *Y Cymro* and *Baner ac Amserau Cymru*, were supportive in north Wales.

The introduction of military conscription in 1916 proved contentious and divisive. Three Liberal MPs voted against the first reading of the Conscription bill on 6 January 1916, and five others originally abstained. From 1916 onwards, it became clear that endorsement of the government was gradually dissipating. Many Liberals came to see conscription as the negation of the libertarian tenets which had underpinned their political creed. As early as 1915, Liberal critics of the war had begun to voice their opposition to belligerent passions. A Peace Society was formed at Bangor in the early part of 1915. The growing publicity given to the plight of conscientious objectors aroused concern in many Liberal and Nonconformist quarters. George Maitland Lloyd

Davies was one saintly figure who suffered lengthy periods of imprisonment for his Christian beliefs. Even in the labour movement, pro-war enthusiasm among miners and industrial workers, who had enjoyed higher wages and improved social conditions, began to fracture as the consequences of war and the control of labour became more apparent. An official strike by Welsh miners in July 1915 for a new standard wage rate heralded a new spirit of opposition. In 1916–17 industrial and political protests merged to campaign for improved working conditions and against the endless fighting. In 1917, the spread of revolution in Russia added a new socialist dimension to anti-war sentiments. In north Wales the conditions of war eroded the traditional bases of Liberal support. Party supporters at all levels differed over such issues as the declaration of war, the introduction of conscription and Lloyd George's coalition government. Liberal support was further undermined by the impact of war on local party structures. An electoral truce and an emphasis on a bipartisan approach to the war ensured that branch and constituency meetings were never convened, with the result that by May 1918 the Liberal Party's structure at constituency level had virtually disintegrated in north Wales. The Great War had produced a seismic crisis of confidence in Welsh Liberalism and undermined the certainties of the older radicalism.

Industrial Unrest

The six-months' coal stoppage of 1898 had inaugurated a new era of industrial relations in south Wales. The old centripetal values of Welshness, Nonconformity, class harmony and communal identification were fractured by the new, centrifugal forces of class struggle and industrial conflict. The 'new unions' had appealed to unskilled workers in south Wales after 1889 and established branches among dockers and general labourers at Swansea, Cardiff and Newport. Trades councils had been set up there and in Merthyr, Aberdare, Briton Ferry and elsewhere. By 1900, the Merthyr and Dowlais trades council claimed to represent 7,000 workers, and in April 1902, the Cardiff trades council had 4,000 members. These new unions and trades councils surmounted early difficulties and survived into the new century to spearhead a new working-class militancy. The trades councils of Merthyr and Aberdare invited Keir Hardie to become the Labour parliamentary candidate for Merthyr Boroughs in 1900. It was also in south Wales that the struggle for the unions' defence of the right to strike without financial penalty took place in the Taff Vale Railway strike of 1900. In north Wales, the Welsh-speaking quarrying districts had become the focus of industrial struggles from 1896 to 1906; but the impoverished quarrymen, by failing to secure recognition for their union, endured a crushing defeat.

From 1908 to 1914 a new wave of industrial conflict and unrest presented a far greater threat to Liberal hegemony in the Edwardian period. The miners signalled their rejection of a Liberal past by voting in 1908 to affiliate to the Labour Party. This was reaffirmed in 1913, when the political levy by trade unions to support the Labour Party was endorsed in a national ballot. The implementation of the Mines' Eight Hours bill in 1909 fuelled the rising level of industrial tension, especially over the miners' demand for a minimum wage. Rationalization in the coal industry and the development of large combines imposed further strain on the coal-mining communities. Also, there were devastating human tragedies during this period, such as the Senghennydd mining disaster of 1913, which claimed the lives of 439 men.

Historians have often referred to the years 1910–13 in Wales as a period of great unrest. On 7 June 1911, 100 workers in a brick factory at Swansea struck in protest at being asked to produce bricks which were thicker than previously agreed. On 11 June 1911, several thousand dock workers and seamen in Swansea and other south Wales ports struck unofficially. In August 1911, 145,000 railwaymen came out on strike for higher pay and union recognition. On 6 September, 500 fuel workers in Swansea started a one-month strike. The Cambrian Combine dispute of 1910 heralded the emergence of south Wales as a storm centre of industrial militancy and unrest. There was a bitter dispute over the price list to be attached to the Upper Five-Foot Seam at the Naval Colliery, when the men refused to accept the price list of 1s. 9d. per ton, plus 1d. per ton of hard stone. On 1 September 1910, 900 men were locked out at the Ely colliery, and by October, all the 12,000 miners in the Cambrian collieries had come out on strike. By the start of November, there were

30,000 men on strike throughout the coalfield. The strike lasted longer than any major strike in living memory, and it led to large-scale and persistent violence. On November 7–8, there was rioting in Tonypandy around the Cambrian pits, in the course of which one man died from a fractured skull, and extra police were mustered under the personal command of the redoubtable chief constable, Captain Lionel Lindsay. On Tuesday, 8 November, a riot erupted and sixty-three shops were destroyed in Tonypandy. Although the crowd was not politically organized, it seemed to share special grievances and communal assumptions about the direction and legitimacy of its actions. The shops were not looted for food, but the targets were symbolic of the crowd's discontent. Winston Churchill, the Home Secretary, after an initially cautious approach, ordered the cavalry into the district. For several weeks detachments of troops patrolled the Rhondda, and on 22 November it was reported that infantry with fixed bayonets had been used at Penygraig after police had been stoned by the local population. Churchill was later castigated for sending troops to Tonypandy in the turbulent year of 1910. During a national railwaymen's strike in the summer of 1911, troops shot and killed two railway workers during the strike at Llanelli. Within twenty-four hours of the Llanelli riots, disturbances were reported in several other parts of the coalfield, with riots at Tredegar, Ebbw Vale, Rhymney, Brynmawr and Bargoed.

The years 1910–13 did witness a significant increase in the level and intensity of strikes throughout the UK. From 1889 to 1913, industrial unrest sprouted in Wales where the numbers of workers participating in industrial disputes and the numbers of strikes were often higher than in other parts of the UK. Occasionally Welsh disputes accounted for the lion's share of British disputes. The miners, who numbered about a third of the labour force, were responsible for half of the total number of strikes in the years before 1901, and for three-quarters of those between 1901 and 1913. At least 80 per cent of all those on strike were miners, and over 80 per cent of all days lost in disputes were in the mining industry. Disputes in the tinplate industry peaked in the period 1899–1905 and subsided thereafter. In north Wales, the quarrymen were largely quiescent after 1906. Miners were eight times more likely to strike than tinplate workers, and a number of reasons were responsible for this: geological factors in south Wales and falling rates of productivity made conditions more difficult; miners reacted angrily to wage reductions; and after 1908, industrial relations in the mining industry concentrated on the operations of the Eight Hours Act and on demands for a minimum wage.

Industrial unrest displayed a pattern of regional variations within the coalfield. While strikes were far more likely to occur in the Glamorgan coalfield than in Monmouthshire, within the Glamorgan coalfield itself the variations were even more marked. In certain registration districts there were substantial increases in the number of workers on strike in the period 1900–13: a 386 per cent increase was recorded in the Rhondda; a 531 per cent increase in the Swansea Valley; 535 per cent in Aberdare; 969 per cent in Pontypridd; and a rise of 1,042 per cent in Maesteg. All the urban areas along the coast from Llanelli to Cardiff experienced a decline, or only insubstantial rises, in the numbers of workers on strike. Recent research seems to confirm that strikes increased significantly among the miners of mid-Glamorgan in these years after 1901.

What explains this pattern of industrial disturbances? Many coalfield communities experienced population increases which were far in excess of the Welsh average of 14.5 per cent in the period 1881–1911. The population of Mountain Ash grew by 310 per cent, Ogmore's by 294 per cent and Bedwellty's by 760 per cent. The population of the Rhondda, which had grown from 3,000 in 1861 to 152,000 in 1911, represented an astonishing augmentation of 5,000 per cent. Yet, not all the coal communities shared in this demographical upsurge; some, such as Aberdare, had high levels of strike activity and low rates of population growth. The mining industry in Aberdare was dominated by one mining combine, the Powell-Duffryn Company, and many other areas with a high incidence of strikes were also controlled by the large combines.

The vast majority of strikes occurred over wages and working conditions. After 1898, workers responded vigorously to changes in their material conditions and working practices, and there was a clear and gradual increase in the proportion of strikes which could be attributed directly to trade-union activity. The early years of the century saw the emergence of a radical critique of union leadership and of the capitalist system. Welsh miners were in the forefront of the Ruskin College strike of March–April 1909. Noah Ablett and Ted Gill argued that workers' education was an essential part of the class struggle and offered challenges to the existing economic and social system. The college rebels eventually set up a new Labour college in north Oxford, which later moved to Regent's Park in London under the name of the Central Labour College. Its impact on the coal-mining communities was considerable, as it produced a cohort of militant union members who were to spearhead developments in trade unionism and Labour politics in the post-Edwardian period.

In January 1909, shortly before the Ruskin strike, Ablett and others had formed the so-called Plebs League, centred on the Rhondda, and committed to class war and industrial action. The Plebs League at Tonypandy became the cynosure of revolutionary syndicalism in the Valleys. It produced a new journal, *Plebs*, and in August 1909 the League held its first 'annual meeting'. The Plebs League was linked to the growth of the Central Labour College movement in south Wales: tutorial classes mushroomed throughout the Valleys and Ablett, Will Mainwaring, Will Hay and others, taught Marxist theory and economics to enthusiastic working-class groups. A whole network of self-educated working-class groups sprouted throughout the Rhondda Valleys, where Arthur Horner, Frank Hodges, Ablett and many other nascent union leaders gravitated towards these educational and political nuclei.

Plebs League members were also prominent in discussions to establish a movement which would be distinct from the formally elected leadership of the South Wales Miners' Federation. In March 1911, an Unofficial Reform Committee, based in Tonypandy, began to prepare a reform programme distinct from that of the SWMF. In November 1912, an open debate took place in Trealaw among miners' leaders on the merits of nationalization or workers' control of the mining industry. The crowd which gathered at the Judges Hall in Trealaw had come to hear two Abertillery miners' leaders, George Barker and Edward Gill, speak in favour of the nationalization of the mines. Noah Ablett, who also participated in the debate, was one of the authors of *The Miners' Next Step*, a pamphlet published early in 1912 by the Unofficial Reform Committee. It rejected the official policy of state ownership of the mines and called for workers' control of the mining industry. This historic document was a classic declaration of syndicalism, with an emphasis on trade unionism, industrial action, industrial democracy and communal ownership for the benefit of the workers. *The Miners' Next Step* was designed to expose what the young militants of the Unofficial Reform Committee saw as the failure of trade-union conciliation in the face of continuing onslaught on the wages and working conditions of the miners. *The Miners' Next Step* was a remarkable document, and it circulated widely. By 1914, however, it was clear that the Plebs League, the Central Labour College movement and the Unofficial Reform Committee had made little impression outside the Rhondda and Aberdare Valleys. Lib–Labism and more orthodox forms of organization predominated in working-class districts. Liberal and Nonconformist values retained their appeal and continued to unite working-class and middle-class communities.

The Rise of Labour

The first phase in the rise of Labour had stretched from 1880 to about 1906. In 1892, the Social Democratic Federation had organized a mission to the western coalfield, and reached Llanelli in December. In 1893, Neath, Landore and Morriston had been targeted by the Federation, and the Treorchy Male Choir had entertained meetings on the Swansea sands. Although the Federation boasted of branches in Cardiff, Pontypridd and Barry in 1897, there were few real successes in Wales. A branch of the Fabian Society was formed in 1886 at Aberystwyth University, but the total Fabian membership in Wales was only twenty-three after twenty years of campaigning. Trade unions made some progress in the period: as we have already seen, new unions had appeared in Cardiff, Newport and Swansea in 1889, and unions were emerging in key industries, such as mining and tinplate.

The Independent Labour Party was formed in February 1893, and after several months there were only eleven contact addresses in Cardiff and one in Newport. Early in March 1894, Keir Hardie launched the ILP in south Wales. A Welsh National Administrative Council was formed, with representatives from Swansea, Neath, Cwmavon, Morriston and Cardiff. A South Wales Federation was established and 20,000 copies of the new constitution were printed. Keir Hardie continued to visit the area and addressed mass meetings as far west as Llanelli. Thereafter, the fortunes of the ILP slumped until the miners' lockout of 1898 brought a campaigner from the north of England to try to organize the ILP in Wales. Willie Wright's inspiration stimulated the formation of thirty-two branches during the summer of 1898. Once he returned to England, enthusiasm waned and the number of branches dropped to seven by 1900. From 1900 to 1905 the ILP struggled to survive, and the South Wales ILP Federation claimed around thirty-five branches in 1903. By 1904, despite Keir Hardie's historic election victory in Merthyr in September 1900, even the Merthyr branch of the ILP was in a perilous state.

The second phase of growth for the Labour movement extended from 1906 to 1914. In 1906, the miners balloted in favour of affiliation to the Labour Representation Committee and, in south Wales, voted 41,843 in favour, as compared to 31,527 against. This was seen as a personal triumph for Keir Hardie who, in the last two general elections, had been returned for Labour in Merthyr Tydfil. It was also a triumph for the ILP, whose forty-nine branches had campaigned in 1906 throughout the coalfield. The 1906 ballot revealed that the miners and other organized trade unionists were already distancing themselves from professional politicians. The ballot encouraged the ILP to accelerate the pace of its activities. In April 1908, at the sixteenth annual conference in Huddersfield, there were thirty-four Welsh delegates in attendance and reports circulated of eighty-four ILP branches in south Wales, and seven in north Wales. The directory of elected members estimated that the ILP could claim four county councillors, twenty-seven urban district councillors, eighteen town councillors, three rural district councillors, eighteen parish councillors and twenty-nine poor law guardians in south Wales. In 1908, the ILP staged its own south Wales conference and claimed that there were 130 branches in Wales. A Swansea Valley Socialist League had appeared, and it seemed as if the affiliated ILP branches were using virtually every school on every evening for lectures and debates. In Cardiff, it was reported that membership had increased by 200 during the previous year.

The growth of the ILP had appeared to be unstoppable. It had created a presence and structure, but had failed to produce a

challenging and effective political organization. In many areas
the ILP branch was seen as a source of propaganda and an
alternative to the chapel as a venue for local concerts, debates
and meetings. The ILP had not yet established itself as a political
powerhouse, from which the control of local government or the
constituency could be planned. The ILP realized that the trade
unions were the essence of the labour movement and that a
socialist bid for power had to be undertaken from the launch pad
of the trade unions. After 1906 the Aberdare ILP displayed a new
sense of urgency. A market stall was rented for the sale of
literature and, in the autumn, an ILP institute was opened with
its own caretaker. Annual teas were organized, as well as a
Socialist Sunday School. In February 1908, a women's branch
was launched and meetings were often held twice a day. The
Cardiff ILP also rented a literature stall at the Market Gallery
and organized regular Sunday meetings. New branches emerged
at Abercrave in 1907 and Bangor in 1908, with forty and thirty-
two members respectively. The ILP attracted supporters from
among the professional classes, with a constellation of academic
stars joining the ranks of the party. Nonconformist ministers
and congregations gravitated towards Labour: the Revd Silyn
Roberts, Blaenau Ffestiniog, was a Methodist; and the Revd
T. E. Nicholas, Glais, a Congregationalist.

Changes within the trade unions contributed to the Labour
breakthrough after 1906. The decision of the law courts in the
Taff Vale judgement of 1902, allowing trade unions to be sued
for damages as a result of strikes, concentrated the minds of the
unions wonderfully. The Osborne case of 1908, which had led to
the ruling that trade unions were not empowered to give money
to the Labour Party, underlined the political importance of trade
unions. In the period 1906–14 the two principal sectional unions
in Wales, the North Wales Quarrymen's Union and the South
Wales Miners' Federation, reflected the burgeoning ideological
conflict between orthodox Liberalism and emergent Socialism.
Based in a predominantly Welsh-speaking Nonconformist community, the NWQU was resolutely opposed to the project of
affiliation to the Labour Party, and it was some time before the
old Liberal contingent was undermined by the younger generation of political activists. It was the recovery and regeneration of
these general unions which provided a fresh impetus for the

Labour movement. Between 1910 and 1914, a surge of union activity swept across the waterfront and industrialized towns. South Wales soon became a stronghold of the Dock, Wharf, Riverside and General Labourers' Union, with 13,000 members in 1911. The Union of Gasworkers and General Labourers and the Workers' Union increased their respective membership rolls. The Amalgamated Society of Railway Servants had a chain of branches from the Severn Tunnel to Neyland in Pembrokeshire. The newly formed National Union of Railwaymen claimed eighty-two branches and over 17,000 members in 1914. It was reported that there were 3,000 members of the NUR in north Wales. Even in rural areas, where resentments and tensions were usually well concealed, there were ominous signs of defiance. Farm servants at Trapp, near Llandeilo, in 1912 threatened to down tools if their demands for shorter hours and better conditions were not met. Murmurs of discontent were heard among the agricultural labourers of Anglesey. At a conference in Llangefni in March 1909, Undeb Gweithwyr Môn was formally launched and, by January 1910, six branches had emerged. By November 1914, it was reported that there were 250,000 trade-union members in south Wales – a formidable base from which to launch a Labour movement.

Another indication of increasing Labour unity after 1906 was the emergence of the trades-councils movement and its strong links to the trade-union movement. In many parts of Wales the most effective agency for political trade unionism was the trades council, a hybrid body consisting of teachers, local government officers, dockers and diverse other groups. Two important trades councils had emerged in Wales in the early days: the Swansea Trades Council was formed in 1873, and Cardiff followed soon after. By 1914, there were at least thirty-three trades councils in existence, twenty-three of which were in Glamorgan and Monmouthshire. Trades councils enabled trade unionists to exert an influence on matters beyond their immediate workplace. Also, they sought to undertake the promotion of unionism among unskilled workers. After 1900, councils emerged in Llanelli (1900), Wrexham (1902), Bangor (1912), Pembroke Dock (1912), North Cardiganshire (1912), Caernarfonshire (1912), Holyhead (1913) and Colwyn Bay (1914). From 1900 onwards the socialists endeavoured to capture the trades councils. Swansea Trades

Council was the first in Britain to affiliate to the new Labour Representation Committee. Cardiff followed in 1908, as did Llanelli, Holyhead and Colwyn Bay. The trades councils provided a wide local network, a cross-section of local opinion and an ideal organizational infrastructure. Caernarfonshire Trades Council on which over 75 per cent of the county's trade unionists were represented, consisted in 1912 of sixty delegates representing thirty-five organizations, including seven ILP branches and one co-operative society.

The next decisive step in the emergence of the Labour movement came with the merger of trades councils, unions and local socialist societies into a Labour Association. The model for south Wales was Swansea, where a well-organized trade-union movement set up a Labour Association in 1906. Similar bodies sprouted in Llanelli, Wrexham, Newport and other urban centres. In many towns the trades council was the only effective forum for socialists. In the mining valleys, ILP branches, miners' lodges, union branches and trades councils often jockeyed for positions of power and scuppered initial attempts at unity: Lib–Lab representatives encouraged these divisive practices in order to prevent the rise of constituency Labour parties.

In the cockpit of industrial discontent and militancy, there was no Rhondda-wide Labour Party until 1911. The responsibilities of the nascent political Labour movement were unequally divided between the Miners' Federation, the Trades and Labour Councils, and the socialist societies and groups. Rhondda's trades councils acted as electoral organizations, propagandist bodies and centres for trade-union co-operation and community concern. By 1910, the Labour movement was on the verge of mounting a serious challenge to the Liberals on Rhondda District Council. Such a challenge had an organizational depth and independence based on the commitment of the SWMF, five trades and labour councils, and eleven ILP branches. Although middle-class Liberals were dominant at all levels of Rhondda society from the 1880s to 1910, and their share of Rhondda local-government seats never fell below three-quarters, independent working-class politics had evolved outside the Liberal fold over this period. It was after the Tonypandy riots and the Cambrian Combine strike that the Liberal edifice collapsed in the Rhondda Valleys. The riots spotlighted the whole of

Rhondda society and fractured the Edwardian illusion of a Liberal consensus. In October 1911, the Rhondda Labour Party was formally launched, but the growth of the Labour Party to a position of local hegemony had already taken place. The organizational structures of the SWMF, the Trades and Labour Councils, and the ILP had nurtured and fuelled this growth over the decades.

Institutional developments had produced working-class leaders in the industrial communities of south Wales. As working-class representatives had become active in local government, the extensive local government framework, which had covered south Wales since the late 1880s, had created opportunities for such representatives. The County Councils Act of 1888, the Local Government Act of 1894 and the reorganization of the Board of Guardians had inaugurated a new era of local-government politics throughout the Principality. As early as 1908, a complaint was tabled at the annual general meeting of the Pontardawe Board of Guardians and District Council that the Labour representatives were determining appointments to the chair and committees in accordance with a plan arranged at a caucus meeting. The first Labour council chairman, David James, JP, epitomized this rising generation of Labour politicians. He participated in the co-operative movement and the ILP, he functioned as an active trade unionist, he sat on the local Board of Guardians and on numerous local government committees, he participated in friendly societies and he served Alltwen Congregational chapel as leader of a burgeoning church orchestra. The growth of trade-union membership in south Wales from the 1890s to 1914 was accompanied by an expansion in the density of trade-union organization. Professional trade unions brought a new career structure at branch and district level. The respected local official could become a checkweigher, and then a miners' agent. They were full-time officials and considered as the voice of Labour in their particular districts.

Labour's domination of south Wales was achieved gradually and in a far from unilinear or uniform manner. As new mining settlements were established in the coalfield after 1880, the process of community formation and community campaigning was led by the young, radical miners who moved into these areas. Pockets of support, in which Labour made steady progress in local government as the voice of these new community values and needs, were established. Even the archetypal 'Lib–Lab' MP, William Abraham ('Mabon'), member for Rhondda from 1885 to 1918 and Rhondda West from 1918 to 1920, had sensed the emerging 'rights of labour' and expressed 'Labourist' concerns in the language he employed as early as 1885.

It would be wholly misleading, however, to exaggerate the coherence and strength of the Labour movement on the eve of the Great War: the Plebs League had been almost entirely confined to the Rhondda Valleys; the turmoil of 1908–14 had ended with the official union leadership in control of events; even ILP activists such as Hartshorn were opponents of syndicalism and industrial violence; and the ILP was still fragile despite the progress it had made since 1898. The prelude to the general elections of 1910 highlighted the problems in south Wales. In the East Carmarthenshire constituency, the local unions chose their own candidate only to find that other organizations did not approve their choice. In Mid Glamorgan, where a constituency Labour Representation Committee had been established, based on the work of two effective ILP branches and Vernon Harts-horn, the Lib–Labs on the Miners' Executive were reluctant to nominate a miners' candidate against Samuel Evans, a prom-inent Liberal and solicitor. Hartshorn was prevented from fighting two by-elections and the first general election of 1910. He was allowed to enter the electoral fray in a March 1910 by-election after Sir Samuel Evans had vacated the seat. Local Liberals, Nonconformists and business interests inveighed against Hartshorn, arguing that they stood for community and not for sector or clique.

In the January and December 1910 elections, Labour candid-ates failed in almost every instance against Liberal opponents. The Welsh Labour members returned in 1910 were wholly of the 'Lib–Lab' persuasion, and almost all of them committed to Welsh national and Nonconformist causes. In the pre-war period, the Liberals were often the aggressive partners in the Labour–Liberal association. Liberal MPs like Clement Edwards and W. F. Phillips launched an anti-socialist crusade in the mining Valleys. A new journal, *Y Gwerinwr*, published in 1912, attacked socialism with gusto and tried to represent all Labour men as Marxists. It was Labour rather than the Liberals that often played a defensive role in industrial south Wales in the immediate pre-war years. The industrial militancy and disturbances of the 1910–14 period seemed to have an adverse effect on the Labour Party, and it was Labour which had to persuade colliers and railwaymen of the merits of gradual, constitutional action. The appeal of Lib–Labism, Nonconformity and Welshness was still strong in the mining Valleys. Between 1910 and 1912 it became difficult to sustain any meaningful party political propaganda. The Great Unrest may well have interrupted socialist propaganda, but it completed the argument for a Labour Party. By 1912, *Llais Llafur*, a Labour paper in Ystalyfera, believed that the local government election results had made heartening reading, with Labour gains in many areas. In May 1912, the ILP held its national conference in Merthyr, attended by seventy-three delegates from fifty-eight Welsh branches, and seats were captured on local and county councils. Even so, when in August 1913 a Labour conference was held in Cardiff, Ramsay MacDonald and Keir Hardie urged the need for organization.

The new Trade Union Act of 1913 regularized and sanctioned political activity, and the South Wales Miners' Federation took advantage of this new dispensation by determining that all future elections fought by miners' candidates would be on 'Labour lines'. The miners were committed to creating Labour parties, and by 1914 the SWMF was spending an increasing amount of time dealing with the local Labour parties. ILP leaders in Caernarfonshire in 1912 established a Labour Council for the county, which held its first conference at Caernarfon in December of that year. By 1913, the North Wales Quarrymen's Union had affiliated to the Labour Council which, in the following year, claimed to represent over 6,000 members in the county. It had two town councillors, seven district councillors and forty parish councillors in Gwynedd. Such was the success of the Caernarfonshire council that it was decided to form a political organization for the whole of north Wales, the North Wales Labour Council, which met in April 1915. It was already possible to detect the reality of a Labour Party presence in many parts of Wales by 1914.

From 1910 to 1914 Labour had made substantial progress throughout industrial Wales. On the threshold of the First World

War the foundations for Labour's post-war advances had been laid: the Labour movement was organizationally prepared and its infrastructure secure. The war brought massive changes to all areas of Welsh life. The original response of most Welsh workers' leaders in the industrial regions had been to support the war effort. Charles Stanton, miners' agent of Aberdare and a leading militant during the Cambrian stoppage, became a recruiting agent. Ted Gill of the Plebs League was a strong supporter of the war. The ILP newspaper, *Llais Llafur*, made an editorial volte-face and wholeheartedly endorsed the patriotic call. Following Keir Hardie's death in 1915, patriotic fever pervaded the election battle at the Merthyr Boroughs in November 1915. Prominent Labour leaders in the Rhondda, including Mabon, appeared on recruiting platforms. Mabon served as president, and T. I. Maerdy Jones as secretary, of the Rhondda Parliamentary Committee working to raise funds for troops and equipment.

The First World War, however, introduced a totally new phase in political and industrial relations. The Labour Party gained in strength, and one key factor in the process was the expansion of the trade unions, which more than doubled in membership from 1914 to 1920. In 1917, the National Union of Railwaymen had 123 branches and 28,628 members in Wales, mainly in the south. The Dockers' Union had over 8,000 members, and the National Union of General Workers 5,000, while the South Wales Miners' Federation, with 150,000 members in 1913, was the most politicized union in Wales. Since 1914 trade unions in south Wales had coalesced under the title of the South Wales Federation of Labour. In the countryside, class relations were sinking to a new low as rural society underwent a momentous transformation. A number of factors contributed to the growing feeling of restlessness: the custom of yearly hirings came to be regarded as a means of holding labourers in bondage; accommodation in unhealthy lofts was a long-standing grievance; the system of tied cottages, which bound the majority of married labourers to the service of an employer, was widely detested; the incidence of tuberculosis in counties such as Cardiganshire and Pembrokeshire was a scandal; the long hours of work – thirteen to sixteen hours a day at haytime and harvest – were a source of grievance; and the relatively low rates of pay at a time of increasing food prices, exacerbated a combustible situation. The

National Union of Railwaymen had already taken an interest in the fate of agricultural workers and inspired local groups to set up trades councils in Milford Haven in 1916 and Fishguard in 1917. From the summer of 1917 onwards scattered revolts erupted in parts of rural Wales. At scores of meetings there was the declared intention of liberating labourers from the evils of poverty and exploitation. Several branches of the National Agricultural Labourers' and Rural Workers' Union were set up in Monmouthshire by the end of 1917; and in Pembrokeshire, and south Cardiganshire, the NALRWU intensified its activities. In Cardiganshire, Nonconformist ministers put on the mantle of leadership and displayed enormous enthusiasm for the plight of the agricultural labourers, with the Revd T. E. Nicholas (Niclas y Glais) in the vanguard of this populist movement. The year 1917 proved significant in the history of the agricultural labourers, as the NALRWU was catapulted into the sphere of industrial relations. Nationwide, it expanded its branches from 249 in 1916 to 402 in 1917, and 1,537 in 1918, as membership soared from 3,676 in 1916 to 40,855 in 1918. In Wales, the NALRWU claimed twenty-nine branches in 1918.

The expansion of trade unionism was of primary importance in the growth of the Labour Party during the war years. Other factors which accounted for the increasing strength of Labour were: the party constitution of 1918 gave a new organizational base in the constituencies; the ideological fervour of the Russian revolutions buttressed Labour's appeal; the Liberals suffered enormous strains in organization and morale during the war, and many Liberal idealists were forced into political isolation or exile; the schism between Asquith and Lloyd George intensified divisions and demoralized Welsh Liberals; and there was the eventual impact of franchise changes and the redistribution of parliamentary seats. The total Welsh electorate increased from 415,786 in January 1910 to 1,018,627 in October 1922. This represented a massive national rise of 145 per cent. Within individual constituencies the augmentation was even more striking, for example, in Carmarthenshire, the electorate grew by 198 per cent in the same period, while in Llanelli the recorded percentage change was 257. The enfranchisement of substantial sections of the Edwardian working classes in 1918 was a fillip to Labour's electoral prospects. The figures in table 3.1 reveal the impact of this process in East Carmarthenshire and Llanelli for the period 1910–23:

Table 3.1

| *Increase in votes and the share of the total vote: %* | | | | | | *% change* | | | |
Party	*Dec. 1910*	*1912*	*1918*	*1922*	*1923*	*1910– 1918*	*1912– 1918*	*1912– 1922*	*1912– 1923*
Liberal	5825	6082	16344	15947	11765	+280	+269	+262	+193
Conservative	2315	3354	–	–	5442	–	–	–	+162
Labour	1176	1089	14409	23213	21063	+1225	+1323	+2131	+1934

The Great War also produced enormous changes in the coalfield, with the mood of industrial relations deteriorating markedly in 1915. There was an official strike in July 1918, declared by the SWMF on behalf of a new and higher standard wage rate. On 20 July, after Lloyd George had made a personal intervention, the miners' and owners' representatives met at the Park Hotel, Cardiff. After a ten days' stoppage, although the miners were granted all their demands, including a standard wage for underground miners, industrial tension showed no sign of abating despite, or possibly because of, these concessions. Miners continued to enlist in the ILP, and the classes of the Central Labour College were rekindled in the Rhondda and Aberdare Valleys. By the end of 1917, there were thirty-one classes active in the Rhondda, with a younger generation of men, such as Horner and Cook, emerging to prominence. The imposition of military conscription in May 1916 was seen as an additional threat to trade-union and civil liberties. The Welsh miners had declared their staunch opposition to military conscription in February 1916, and had only narrowly failed to persuade the Miners' Federation of Great Britain to oppose it. In the summer of 1917, the Lloyd George government revealed its concern over the worsening state of labour relations when it appointed a Commission of Industrial Unrest under the chairmanship of Daniel Lleufer Thomas. The Commission painted a depressing picture of conditions in south Wales, but its recommendations, though well-meaning and wide-ranging, were largely irrelevant in the new arena of class politics. In 1918, the miners responded angrily to soaring rents and food shortages.

With the appearance of the new Labour Party constitution in June 1918, constituency Labour Parties sprouted throughout the coalfield, and in industrial north Wales.

Women's Reform Movements

A number of factors proved conducive to the development of women's political organizations in the early years of the century: the Reform Acts of 1867 and 1884 had produced mass party organizations which enabled women to become more closely involved with political activities; expanding educational opportunities, especially after the 1889 Intermediate Education Act, had created a network of intermediate schools and promoted women's status in society; the Liberal Party, which had begun to establish organizations for women in 1890, claimed that there were 9,000 women in the Welsh Union of Women's Liberal Associations by 1895; a host of non-party pressure groups sprang up to promote women's suffrage, with the National Union of Women's Suffrage Societies appearing in 1897, and the Women's Social and Political Union in 1903; finally, the First World War enhanced the position of women, providing opportunities for employment and participation in state institutions.

The first organization for women's suffrage in Wales was established in 1907 at Llandudno, where the presence of a sizeable English middle-class contingent in the seaside town encouraged its development. In 1909, the Women's Social and Political Union disrupted the Welsh National Eisteddfod held in the Albert Hall, London. In July 1908, the Cardiff and District Women's Suffrage Society was formed with the intention of securing equal voting rights for women, and in the same year the WSPU and the NUWSS were active in south-west Wales. Mrs Pankhurst held a number of meetings during a by-election in Pembrokeshire in July of that year. The WSPU campaigned vigorously against the Liberals, believing that the Tories were far more likely to concede their demands. In 1909, delegates from Liverpool imported the cause of women's suffrage into Anglesey. Militants intervened in the 1910 elections by harassing candidates who were perceived to be hostile to the suffragette movement. Lloyd George was a favourite target on several occasions.

Non-militant Women's Suffrage Societies sprang up along the north Wales coast in tourist centres such as Cricieth, Llanfairfechan, Pwllheli and Porthmadog, and at Llandudno 700 people out of a total electorate of barely 1,500 signed a suffrage petition. In south Wales the non-militant movement spread beyond Cardiff to Bargoed, Kidwelly, Pontypool and the Rhondda. By 1913–4 there were more than 1,200 members in the Cardiff and District society. Militant activities also persisted in the south with violent scenes at Cardiff in November 1909, when three women endeavoured to speak in the heart of the commercial district. Both the militant and non-militant factions of the movement seemed to have suffered from the outbreaks of violence. In 1912, Mrs Gladstone Solomon reacted vigorously to the suffragette activities by establishing a branch of the National League for Opposing Women's Suffrage at Bangor. By 1917, there were seventeen branches throughout Wales. In the immediate pre-war years the NUWSS responded by concentrating on educational and propaganda campaigns in north Wales. Many local branches participated in the march to London in July 1913, as did a sizeable contingent from Cardiff.

The non-militant societies proceeded steadily with their campaigns. The NUWSS organized one of its summer schools at Tal-y-Bont in the Conwy Valley in 1913, while in south Wales there were clear indications of working-class involvement with the societies through the work of the Women's Co-operative Guild. The first guild was established at Tonpentre in 1914, with Elizabeth Andrews, the Labour Party's women's organizer for Wales, as its first secretary. With the outbreak of war in 1914, the various suffragette factions united in support of the war effort and engaged in voluntary work. At Bangor, the propaganda campaign was halted as women immersed themselves in pro-war activities. By 1916, the Cardiff and District Suffrage Society had suspended political action in favour of relief work, which actually helped to bind them together in a common cause for the duration of the hostilities. The impact of war certainly weakened the movement and undermined the initial enthusiasm of many branches. The NUWSS branch at Llangollen disappeared by 1921, while in Cardiff the society proved sufficiently resilient to continue its campaign into the post-war years. On the whole, women in Wales were excluded from waged work in the pre-war years, leading to a lack of economic power which probably restricted the public impact of the suffragette movement and prevented many women from embracing the suffrage issue. Other factors which hindered the movement in the Principality were the powerful and pervasive influences of Liberalism and Nonconformity.

The Years 1918–1945

Industrial Relations

The end of military conflict saw the government embark on a period of reformist zeal. New subsidized council houses, new schools, provision for public health, increased pensions and a comprehensive system for unemployment insurance flowed from the corridors of power. The flood-gates of governmental generosity were soon obstructed by the over-powerful prudence of the treasury: the housing drive was blocked after Addison's resignation in 1921, while much of the rest of social policy was cut down by the Geddes 'Axe' in 1922. In the realm of industrial relations the government sought to maintain the harmony and consensus which had prevailed during the war years. A National Industrial Conference, which was convened in April 1919, purported to embody the industrial harmony of that time.

The veneer of consensus and conciliation was superficial: the National Industrial Conference collapsed in a mood of recrimination; the Sankey Commission failed to persuade the government to accept nationalization of the mines in August 1919; and the breakdown of negotiations produced the miners' lockout from April to July 1921. In Welsh society there were clear indications of a new temper of industrial relations. The Commission on Industrial Unrest in 1917 had graphically illustrated the deteriorating relations between miners and coalowners. A secret report prepared for the government in September 1919 on the extent of 'direct action' movements highlighted the explosive nature of the south Wales district. Clydach, the base of Mond's nickel works, was portrayed as a hotbed of Bolshevism, while the Rhondda was depicted as a powerhouse of extreme syndicalism. After 1918, south Wales miners had continued to enjoy the benefits emanating from government control of the industry and the post-war boom. Employment in the coalfield had risen to a peak of 271,516 in 1920, and average earnings were more than treble those of 1914. The prosperity was, however, short-lived and fragile, with south Wales coal being produced at a loss of 6s. per ton by 1921, and once the coalfield was returned to private control in 1921, average earnings halved. Even the moderate miners' leader, Vernon Hartshorn, said that the miners felt betrayed by the government's decision to decontrol the mines. In 1920, the south Wales district voted several times for a national strike, with the majority in south Wales for a miners' strike of 141,721 to 40,047 in September. When a national stoppage did occur from March to July 1921, there was widespread solidarity in south Wales. The miners were moving increasingly to the left under more militant leaders such as S. O. Davies, who was elected agent for the Merthyr miners in 1918, and Arthur Cook, who became agent for the Rhondda No.1 District in 1919. Davies was a committed Marxist, and Cook a member of the Communist Party until 1921. The realization that affluent times had ended, that there was a massive loss of trade and soaring unemployment from 1920, and that private ownership was in the ascendant intensified the sense of bitterness in the coal-mining districts. One indication of the changing mood in the coalfield was the regeneration of the Central Labour College movement, whose classes were expanded in the Rhondda, Aberdare and Neath valleys. A new race of militant leaders emanated from the college in the 1920s: there was Lewis Jones, who later published novels on mining life; Ness Edwards, a coalfield activist, Labour MP for Caerphilly and a member of the Attlee government after 1945, had attended the College from 1919 to 1921; James Griffiths, an ILP activist in the Ammanford anthracite area, president of the SWMF, Labour member for Llanelli, a Cabinet member of the Attlee and Wilson governments, and the first secretary of state for Wales, had been a contemporary of Edwards at the college; and there was the coruscating presence and genius of Aneurin Bevan, who attended the college from 1919 to 1921. This coterie of intelligent and militant young miners reflected the extraordinary transmogrification in the mood of south Wales in the post-war years.

The miners' defeat after the collapse of the national coal strike in 1921 inaugurated a fairly quiescent period until 1925, when the anthracite coalfield of west Wales erupted in turmoil. This unusual outburst, in a Welsh-speaking and fairly eirenic corner of the Principality, occurred after a series of attacks by the new combines, the Amalgamated Anthracite and United Anthracite, on the traditional working practices in the anthracite pits. From the beginning of July 1925, all the miners from Ammanford to Abercrave went on strike after the dismissal of the miners who refused to be moved from their traditional places of work. The violence and rioting which ensued resulted in the prosecution of almost 200 miners. At the end of August the miners were forced to return to work. A period of mass victimization followed as the coalowners trampled on the old working practices of these normally peaceful, Welsh-speaking and chapel-going communities.

When the General Strike, which originated from a national miners' strike, took place on 3 May 1926, the Welsh miners were heavily involved. Within the actual mining Valleys of south Wales the strike was largely a non-event. The Valleys were dominated by the miners and their families, and the villages were run by the strikers for the nine-day period. It would have been unthinkable not to express support for the strike in these close-knit communities. In the large coal-exporting towns to the south of the coalfield, the more revolutionary and broader-based Councils of Action of the Valleys gave way to the TUC-style Central Strike Committees at Newport, Cardiff, Penarth, Barry and Swansea. The miners hardly interfered in these towns and the nature of the stoppage was entirely different. The authorities were so concerned about transportation and communications at the ports that a military and naval presence was deemed necessary. A battalion was stationed on the outskirts of Cardiff, while 200 special constables were enrolled to patrol the commercial and financial centres. The cruiser *HMS Cleopatra* arrived, and three potato boats were unloaded under police protection. Foodstuffs were freely distributed to Neath, Swansea and the hinterland. There were instances of clashes with the police and reports of four men and one woman jailed at Cardiff under the Emergency Powers Regulations. At Newport and Cardiff, the Labour movement remained loyal to the TUC, with the suspension of work in factories, docks, and on tramways and buses. The destroyer *HMS Tetrarch* arrived in Swansea on 6 May, and there were attempts to break the strike by employing volunteers at the docks. At Llanelli, all essential services were stopped. Even the police stations and market were command-eered by the Council of Action. Such was the extent of the Council of Action's control that the local Board of Guardians took the unprecedented decision to relieve all strikers on full rates. Although the General Strike ended on 13 May, the author-ities considered that a naval presence was necessary until 19 May 1926. Support for the strike was so overwhelming in the coalfield that not a single prosecution occurred during the nine days, and one 'blackleg' miner was hospitalized for the duration of the strike.

For the nine days of May, the Welsh miners were solid in their support, as they were to be for several months after May 1926, until those still remaining on strike were eventually forced back to work by starvation. There were communal kitchens in the institutes and chapels, and some authorities expended consider-able sums to relieve hardship. Rhondda's programme for the whole lock-out cost £57,708, with as many as 18,050 children being fed during the week ending 26 June; its schools medical officer taking pride that 5,986,257 meals were provided from public funds during the lockout.

The combined defeats of 1921 and 1926 resulted in a massive shift of power away from the miners. Union and political activists were subjected to widespread victimization, wages were cut, hours extended, conditions of work worsened and employment in the coal industry fell steadily every year from 1926 to 1937. Non-unionism became rife, and from 1929 to 1933 fewer than half of the coal industry's employees were members of the SWMF, whose membership fell from 136,000 in the early 1920s to 60,000 in 1932. Between 1921 and 1936, 241 mines closed in south Wales, and the workforce plummeted from 271,516 in 1920 to 126,233 in 1936. The growing influence of large combines enveloped the area between the Rhondda and the Rhymney Valleys: there were twenty-seven companies operating 121 col-lieries and employing 98,000 men in 1920; by 1938 one com-bine operated forty-nine pits and employed 37,000 workers. Whereas in the anthracite area there were a hundred separate companies in 1913, by 1928, the two principal companies had amalgamated and controlled 80 per cent of production. New unions also emerged to challenge the declining supremacy of the SWMF. The South Wales Miners' Industrial Union was to plague the Miners' Federation from 1926 until its extinction in 1938.

In the period from 1926 to 1934 the SWMF adopted a defensive posture and largely eschewed industrial action. There were the endemic dangers of further defeat and fragmentation of an already beleaguered union. The only coalfield strike of the 1930s began on 1 January 1931 and ended in ignominious defeat. The existence and viability of the SWMF were increasingly questioned in the early 1930s by the SWMIU and other trade unions. As the SWMF settled into a period of consolidation and regeneration from 1927 to the mid-1930s, there were indications of new forms of political radicalism throughout the south Wales coalfield. The first sign of extra-parliamentary activity was the Hunger March from south Wales in the autumn of 1927; a protest against the Ministry of Health's grip on the local Board of Guardians. Over 270 marchers were drawn from the Rhondda Valleys, Aberdare, Merthyr, Pontypridd, Tonyrefail, Ogmore and Nantyglo. Other erstwhile lodge militants were attracted to the National Unemployed Workers' Movement, which epitomized the extra-parliamentary movement in south Wales. Following the National government's 10 per cent cut in unemployment benefit in September 1931, the NUWM organized a South Wales Hunger March to the TUC at Bristol. A series of localized marches was also mounted by the NUWM in 1932.

The election of James Griffiths as president of the SWMF in 1934 heralded a more successful period for the miners' union. The SWMF had been restructured in 1933, with eight 'areas' replacing the old nineteen districts. The union, which emerged in a more confident and buoyant mood, was soon to be tested by Neville Chamberlain's 1934 Unemployment Act. This measure removed financial control of Treasury funds from local bodies and Public Assistance Committees, which had hitherto administered unemployment benefit, and transferred the responsibilities of applying the infamous 'means test' and distributing benefit to the offices of a new Unemployment Assistance Board. The SWMF ascended like a phoenix from the ashes of defeat to co-ordinate the groundswell of protest that was emerging throughout the coalfield. It summoned a conference of all interested parties in south Wales, which met on 26 January 1935 with 1,600 delegates from the trade unions, co-operative societies and Labour Party organizations, and marches followed, with around 300,000 reputedly participating. Eventually the government unexpectedly announced that the new scales would be suspended. It was a momentous victory against the 1935 means test: the only occasion in the 1930s when direct action caused a government to change its course of action and capitulate to demands from outside Parliament.

The politicization of the coalfield also manifested itself in support for the cause of overseas socialists. The outbreak of the Spanish Civil War in July 1936 coincided with social unrest and intensified political activity in the south Wales coalfield. Unemployed mining communities showed an enhanced propensity to participate in social disturbances throughout the 1930s: disturbances occurred at Maerdy in 1932 against rates eviction; at Bedwas in 1933 and Bedlinog in 1935 against company unionism; at Merthyr in 1935, and at Abertillery, Nantyglo and Blaina in 1935 in opposition to the means test; at Ammanford in 1935 during a transport dispute; and at Tonypandy in response to Fascism. Support for the Republican cause in Spain took three forms: individual miners enlisted; mining communities displayed wholehearted support; and there was assistance at all levels of the SWMF. Although the military insurrection began in Spain in July 1936, no Welsh miners volunteered for the International Brigades until the beginning of December 1936. Of the 174 Welsh volunteers who fought in Spain, 122 were miners. Over 72 per cent were Communist Party members, and a quarter of the total volunteers were union officials. Enthusiasm for the Republican cause reflected the maturing political consciousness of industrial Wales in the mid-1930s.

In rural Wales, agricultural labourers were rarely a militant group, but in 1919 they displayed a more belligerent mood. Farmers and labourers had been at loggerheads in the Vale of Glamorgan before the eruption of a four-week strike by 300 men in June and July 1919. Members of the NUR and SWMF had rendered financial assistance to the strikers, who were campaigning for an increased minimum wage. By 1920, the National Union of Agricultural Workers claimed 158 branches in

Wales, and in the same period the Workers' Union recognized 116 branches in the agricultural areas. The NUAW had four, and the Workers' Union six full-time union organizers in Wales by 1920. Thereafter, a number of factors began to militate against the agricultural workers: agriculture decontrol became effective from 1 October 1921 and prices tumbled to their 1916 values; the removal of government subsidies forced farmers to cut labour costs; the Corn Production Act was repealed; and Agricultural Wages Boards and district wages committees were abolished. The decontrolling process destroyed trade-union strength and severely affected the plight of agricultural labourers. From 1921 to 1923 the Workers' Union and the NUAW suffered huge reductions in membership, so that by 1923 the NUAW was almost sounding the retreat in Wales. Already by 1922 the number of NUAW branches had plunged from 140 to 82, and by 1924 only 37 were left in Wales, with about 56 Workers' Union branches having disappeared by 1923. The process of decline continued unabated so that only twelve NUAW branches operated in 1929. The cumulative effects of government legislation, unemployment, economic depression and trade-union rivalry had seriously impeded the farm workers' cause in Wales.

Political Parties in the Inter-War Period

The Collapse of Liberalism and the Growing Ascendancy of Labour
No sooner had an armistice been declared on 11 November 1918 than Lloyd George decided to call a snap election for December 1918, to endorse his coalition government of Unionists, Liberals and patriotic Labour members, its 'couponed' candidates standing as the representatives of national unity. Lloyd George was characterized as the greatest Welshman of his day and the most gifted Liberal of the century. In Wales, the election was fought in an atmosphere of national euphoria, and anti-government candidates were castigated for being unpatriotic. The eventual result was a huge endorsement for Lloyd George's coalition government with 526 of its supporters returned: in Wales, twenty-five supporters were elected of whom twenty were coalition Liberals, four Unionist and one Asquithian Liberal; one represented the patriotic Labour 'National Democratic Party', and ten were Labour.

The frenzy of the 'coupon' election and the apparent ascendancy of the coalition government concealed the massive changes that were about to take place in Welsh politics. The hegemony of the Liberal Party, which had been the dominant feature of Welsh politics since the *annus mirabilis* of 1868, was about to be shattered. The coalition government, which lasted from 1918 to 1922, merely disguised and delayed the inevitable. A number of factors were fragmenting the Liberal Party: a growing disenchantment with the aftermath of the war undermined Liberal strength; the very existence of a coalition government, with its Tory alliance, sapped Liberal confidence; the transitory period of social reform was soon splintered under the Geddes Axe; and the belligerent policy adopted by the government against Sinn Fein in Ireland caused considerable anxiety in Liberal circles. In Wales, there was dismay at the government's failure to support measures of devolution, and to combat growing unemployment in the mining Valleys of the south. In February 1921, the Asquithian 'Independent Liberals' recorded a significant result in the Cardiganshire by-election. Despite the coalition victory, the government witnessed a creeping paralysis which eroded coalition support all over Wales. Liberal Associations began defecting to Independent Liberalism, or simply disappeared from the political landscape. The collapse of Welsh Liberalism was confirmed in the general elections of 1922, 1923 and 1924.

The main threat to the coalition was the external challenge of Labour, which captured several seats in south Wales by-elections from 1919 to 1922. In the 1922 general election Labour won eighteen out of the thirty-six seats in Wales, mainly in the coalfield, but with victories also in Caernarfonshire in the northern quarry districts and in Wrexham. In the 1923 election, Labour won twenty Welsh seats. In some constituencies the Liberals formed a clear anti-Labour pact with the Conservatives. Labour's growing challenge in the industrial south was manifested in Swansea West where Walter Samuel, an ex-miner, defeated Sir Alfred Mond. By 1924, the traditional values of Welsh Liberalism had become increasingly outdated. Disestablishment of the Welsh Church had been achieved in 1920, while other shibboleths, such as Home Rule or temperance, evoked little enthusiasm in the post-war scene. The general election of 1924 was less successful for the Labour Party, with only sixteen Labour members returned, an aberration which resulted from the disastrous end of the first Labour government. The Conservatives captured nine seats, their best performance since 1895. The Liberals, with eleven seats, recaptured Swansea West and the university seat, but by 1924 the Liberals had virtually abandoned south Wales. There was no Liberal seat in Glamorgan or Monmouthshire, apart from Swansea West. In the last three general elections, the Liberals had fought with an anachronistic and anti-Bolshevist programme. Meanwhile, a new generation of leaders was emerging for the Labour Party from the Central Labour College: Aneurin Bevan, Morgan Phillips, Ness Edwards and James Griffiths would spearhead the Labour movement in the 1930s and 1940s.

Despite suffering an electoral setback in 1924, Labour's fortunes were hardly catastrophic. Its total vote had increased by more than 1 million, and it had shown its ability to benefit from the crushing defeats inflicted upon the Liberals. In the south Wales coalfield, the Labour Party had won all the sixteen seats and 56.6 per cent of the total vote. The steady growth of Labour reflected economic and sociological transformations in the Labour hinterland. The advance of Labour displayed the growing influence of the trade unions, and especially the miners. Of the sixteen Welsh Labour MPs returned at the 1924 general election, thirteen were, or had been, prominent trade-union officials: twelve of these were miners. They were chosen for their loyalty and devotion to the trade-union movement, as representatives of their communities and as symbols of the working-class proletariat of the coalfield.

Although Labour scored well in the coal-mining communities, outside the coalfield its position had deteriorated. It lost the three marginal seats of Cardiff South, Swansea West and Wrexham; losses that were largely attributable to the issues upon which Labour had fought the election. The Labour Party had entered the campaign charged with recklessness, and accused of harbouring pro-Russian and pro-communist sympathies. The 1924 election was fought in Wales, as elsewhere, on the key issue of Labour's extremism – 'Constitutionalism' and 'Anti-Constitutionalism' were the overarching themes. If Labour wanted to be elected as a majority government, it needed to transform its ideas and image in the eyes of the electorate. Perhaps the single most influential event during these years in the development of the political parties was the impact of the 1926 General Strike. In the aftermath of its failure there emerged a distinct move towards political, as opposed to industrial, action. The notion of the unions taking solitary and independent industrial action was largely discredited. The cleavage between industrial and political action was to evaporate during the sequel to the 1926 strike. In the 1920s the Labour Party benefited from this process and witnessed a vast growth in the numbers of local divisional parties. The total number of divisional Labour Parties, local Labour Parties and trades councils expanded from 2,653 in October 1923 to 3,314 in October 1926, and to 3,500 by 1929. In Wales, there was no divisional Labour Party before 1923 in Cardigan, Merioneth and Carmarthen, nor in Anglesey, Denbigh and Caernarfon Boroughs before 1924. By 1924, however, every constituency in Wales possessed a divisional party, and in the 1920s the number of agents increased from five in 1923 to eight in 1926.

In the 1929 election campaign Labour emphasized moderation and constitutionalism, and launched quite savage attacks upon the Communist Party. Labour candidates deliberately refrained from referring to nationalization in their speeches, with the official manifesto containing only one reference to the subject. At the 1929 election, Labour captured twenty-five Welsh seats. In addition to the sixteen coalfield seats, Labour gained the southern constituencies of Newport, Swansea West, Llandaff, Barry and the three Cardiff seats, Brecon and Radnor, Carmarthen, and Wrexham. The victories confirmed the steady advance of Labour against a radical and challenging Liberal programme. The Liberals had captured eleven Welsh seats in 1924, and in the mid-1920s Lloyd George had launched a new dynamic programme designed to capture the imagination of modern voters. The 'green book' on land in 1925, the 'yellow book' on industrial recovery in 1928, and the 'orange book' on unemployment in 1929, were the fruits of recent economic thinking, and they were presented as powerful responses to endemic socio-economic problems. For the first time, a party in Wales had a radical, progressive, economic programme and an impressive range of policies for ameliorating Welsh society. Notwithstanding Lloyd George's personal appeal and his efforts to rejuvenate Welsh political life, the Liberals secured only ten seats, one fewer than in 1924. The three seats in industrial or urban areas transferred to Labour, as Carmarthen, Swansea West and Wrexham left the Liberal fold.

The 1929 general election seemed to confirm the final eclipse of Welsh Liberalism. Although the Liberals had increased their proportion of the Welsh poll from 30 per cent in 1924 to 33.5 per cent in 1929, the electorate had decisively rebuffed the new radical programme. Although Labour seemed to have established a stable electoral foundation for future triumphs, the victory in 1929 did reveal, however, some possible limitations to its electoral success: first, not one of the seats won by Labour was really a rural constituency, because Carmarthen, and Brecon and Radnor contained sizeable mining communities within their constituency boundaries. Secondly, Labour did not win a majority of the votes cast in any Welsh division outside the coalfield block, and many of the Labour victories in Wales were marginal and precarious. In Brecon and Radnor a wafer-thin total of 330 votes separated the candidates, while the southern coastal constituencies were just as insecure. At the 1931 general election all the coastal seats surrendered to supporters of the National government.

This cleavage between the coastal belt and the coalfield heartland was significant for Labour between 1918 and 1935. The three counties of Glamorgan, Monmouthshire and Carmarthen gave Labour the appearance of domination in Wales in the years before 1935. In fact, not a single rural constituency returned a Labour member in any general election from 1918 to 1935. The outstanding characteristic of Welsh politics at this time was clearly the intense loyalty of this large block of south Wales mining seats to Labour. It provided a definition of the Welsh working class and of Welsh identity in the inter-war years, enabling the Labour Party to become the dominant voice of protest in Wales.

The general election of 1931 followed the disastrous collapse of the economy, with mass unemployment and the run on the pound in July–August 1931. The second Labour government resigned, and Ramsay MacDonald emerged as the head of a new 'National' government, which almost all his party rejected. In all, only 46 Labour and 5 ILP members were returned, in place of the 289 elected in 1929. Although Labour lost 8 seats in Wales, with 5 falling to the Conservatives, with 16 Welsh seats remaining in Labour hands, the party had actually improved its share of the poll from 43.9 per cent in 1929 to 44.1 per cent in 1931. In the 1935 election, as unemployment and stagnation scarred the landscape, Labour won 18 out of the 36 Welsh seats. James Griffiths, the president of the South Wales Miners' Federation, was elected for Llanelli at a by-election in 1936; S. O. Davies had entered Parliament at a Merthyr by-election in 1934; and Aneurin Bevan was deploying his gargantuan talents as a powerful orator and critic of the capitalist system. In the 1935 election, only seven Independent Liberals were elected in Wales, six in rural areas and the seventh in the University of Wales. By now, it was clear that Liberalism had been ousted from the industrial and urban areas of Wales. It could only muster a challenge to Labour in rural areas of declining population.

Labour's Political Rivals

The one serious challenger to Labour was the Communist Party, which had made inroads in Wales since its inception in 1920. The most important Welsh Communist was Arthur Horner, a founder member of the party, who stood for Rhondda East in 1931 and polled 30 per cent of the vote. In 1933, he stood again in a Rhondda East by-election against Labour's William Mainwaring, an erstwhile co-author of *The Miners' Next Step*, who triumphed with a majority of 2,899. In the years before the disaffiliation crisis of 1927, when the Communist Party of Great Britain decided to sever its links with the Labour Party, the results of parliamentary contests in the Rhondda had been determined largely by the selection procedures of the Rhondda Labour Party. The division in 1927 had marked the beginning of a new phase as the Communist Party mounted challenges in Rhondda constituencies. In thirteen parliamentary elections in Rhondda East and West from 1929 to 1951, eight saw the appearance of Communist Party candidates. In 1933 and 1945 in Rhondda East, Labour's percentage margin of victory was reduced to single figures by the emergence of Communist Party candidates. In 1945, Harry Pollitt, editor of the *Daily Worker*, came within one thousand votes of defeating the sitting Labour

MP, William Mainwaring. No other party could match the Communist challenge to Labour in the coalfield but, after 1945, with the spread of popular anti-communism and the impact of the Cold War, the Communist challenge gradually subsided.

The history of the Conservative Party in Wales in the years before 1935 was a chronicle of electoral defeat. In the period before 1914 defeats could largely be explained by the uncompromising Tory opposition to Church disestablishment. In the Liberal landslide of 1906 not one Conservative was returned from Wales. The 1918 electoral boundary changes and the extension of the franchise confirmed the minority position of the Conservatives. From 1918 to 1935, the party secured only thirty-seven election victories in the thirty-six Welsh constituencies. Unsurprisingly, the Conservative percentage of the vote, which had hovered at around 37 per cent between 1885 and 1910, fell to 21.4 per cent in the inter-war period. The advent of three-party politics and the formation of anti-socialist agreements with Liberals probably accounted for this diminution. An additional factor was the exceptionally poor organization of Welsh Conservatives, who, in the years before 1918, could muster only six qualified party agents in Wales. There was some improvement in 1921 with the formation of the Wales and Monmouthshire National Conservative Council. In October 1923, an associated women's section followed, and by 1925, there were twenty-eight central constituency ladies' Tory associations in existence. Significantly, there were no such associations in the mining divisions of Aberdare, Abertillery, Bedwellty and Merthyr Tydfil, nor in Caernarfonshire and Cardiganshire. A factor which exacerbated the plight of the Conservative Party in Wales was its apparent identification with Englishness, as its parliamentary candidates were invariably selected from outside Wales. Of the fifteen Tory members elected from 1918 to 1935, almost all had originated from the landowning and commercial classes, only one was classified as a Welsh-speaker, and all were elected for heavily Anglicized constituencies. Throughout most of the period, and mainly because of the Conservative Party's failure to project a Welsh image, the Liberals easily captured Conservative votes in the Principality.

The main area of organized Fascist activity was in Glamorgan, with isolated instances of support in Ebbw Vale, Wrexham and

Pembrokeshire. There was no tradition of political anti-Semitism in Wales from which the British Union of Fascists could benefit. The 1911 anti-Jewish riots had been a response to the combined effects of food price rises and the particular truck arrangements of certain Jewish landlords. Jewish communities scattered throughout Wales were small and incapable of igniting the ugliest forms of racial hostility. Mosley's New Party had fought two parliamentary seats in Glamorgan in the 1931 general election, and by 1934, it was claiming active branches in Barry, Swansea, Merthyr, Rhondda, Bridgend, Bargoed and Newport, with around 200–300 members in total. From 1936 to 1939 there were signs of heightened activity with the arrival in Cardiff of Tommy Moran, an ex-miner and boxing champion of the Royal Navy. In June 1936, he spoke at a rally in Tonypandy, when 6,000 people are reputed to have attended. By 1936, the Fascist traders of Cardiff were organized into a local BUF organization called the National Traders' Protection Society. This declared that the small traders of Britain were being threatened by the encroachments of chain stores, like Marks and Spencer, Lyons and Boots. The organization of street meetings and parades was prevented by the police under the 1936 Public Order Act. Hardly any Fascists were interned in 1940, apart from one Pembrokeshire farmer and his daughter. In fact, there were few BUF successes in Wales: there were no real leaders; the Labour Party dominated the coalfield; and the BUF was seen as a particularly unpleasant and extreme form of English nationalism.

The Arrival of the Welsh Nationalist Party

In the period when the greatest Welshman of his day dominated British politics, little was done for the cause of nationhood in Wales. The interest of the Welsh in their nationality and national community seemed to be overtaken by a concern for economic and social problems and for relations between employers and workers. The decline of the Liberals and the refusal of the Nonconformists to embrace social issues in the depressed industrial communities inaugurated a new era in Welsh political life. The arrival of mass unemployment and industrial unrest merely confirmed the political transformation that was taking place in the industrial regions of Wales.

There were some Welsh men and women who avoided the lure of industrial politics and sought refuge in a new, and possibly more cerebral form of nationalism. The cause was rekindled by *Welsh Outlook* and by the continuing activities of E. T. John. At a parliamentary level, a Speaker's Conference on the government of Scotland and Wales, which was set up in 1919 to consider a scheme for legislative and administrative devolution in the UK, could not agree on the composition or method of election. Questions were asked by individual MPs in 1928 and 1930 about the possibility of a secretary of state for Wales, but they aroused little interest. A Government of Wales bill, introduced by Sir Robert Thomas, Liberal MP for Wrexham, on 28 April 1922, was talked out on its first reading. There was some discussion of nationalist demands in 1936 when two Liberal MPs sponsored an unsuccessful Secretary of State for Wales bill in 1937. The position with regard to administrative devolution was also disappointing. The national arrangements made for Wales under the Ministry of Pensions had been abolished. Probate work for north Wales was by 1925 administered from Chester, and not from Bangor as previously. In the field of education, the Central Welsh Board, after years of conflict with the Welsh department of the Board of Education, had ceded many of its powers to Whitehall. The Welsh Board of Health did manage to expand its powers, and in 1931 assumed the general functions of the ministry in co-ordinating and supervising public health services in Wales. Notwithstanding this notable exception, these were depressing years for nationalists and supporters of some form of devolution.

However, a combination of forces was beginning to revive the nationalist cause: a widespread disillusionment with the performance of the Liberal Party and the promises of Labour was pushing some intellectuals into the nationalist ranks; the creation of the Irish Free State in 1922 stimulated the Welsh supporters of nationalism; the settlement of the First World War, and President Woodrow Wilson's Fourteen Points, and the observance of the principle of nationality in the formation of the new European states were important factors, as was the desire of many enthusiasts to found a party that would defend the Welsh culture and identity. The result was the formation of the Welsh Nationalist Party in 1925 in a temperance hall during the Pwllheli National Eisteddfod.

It was the product of the merger of three different nationalist groups based mainly in the University of Wales. The six founder-members were the Revd Lewis Valentine, Moses Gruffydd, H. R. Jones, Fred Jones, D. J. Williams, and the dominant figure in the movement, Saunders Lewis. A celebrated writer and intellectual, he became Plaid Cymru's president in 1926 and served as its outstanding thinker and ideologue. He was attracted to medieval Christian ideals of an organic community and eventually joined the Roman Catholic Church. For Saunders Lewis the language was more important than self-government. He believed that the Welsh people should regard themselves as members of one of the founder nations of the civilization of Europe. As such, the Welsh had claims to nationhood which were as authentic as those of the English. At first, Plaid Cymru was a pressure group concerned mainly with preserving the Welsh language and culture. Welsh Nationalists in 1926 stood for specific values and a specific way of life, religious, co-operative, highly individualist, and opposed to the consequences of urbanization and industrialization. Plaid began as a cultural, intellectual and moral movement, whose principal concerns from the outset were the Welsh language, Welsh identity and Christianity in Wales.

The inter-war years were not a period of great activity for the Welsh Nationalists. The only memorable event in the Nationalist calendar was the annual summer school, at which the leading Welsh intellectuals would deliver powerful addresses to the party followers. In the early days, Plaid Cymru was not formally committed to self-government for Wales, its main party object-ives being the preservation and protection of the Welsh language. After 1932, however, all Plaid members were required to agree to three principal objectives: self-government; the preservation of the Welsh language and culture; and representation for Wales at the League of Nations (later the United Nations).

Plaid founded its first newspaper, *Y Ddraig Goch*, in 1926, followed in 1932 by an English-language newspaper, *The Welsh Nationalist*. In 1929, the party fought Caernarfon in the general election, when its candidate secured barely 1 per cent of the vote. The vote did improve in the 1931 and 1935 elections, though the candidate lost his deposit on each occasion. In 1931, Saunders Lewis fought the University of Wales seat, but he managed to poll only 914 votes.

Table 3.2

Plaid Cymru membership		Number of party branches	
Year	*Number*	*Year*	*Number*
1925	6	1933	52
1930	500	1935	67
1939	2000	1937	94
1945	2500	1944	137

Lewis eventually came to realize that the Welsh Nationalist Party needed a social and economic policy. He condemned large-scale capitalism which, he argued, had created *ffatriaeth* (factoryism). For south Wales, with its appalling record of unemployment, Saunders Lewis advocated the drastic solution of de-industrialization. Rural life, on the other hand, with its family farms, contained many elements of Lewis's ideal society. Lewis espoused a distributivist philosophy and a form of economic organization which he called *perchentyaeth*: property should remain in small, individually owned units. To establish a Welsh-speaking Wales would be the best way of counteracting the oppressive force of international capitalism.

These economic ideas failed to enlarge the party's appeal in the inter-war period. Plaid did, however, spring into prominence in September 1936 when three senior members, Saunders Lewis, the Revd Lewis Valentine and D. J. Williams, set fire to an RAF bombing school at Pen-y-berth aerodrome in the Llŷn peninsula in Caernarfonshire. They objected to the school on nationalist, cultural and environmentalist grounds. They surrendered themselves to the authorities, and they were sent for trial, first in Caernarfon, and then at the Old Bailey. The three were imprisoned for several months in Wormwood Scrubs, and Lewis lost his post as a university lecturer at Swansea. Plaid Cymru had produced its first martyrs, and party membership figures began to climb slowly. The number of party branches increased from 72 to 111 in two years.

The outbreak of the Second World War soon dampened nationalist activities. The party adopted a neutral standpoint and encouraged conscientious objection to war service. Plaid was frequently accused of leaning towards Fascism, a charge that had often been levelled at Nationalist leaders in the 1930s. Both Ambrose Bebb and Saunders Lewis had been much influenced by right-wing French Catholic nationalist writers such as Maurice Barrès and Charles Maurras of *Action Française*. Lewis was also unfairly accused of showing sympathy for Mussolini's corporate state and the anti-democratic tendencies in Italian and German Fascism. Undoubtedly, this was one potent factor which prevented Plaid Cymru from widening the base of its appeal in the years before 1939. Other factors which impeded the expansion of the party were: Plaid seemed far too rooted in intellectual, cultural and literary circles within the university; it failed to appeal to the mass of working people during the depression years; the concept of Home Rule for Wales appeared anachronistic in the turbulent world of industrial politics; and Saunders Lewis's eccentric ideas often provoked hostile responses from many quarters throughout the Principality.

The Impact of War

The Second World War did not generate a crisis of conscience for Welshmen, since Welsh opinion seems to have been over-whelmingly in support of the war effort. In south Wales, Labour experienced few doubts about the 'just' nature of war and immediately took the lead in organizing the community for the new challenges. The Rhondda Borough Labour Party deter-mined that each ward Labour Party should establish committees to deal with food control, rents, the cost of living, and with assistance in the form of unemployment and social insurance. Later, Labour also supported the Rhondda Spitfire Fund, War Weapons Week and the establishment of a War Effort Com-mittee.

There was little enthusiasm for peace movements in Wales from 1939 to 1945. Christian pacifists of *Heddychwyr Cymru* con-tinued their activities on behalf of an immediate armistice. Their new pamphlet series in 1941 comprised a dozen distinguished contributors, including Ben Bowen Thomas, the first warden of Coleg Harlech, and academic notables such as Iorwerth Peate and the philosopher, Hywel D. Lewis. In 1942, the Welsh Con-gregational Union passed a resolution in favour of immediate peace negotiations, and resilient pacifists such as the Revd W. J.

Rees, Alltwen, quietly denounced military actions from their Sunday pulpits. In 1944, a new Welsh Council of Peace was formed to co-ordinate the activities of various pacifist groups. Conscientious objectors were treated with more sensitivity during the Second World War. The numbers imprisoned in Wales by late August 1944 were only 47 males and 20 females. Even so, anti-war protesters were often harassed by local authorities: some pacifist teachers were dismissed in Cardiff; members of the Communist Party were severely treated by the local police in 1939–40, and the veteran Revd T. E. Nicholas was imprisoned in Swansea and Brixton prisons. Groups of Welsh Nationalists refused to participate in an English war, and about two dozen objectors were brought before the courts.

The impact of anti-Fascism and the devastating effects of hostilities on the home front united most Welsh people during the war years. The bombing raids on Swansea, Cardiff and Newport left an indelible impression on these communities, when 985 civilians were killed in 1941 alone. The worst-affected area was Swansea, where rumours abounded in 1940 of German landings at Fairwood airport and of a Panzer division occupying Oystermouth Castle in Mumbles. Sandbags lined every road junction and public building; soldiers lived under canvas in the grounds of Singleton Park; and searchlights were installed in St Helen's cricket ground. Swansea was subjected to five air raids in July 1940, and thirteen people were killed in a raid on 10 April 1940. The first major raid occurred on the night of 1 September 1940, when thirty-three people were killed and 105 injured. People trekked at night to the nearby rural areas in Mumbles, and to the Gower peninsula, in search of refuge in tents and huts, or in parked cars and lorries on open land around Swansea. The most severe raids came on the nights of 19–21 February 1941, when 240 people were killed and a further 409 were injured. Incendiary and high-explosive bombs rained down on the town lit by parachute flares, and its centre was almost completely destroyed. In early March, Cardiff was also heavily raided, and by the end of October 1941, 600 houses had been destroyed and 29,998 damaged in the blitz. Llandaff Cathedral and Cardiff Castle were among the historic buildings to suffer from the bombing.

The arrival of evacuees brought the reality of war to communities in more sheltered parts of Wales. In north Wales,

Denbighshire took in 17,721 evacuees, while Anglesey hosted 2,468 elementary-school pupils. There was a steady flow of evacuees to and from Wales during the war years. By January 1940, 60 per cent of the evacuees sent to Flintshire had returned home. In Denbighshire, of the 6,400 received by Wrexham Rural District, 4,066 had departed by the end of 1939. Many returned home because of the perceived lack of danger in the home areas, or as a result of the cultural and social mismatching that often occurred, or simply on account of homesickness. The first government evacuation scheme had been something of a revelation: townspeople had met country folk; urban poor had encountered rich rural inhabitants; Catholics and Protestants had been assembled in one community; and English people had often met Welshmen for the first time.

There were many different experiences of collectivism at work. The Essential Work Order of 1941 had directed work to industries working on the war effort. There was direct control of private industry by the state, and especially in the coal mines. Welsh politicians became increasingly involved in the new surge of reform during the war and in the longer-term crusade for social and economic reconstruction. It was James Griffiths, Labour MP for Llanelli, who criticized the Churchill government in February 1943 for refusing to commit itself to an early implementation of the Beveridge report on social insurance. Aneurin Bevan, a persistent critic of the government, published an onslaught on its attitude to social questions in his book, *Why Not Trust the Tories*, in 1944. Welsh Labour MPs, such as Griffiths, were prominent in the Welsh advisory panel of the Ministry of Reconstruction, which issued a report in 1944 on the social and economic stagnation in Wales. A concern for a post-war programme of reconstruction and regeneration permeated the discussions of the Welsh advisory panel from 1942 to 1944. A comprehensive social security system, housing and a national health service emerged as dominant issues for the post-war world of politics.

SUGGESTED READING

K. D. Brown (ed.), *The First Labour Party* (London, 1985).
M. Francis (ed.), *The Conservatives and British Society, 1880–1990* (Cardiff, 1996).

Gareth Elwyn Jones, *Modern Wales: A Concise History* (Cambridge, 1994).
Trevor Herbert and Gareth Elwyn Jones (eds.), *Wales Between the Wars* (Cardiff, 1988).
Philip Jenkins, *A History of Modern Wales, 1536–1990* (London, 1992).
Kenneth O. Morgan, *Rebirth of a Nation: Wales 1880–1980* (Oxford, 1981).
Kenneth O. Morgan, *Wales in British Politics, 1868–1922* (Cardiff, 1991).
Prys Morgan (ed.), *Glamorgan County History, vol. VI* (Cardiff, 1988).
Hywel Francis and David Smith, *The Fed: A History of the South Wales Miners in the Twentieth Century* (London, 1980).
C. Williams, *Democratic Rhondda, 1885–1951* (Cardiff, 1996).

4. Education and Cultural Life

Education

Schooling in the Years 1906–1914

SINCE the 1880s higher-grade schools had been set up in urban and industrial districts with populations of over 5,000: one school was founded at Cardiff in 1884, two others in the Rhondda in 1893 and one at Llanelli in 1891. These quasi-secondary schools, which became increasingly attractive to working-class parents, as tuition fees had been abolished in the Swansea, Rhondda and Merthyr Tydfil areas well before the First World War, were seen as an independent working-class sector by the Tory governments. With the disappearance of the School Boards after 1902, the majority of these higher-grade schools were assimilated into the municipal secondary school organization, but only after many had suffered the humiliation of being called higher elementary schools. By 1920, there were at least twenty of these schools in Wales. Although they provided admirable sources of entry for working-class pupils and the tuition was free, they were not administered by the Central Welsh Board and never enjoyed the financial benefits of the schools in the new intermediate system. For years they endured a Sisyphean struggle to secure parity of esteem with the intermediate schools, while the most successful pupils usually chose the intermediate ahead of the municipal secondary school.

The Report of the Aberdare Committee in 1881 had high-lighted the inadequacy of secondary education in Wales. There were places for only 4,000 pupils in all types of secondary schools, when there should have been provision for 15,700. The endowed grammar schools provided only 1,540 of these places. The pattern of Welsh secondary education before 1914 was largely deter-mined by the Welsh Intermediate Education Act of 1889.

It was assumed in the Act that the parents of pupils who wanted a secondary education should pay for it, but it was accepted that there should be some opportunity for clever working-class pupils to have access to the secondary sector. A scholarship system was built into the county schemes so that 10–20 per cent of pupils were given scholarships. McKenna's bill of 1907 made a major concession to working-class parents by imposing a minimum of 25 per cent free places on any secondary school grant-aided by the state. By 1902, ninety-five of the new intermediate schools had been established throughout Wales.

Glamorgan's intermediate scheme was approved in 1896, the last in Wales because of the protracted negotiations over Cowbridge school. The provision of schools was the least satisfactory aspect of the 1889 Act. Since 1900 there had been a growing demand for secondary places and a steady increase in the number of pupils receiving secondary education. In Merioneth, from 1896 to 1919 the numbers had trebled, while in industrial Glamorgan the increase had been almost as large. The average size of the population in intermediate school districts in Wales was 8,000, compared with 35,000 in Glamorgan and 88,350 in Porth. In 1902, the School Boards had been abolished in Balfour's Act so as to ensure that secondary education would be preserved for the middle classes in fee-paying schools under the aegis of the county and county borough councils. Urban district councils in Aberdare, Mountain Ash, Pontypridd, Neath, Barry and Rhondda were intended to control only the elementary schools. As a result of the 1902 Act the higher elementary schools were transformed into the municipal secondary schools, thereby creating a dual administrative system in secondary education. By 1920, there were twelve of these schools in Glamorgan alone. A dual secondary system tended to reinforce class awareness, as the mass of Glamorgan's schoolchildren attended elementary schools, while an élite minority benefited from a secondary education which provided a degree of occupational mobility. In Pembroke's schools there seemed to be no difficulty in attracting pupils, but it was almost impossible to ensure that they would complete the four-year course leading to the School Certificate. From 1895 to 1902, for example, a total of 292 girls attended Tasker's School, 140 of whom stayed less than two years. The majority of Welsh parents were poor, and pupils, once they had reached the age of fourteen, tended to leave in search of employment. The Board of Education and the Welsh Department tried to control the deteriorating situation by requiring parents to sign legal agreements which would ensure that their children completed the four-year course.

The parameters of intermediate school development were set by central government, and the schools themselves usually reflected the perceived virtues of the endowed-school system: fees were charged, a prefectorial system would be introduced, staff would be gowned, prize days and detention systems prevailed, and headteachers were usually enlisted from the older universities, with over a half of them coming from outside the Principality. Regulations were firmly entrenched by 1904 to ensure an upper age limit of fifteen for the higher elementary school. The Welsh Intermediate schools were securely placed on the secondary side of this binary line. Within the secondary sector, a rigid and hierarchical education system reflected the aristocratic and upper-middle-class public-school ethos. The lower middle classes seemed just as anxious as their social superiors to ensure that their privileged access to secondary schools should be maintained at the expense of the working classes, whose free education in the deliberately named elementary schools was an act of charity on the part of the state. The secondary schools of Wales were intended to be low in the pecking order. It was assumed in the 1880s that very few secondary schools were required in the poorer circumstances of Wales, and that a preponderant number of Welsh schools would be third-grade. Fees were imposed, but at a low level compared with those of the English grammar schools. Gradations within the school system were considered essential and carried connotations of social class. Differentiation of secondary provision was not deemed to be a matter of educational priority, but of social distinction. The Welsh Intermediate Education Act of 1889 and its attendant school system were intended to promote the interests of the Welsh middle classes. The whole tone of the curriculum was humanistic and academic, and from 1906 to 1916 only eighteen technical and fifteen commercial certificates were awarded by the Central Welsh Board for all its schools. Welsh was taught in no more than 47 of the 95 intermediate schools by 1907, a state of affairs deeply deplored by the distinguished Welsh scholar and writer Dr Kate Roberts when she taught at Ystalyfera Intermediate School in the Swansea Valley in the early decades of the century.

As a result of the two Acts of 1889 and 1902, Wales had a dual system of secondary education which was to remain until 1944. Since fee-paying was regarded as an essential characteristic of secondary schooling, the municipal secondary schools had to compensate by concentrating on the other symbol of secondary status, the academically orientated curriculum. It was on this that the two systems converged, as the municipal secondary schools aspired to teach a humanistic, academic curriculum.

In April 1906, Birrell introduced a new education bill into the House of Commons in an attempt to quell the age-old education controversies and to satisfy Nonconformist expectations. It recommended that all public elementary schools were to be controlled by the local authority and that teachers should not be compelled to provide religious instruction. Part IV of the bill proposed a national council for Wales, with representatives from county, county borough and urban district councils. Although the bill eventually passed through the Commons on 30 July, it encountered inevitable defeat in the House of Lords, where their lordships insisted on their amendments and the bill was withdrawn. The government did introduce a moderate scheme for a Welsh department in the Board of Education in February 1907. A. T. Davies, a Flintshire solicitor, was appointed permanent secretary, with O. M. Edwards as chief inspector of schools. Edwards was a distinguished scholar of Balliol College, Oxford, and a Fellow of Lincoln College, whose educational views reflected his idyllic upbringing in rural Merioneth. Influenced by John Ruskin and Rousseau, Edwards's vision of Wales was romantic and noble. Believing in the virtues of craft labour and a classless community, he was convinced that the educational system should fortify the national life of Wales, producing honest craftsmen and learned men. Welsh should be the language of the hearth, of the early school years and taught throughout the secondary school. He promoted the belief that subjects such as history should be taught through the medium of Welsh, and that the language and literature of Wales should be prominent in the school curriculum. While A. T. Davies concentrated on the administrative skirmishes, O. M. Edwards battled on the educational front. As soon as the Welsh department was created in 1907, the Central Welsh Board, which had operated the new educational system since its inception in 1896 and provided for the inspection of schools, became increasingly protective of its administrative and territorial jurisdiction. Clashes occurred over the right to separate identities, with the Central Welsh Board jealously guarding its privileged position as a representative body of the Welsh people through the county and county borough councils.

For O. M. Edwards, the English secondary-grammar schools, with their promotion of a literary and academic curriculum, were entirely inappropriate for Wales. He castigated the Central Welsh Board examination system with its undue emphasis on memorizing facts and rote learning, and for distorting the true purposes of Welsh secondary-school education. In 1911, the Central Welsh Board operated four examinations: the Junior Examination commenced in 1899 and continued officially until 1924; the Senior Examination became the School Certificate in 1923, and lasted until the Second World War; the Higher Certificate, set up in 1911, was taken one year after the School Certificate; and an Honours Certificate, for those abler candidates who were likely to take scholarships at universities, lasted until the First World War. The Higher and Honours certificates were amalgamated in 1917, when the Secondary Schools Examinations Council was established, with a new portfolio of examinations. The first School Certificate examination was taken at sixteen, while a Second School Examination was set for pupils aged about eighteen. There were to be three subject groups – English subjects, foreign languages, science and mathematics – and candidates were expected to pass in the three groups.

By 1900, intermediate education had permeated the whole of Wales. The number of pupils in Welsh intermediate schools had risen from 6,427 in 1897 to over 13,000 in 1910–11, paying an average fee which ranged from £4 to £5 per annum. Local authorities in the industrial areas sometimes provided far in excess of the 25 per cent minimum of free places, though the actual extent of their generosity depended upon the councils' prosperity. Merthyr County Borough Council ensured that one-third to one-half of the places in its intermediate schools were free in the years before the First World War.

Impact of the First World War

In 1914, there were 117 recognized secondary schools in Wales, ninety-nine of which had been set up under the Welsh Intermediate Education Act of 1889, eight were provided by county borough councils, two by a county council, two by an urban district council, and there were six small private schools. The system of secondary education lacked coherence, with marked contrasts in the pattern of provision of schools in rural and industrial Wales. In much of rural Wales, secondary education functioned almost entirely under the county schemes which had been established by the 1889 Act. In industrial south Wales the picture was different: in Glamorgan, the intermediate schools tended to be the main providers of secondary education, though Maesteg, Ferndale and Pentre schools were outside this system. Monmouthshire had the largest concentration of ancient foundations, with King Henry VIII Grammar School, Abergavenny, Monmouth Grammar School and Monmouth High School for Girls. In the county boroughs, Cardiff had four municipal secondary schools, and two intermediate schools, Swansea had two intermediate and two municipal secondary schools, and Merthyr had two municipal secondary schools and one intermediate school. The average size of schools also differed: in rural Wales, numbers were usually small, with nine schools for 570 pupils in Montgomeryshire, whereas by contrast, 7,827 pupils were accommodated in the thirty-seven secondary schools of Glamorgan. The scale of school provision fluctuated as between rural and industrial schools: in 1917, there were 19.75 pupils per 1,000 population in Merioneth, 15.69 in Cardiganshire, 6.92 in Glamorgan and 6.76 in Monmouthshire.

With the outbreak of hostilities in 1914 the Welsh secondary school system suffered considerable disruption. Some schools in Caernarfonshire were commandeered for billeting soldiers, while in Cardiff, Howard Gardens Secondary School was used as a military hospital. Teachers were soon recruited into the armed services and, by 1916, 204 secondary school teachers had enlisted. In some county schools, such as Greenhill, Tenby, there were no male members of staff left by 1915–16. In 1925, an HMI report observed that Friars Bangor County Boys' School had been adversely affected by the departure of experienced staff to the armed forces and the use of thirty-five assistants during the war years. Wartime conditions resulted in reduced medical services, school closures, teacher shortages and social strains. School gardens were often used to grow potatoes and other vegetables; in Caernarfonshire, for instance, seed potatoes were supplied to fourteen schools. Schoolboy labour was frequently employed on the land, and school holidays were organized so that children in rural areas could assist with the harvest. Economy was insisted upon in schools: there was no fuel on school fires after 1p.m.; and there were no further orders for school pictures or sewing machines. School buildings or extensions were peremptorily curtailed, despite the indications of an increased demand for places. In 1915–16, there was a 5.2 per cent increase in the number of school admissions, and a further 7 per cent spurt by 1917. There were some unfortunate records of concessions to jingoism, with the pupils in Llangefni school being sent on route marches.

After the war, the school population continued to grow, with an 8.7 per cent increase by 1919. The post-war growth was caused by pupils staying on longer at school and by a 50 per cent increase in the number of boys over sixteen. Yet, paradoxically, early leaving was still a problem, with 63.2 per cent of boys and 51.2 per cent of girls leaving Welsh county schools before the age of sixteen in the period 1918–20.

Secondary Education in the Inter-War Period

The Fisher Education Act of 1918 had proved to be a disappointment in Wales. While it encouraged further co-operation between central and local government, and extended the provisions for further education, there was no reference to a Welsh national council. In 1918, Glamorgan had responded vigorously to the Act and drawn up a blueprint for educational development, which, in many ways, demonstrated the supreme confidence of the county at the height of its prosperity. Glamorgan county council had responsibility for 207,000 pupils aged from five to sixteen, and it had become increasingly concerned over the differences in provision between industrial south Wales and rural Wales. The Glamorgan education plan of 1918 was innovative and highly ambitious. It intended abolishing the dual system whereby the great majority of pupils were restricted to elementary-school education and the chosen few destined for secondary schools. It envisaged that all pupils should transfer to secondary schools for a free education from twelve to sixteen years of age, while intermediate schools would continue to prepare pupils for university and the professions. The other secondary schools, thirty-three in all, would provide a progressive course of general education almost up to matriculation standard.

With the onset of post-war depression, Glamorgan's plans were shelved. From 1921 onwards, financial restraints slaughtered the nascent developments foreshadowed in Fisher's Act. Economies were imposed on local authorities and the perennial disincentives to secondary education remained firmly in place. Early leaving was a continuing problem throughout the early 1920s, though there were marginal improvements. In 1913, the average length of school life was under three years, but by 1925–6 it was just over three and a half years. Between 1926 and 1929, the Conservative government was demanding further cuts in education, and considered the possibility of levying a charge of 3*d.* per week for each child in school, at a time when unemployment was creeping up over 20 per cent. Labour councils were desperate to protect their hard-won gains, but Merthyr authority failed to open Quaker's Yard as a free secondary school until the Labour government came to power in 1924. Cardiff also had to wait until 1924 before Sir Charles Trevelyan allowed free education in its municipal secondary schools. Economic devastation prompted the second Labour government to commission a committee to report on the education problems of the south Wales coalfield. The committee condemned the inadequacy of technical education and encouraged the establishment of the Advisory Council for Technical Education in south Wales and Monmouthshire. Between 1929 and 1931 five mining institutes were opened in Glamorgan, fed by eighty-four junior centres providing over 350 separate classes. From these institutes, students could proceed to technical colleges in Cardiff or Swansea, or to the School of Mines at Treforest.

In the 1920s a number of reports appeared on the position of the Welsh language and Welsh teaching: *Welsh in Education and Life* was published in 1927, followed by *Language Teaching in the Schools of Wales* in 1929 and *Entrance Tests for Admission to Secondary*

Schools in 1930. The departmental committee of the Welsh Department concluded in its 1927 report that the Welsh language suffered as a result of the perceived economic potential of English. Of the 135 secondary schools surveyed by the committee, seventeen did not teach Welsh in the curriculum, and nowhere was Welsh regarded as the exemplary language of the school. The contrast between the contribution of the official educational system and that of Urdd Gobaith Cymru was quite astonishing. The Urdd (Welsh League of Youth) was founded by Ifan ab Owen Edwards, and its purpose was to infuse among young people a love of the native language and culture. From its foundation in 1922, it spread rapidly, as branches emerged in schools, colleges and chapels throughout the land. There were summer camps, with eisteddfodau, competitive sports and publications. In 1927, the Urdd had 5,000 members, and by 1934, 50,000. The first Welsh-language school was founded at Aberystwyth in 1939 by the Urdd. It was essentially a children's and young people's movement, contributing a whole educational programme in the Welsh language and emphasizing the virtues of community and Welshness.

The depression of the 1930s, the policies of the National government and the savage cuts proposed by the May Committee, which reported in July 1931, exacerbated the plight of local authorities. As depopulation and migration followed in the worst-affected industrial areas, in north Wales there was a fall of 13.3 per cent in the secondary age group (ten to fourteen), and in south Wales, the figures were even more disturbing: a fall of 28 per cent in the age group under five; 11.8 per cent in the 5–9 age cohort; 11.4 per cent in the 10–14 group; and 13.3 per cent in the 15–19 age group. In Merthyr Tydfil, from 1921 to 1931 the number of children in the age group under five fell by an astounding 36.4 per cent. From 1928 to 1936 the school population of Wales fell by 14 per cent. Nevertheless, the combined effects of emigration, and determined campaigns by authorities to expand the secondary sector, produced dramatic improvements in secondary educational opportunities during the depression years: proportions increased to 20 per 1,000 in the Rhondda, 19.9 per 1,000 in Cardiff and 16.9 per 1,000 in Glamorgan county by 1938. Glamorgan built or took over twenty-two schools in the inter-war period. In 1931, 19.33 per cent of elementary school pupils in Wales aged eleven and twelve entered secondary schools, as compared with the English figure of 9.58 per cent. As twenty-six of the local education authorities had charged no fees, the imposition of means-tested places in September 1932 produced a passionate outcry in Wales. Glamorgan education authority fought bravely to defeat the proposal and presented a plan, which proved totally unacceptable, to make all the county's secondary education free. Although forced into submission, it received 100 per cent special places, ensuring that access to secondary schools was wholly on merit. Brecon, Monmouthshire, Cardiff, Merthyr and Swansea were also granted 100 per cent special places, and Flintshire secured 80 per cent. Overall, 67.5 per cent of places in Welsh secondary schools were free in 1932, a figure which improved to 69.1 per cent in 1934, and remained at 64 per cent in 1939. Ironically, the depression and the harsh economic measures of 1932 had engendered a movement in Wales towards the fulfilment of Labour's policy of admission to secondary schools based on talent rather than the ability to pay.

The Spens Report of 1938 recommended a tripartite system of education, with secondary grammar, secondary modern and technical-commercial schools. It proposed a common curriculum up to thirteen, and a common code and parity of esteem. The government shelved the report, arguing that financial constraints hampered educational reforms. In 1941, however, an unofficial group of senior civil servants considered the nature of post-war reconstruction, although no Welsh delegates were invited to contribute to these historic discussions on secondary-school reorganization. The shape of post-war secondary education was initially decided by this coterie of senior civil servants on the tripartite model. On the eve of the Second World War, the Welsh secondary system was essentially the same as in 1914: the intermediate sector had experienced little change; the municipal sector had grown from twelve schools in 1914 to forty-two in 1939; the average size of schools had increased; the whole basis of fee income had been transformed by the 1933 special-places scheme; Welsh elementary and secondary systems had always been well integrated, and by 1939, 95.5 per cent of all pupils admitted to secondary schools came from elementary schools; the content of education was essentially the same – academic and arts subjects dominated the Welsh secondary and grammar schools in 1939, as in 1915.

Wales and the 1944 Education Act

The Second World War had brought further disruption to Welsh education. Evacuees descended upon the local authorities, with whole schools transferring from London, Liverpool and the major cities to parts of Wales. Male staff were lost once more to the armed forces, and pupils tended to leave school before completing their normal four-year courses. The Welsh Department actually transferred to Bournemouth, symbolizing the alien nature of that agency. In July 1941, R. A. Butler was appointed to the Board of Education and thoughts soon began to turn to post-war reconstruction and an improved society. The 1944 Education (Butler) Act laid the foundations for the post-war development of secondary education. The three progressive stages at the heart of the new Act represented a significant improvement: 'The statutory system of public education should be organized in three progressive stages to be known as primary education, secondary education, and further education . . .' Hitherto, most Welsh pupils had been educated in the elementary schools. The latter had tended to reflect a presupposition among the ruling classes that the great majority of the working classes required a charity-based schooling, suitable for the low-level, unskilled forms of labour which they were likely to inherit. The 1944 Act did little to change the prevailing attitudes to education among the ruling élites. In fact, it provided the framework within which civil servants, administrators and governments could perpetuate the divisions of society. Professor Gareth Elwyn Jones has shown that the 1944 Act's provision of secondary education for 'age, aptitude and ability' disguised a decision taken in 1941 by the Board of Education's senior civil servants to perpetuate the bipartite discriminatory post-eleven provision. Conservative governments endorsed the selective system manufactured for them by those mandarins who were themselves products of prestigious public schools. Professor Jones has succeeded in demythologizing the 1944 Act, showing that its apparent progressivism was a veneer which concealed Norwood-type notions of children possessing different types of minds: the grammar-school type and the secondary-modern type. R. A. Butler, the so-called radical author of the 1944 Act, actually produced a list of savings for Cabinet colleagues in 1953, which included levying fees in state schools, raising the age of entry to six and lowering the leaving age to fourteen. The 1944 Act required local authorities to submit development plans within twelve months, but this aspect will be discussed in the final chapter on educational developments after 1945.

Adult Education in Wales

In the first half of the century there were various traditions existing throughout Wales, with visions of educational improvement, personal enhancement and communal enlargement. One such tradition was the university extension movement, whereby university teachers brought their talents and interests to the communities of Wales. During the depression years there were nine full educational settlements operating in the east of the south Wales coalfield, the largest of which, Maes-yr-Haf in the Rhondda, catered for hundreds of students. In 1934, there were thirty-four adult education courses in this settlement alone, helping with industrial retraining for redundant miners, and setting up workshops. The University Extension Board, in conjunction with the University Press Board, had arranged for a series of books to be published called 'Cyfres y Brifysgol a'r Werin' (the University and the People series) to meet the needs of adult education. By 1940, nineteen volumes had appeared. From 1921 to 1939 the number of classes held under the auspices of the four colleges had increased from eighty-two to 201. An alternative branch of the university extension movement promoted the virtues of citizenship. It evolved rapidly among those active in adult education in south Wales in the period after 1906, as the nascent Labour movement began to exercise its political and industrial muscle. The *South Wales Daily News* (Liberal newspaper) was one prominent advocate of the need to promote ideals of citizenship.

From the outset, the concept of workers' education was splintered into two: one group demanded that the universities should extend their educational facilities to the working people and welcomed the contributions of middle-class academic staff; a more radical group argued that the universities should be avoided. For the latter, university courses for working people were a ploy designed to protect the existing social order, to reinforce property rights and to undermine the aspirations of the Labour movement. The Workers' Educational Association emerged as a collaborationist body and tended to express the views of the first group. By 1933, the WEA had become a major cultural institution and a powerful political and social base in south Wales, with over 200 WEA classes and more than 4,000 students. The WEA, with its non-party-political stance, benefited from monies which were made available through the social-service responses to heavy unemployment.

The most impressive example of the collaborative approach was the founding of Coleg Harlech in 1927. Its main inspiration was Thomas Jones, who had pirouetted in Whitehall circles for years. Through his friendships with the philanthropic coalowner David Davies, Llandinam, the poet Silyn Roberts and Percy Watkins, secretary of the Welsh Board of Health, Thomas Jones sought to establish an agency that would reconcile capital and labour in the mining districts and promote peaceful methods of industrial reform. Jones and his collaborators secured financial assistance from the Carnegie Trust, from Sir Alfred Mond, Lord Astor and Lord Haldane, and bought Wern Fawr, an imposing house at Harlech. With the assistance of the WEA and the university colleges, and Ben Bowen Thomas as its first warden, the new college for working men opened in 1927, when ten students were admitted. By the later 1930s Coleg Harlech had become a thriving and expanding institution: 220 students had attended the college, 209 of whom were Welsh, and 91 were miners.

There also emerged a separate workers' tradition, which was associated with an independent working-class education (IWCE). This stressed that only independent working-class education, based on Marxian doctrine, was of any benefit to the working classes. Through the Labour College movement and the propaganda of the Plebs League, the south Wales Valleys became one of the distinctive centres of IWCE activity. The Central Labour College exercised an enormous influence on the organized working-class movement in south Wales and on the south Wales miners' union. By the 1930s the executive committee and its senior positions were already well staffed by ex-students and tutors of the Labour College. The coalfield, by 1945, was represented by thirteen MPs, sponsored by the miners' union, eight of whom were former students of the Central Labour College, two of whom became Cabinet ministers – James Griffiths and Aneurin Bevan. There were ex-Labour College men like Lewis Jones, the first Communist to be elected to Glamorgan County Council, who provided graphic illustrations of coalfield activists in the 1930s through his novels *Cwmardy* and *We Live*. In the 1930s there were over forty Central Labour College classes operating in the Valleys towns of south Wales, with aggregate enrolments of about 1,000. In the era of revolutionary posturing, between 1916 and 1921, it had seemed as if the Labour College might overwhelm the WEA; but the damaging effects of industrial defeats in 1921 and 1926 highlighted the strategic limitations of independence. The decade of heavy structural unemployment gave the WEA a fresh opportunity and an added fillip.

Developments in Higher Education

In the early years of the century the University of Wales served as a powerful symbol of popular achievement and national status. There were three colleges already in existence: Aberystwyth, established in 1872; the University College of South Wales and Monmouthshire founded in Cathays Park, Cardiff in 1883; and the University College of North Wales, established at Bangor in 1884. St David's College, Lampeter, founded in 1827, remained an Anglican preserve concerned with the training of ordinands. At the end of 1893, the University of Wales had received the royal assent, and in 1896 it came into being as a federal structure.

The outbreak of war in 1914 severely disrupted the new seats of learning, but the colleges adjusted as best they could to wartime conditions. Rooms were set aside as military hospitals at Bangor, and two acres of playing fields converted into allotments. Belgian refugees settled at Aberystwyth, and Serbians began arriving in Wales towards the end of the war. Courses were soon disrupted and a substantial decline in student numbers produced a corresponding fall in fees. Students of engineering at Cardiff were encouraged to devote two days to making munitions. The university recognized two days' weekly training by members of the Officer Training Corps as part of their degree course. The advent of conscription in 1916 intensified the pressure on all male students to enlist; not even theological students being exempt from the draconian measure. Those who harboured reservations about the military cause were told to serve in the Royal Army Medical Corps, the Army Service Corps or the YMCA. Conscientious objectors faced tribunals, public scorn and certain imprisonment. T. H. Parry-Williams and T. Gwynn Jones supported *Y Wawr*, a student publication opposed to the war. At Bangor, Thomas Rees, principal of Bala-Bangor Theological College, stood firm in defence of conscientious objectors. In general, however, there was overwhelming euphoria at the outbreak of hostilities and widespread support for the war effort. In September 1914, the principal of St David's College, Lampeter, a theological oasis in idyllic rural Wales, sent a circular to all students urging them to enlist.

In 1916, a royal commission, under the chairmanship of Haldane, was set up to investigate the University of Wales. It confirmed the federal, national structure of the university and recommended more autonomy for the individual colleges. The 1918 Representation of the People Act also granted the university a member of Parliament. In December 1916, Swansea's advocates appeared before the Haldane Commission to plead its case for the siting, in the town, of a constituent college of the university. In January 1916, the college received its charter, and the new university college opened its doors to science students at Mount Pleasant in October 1920, although arts students had to wait another year for admission. In 1925, the University Court approved a resolution to constitute an independent School of Medicine of the University. The Welsh National School of Medicine was finally granted its charter by the Privy Council in February 1931. The establishment in 1922 of a Board of Celtic Studies and a Press Board of the university was testimony both to the flowering national culture and to the encouragement of it.

The federal university now consisted of four constituent colleges, but links between Lampeter and the university remained tenuous throughout the inter-war period. In 1927, St David's College held its centenary celebrations, attended by the Archbishop of Canterbury. By 1939, there was a student body of over 200 in Lampeter, whereas Leicester had only 82 students and Hull 162. The majority of students in the university had come from Wales: the proportion of students from outside Wales at Aberystwyth before 1939 was no larger than 13 per cent; while Cardiff had only 3 per cent of non-Welsh students in 1938. As for the distribution of students from within Wales, the vast majority of undergraduates attended their local colleges. Of all Cardiganshire students in the university, 88 per cent enrolled in Aberystwyth; over 85 per cent of Caernarfonshire's students flocked to Bangor, and 87 per cent of students from the Cardiff County Borough trooped to Cardiff. Students at Aberystwyth were far more representative of the Welsh population generally, with 33 per cent emanating from Glamorgan and Monmouthshire, 21 per cent from north Wales and 37 per cent from Cardiganshire and Carmarthenshire.

It seems that, in 1911, the number of boys proceeding from Welsh intermediate schools to universities was 4.3 per cent, compared with 1.9 per cent from English 'council' schools. In the large, populous counties of Glamorgan and Monmouthshire, it had been possible to offer a substantial number of free studentships to impecunious working-class children. Before 1914, it was estimated that an arts student could survive on £38 per annum, and a science student on £42. Student numbers had reached their peak in the years 1933–5, but between 1934–5 and 1938, numbers dropped from 3,521 to 2,779. On the eve of war, 26 per cent of students lived in hostels at Aberystwyth, 37 per cent at Bangor, 11 per cent at Cardiff, and 4 per cent at Swansea. Those living at home amounted to 12.7 per cent at Aberystwyth, 22 per cent at Bangor, 60 per cent at Cardiff and 83 per cent at Swansea.

Women's position within the university was ambiguous. In 1924, women represented 40 per cent of the student population, a figure far in excess of the English and Scottish proportions. Thereafter, there was a decline in Wales to 28 per cent, and a further fall to 27 per cent in 1938. Women seem to have been regarded as separate, but not equal, within the university. There were few women professors in the University of Wales between 1893 and 1939: three at Cardiff, two at Swansea, one at Aberystwyth and none at Bangor. At Swansea, women were not even permitted to be members of the Senior Common Room until after 1945. The sharp decline in the number of women students during the 1930s may be attributed to the reduced grants for teachers and increased competition for posts. There were other contributory factors: at Bangor, for example, fees in women's halls of residence ranged from £51 to £61 per session, while those for men averaged £43. Grants to prospective teachers in hostels were also discriminatory – £43 for men, and £34 for women.

The outbreak of the Second World War in 1939 impeded further progress in the university. Cardiff suffered serious air attacks and the college took a direct hit on 17 February 1941, when the students' union refectory was destroyed. At Swansea, the sports pavilion, the gymnasium, playing fields and a large portion of Singleton Park were requisitioned by the military, the Royal Artillery being encamped in huts in front of the college. The arrival of evacuee departments soon transformed the pre-war college: in September 1939 the department of explosives research came from Woolwich Arsenal; while in 1940 students from the department of metallurgy of the Royal School of Mines at Imperial College, London, arrived. The blitz, which virtually demolished Swansea's town centre, hardly affected college buildings. Aberystwyth was considered a safe haven for staff and 600 students from University College, London, while by 1940, Bangor had welcomed 197 science students from London. Lampeter remained as a theological and arts college during the war years, and, though there were discussions between Lampeter and university officers concerning a more formal relationship, the outcome was unsuccessful. Nonconformist doubts, which still prevailed, effectively blocked a rapprochement.

Cultural Life

Literary Revival 1906–1918

The Edwardian period, which witnessed increasing economic affluence and growing political confidence in Wales, was also a time of passionate national awareness and cultural revitalization. Cultural regeneration began to emerge in the 1880s and grew to fruition in the early part of the twentieth century. One formative influence was O. M. Edwards, the distinguished Fellow of Lincoln College, Oxford, and educationalist, who represented the ideal of the *werin*, the ordinary folk, and their passionate desire for self-improvement through educational channels. He used his coruscating academic achievements, and his status as chief inspector of schools from 1907 onwards, to promote the history and culture of Wales. He believed that the Welsh *werin* had progressed from poverty and serfdom to a position of freedom and nobility. As we saw in an earlier section on developments in education, O. M. Edwards fought valiantly to promote the teaching of Welsh in schools and to further the cause of Welsh-medium teaching. The impact of men like Edwards and John Morris-Jones was undeniably pervasive at this time. The original interests of Morris-Jones, also a product of Oxford, had been in mathematics, but philology soon became his consuming passion. His position as professor of Welsh at University College of North Wales, Bangor, from 1893 gave him the authority to play a leading role in the new literary movement as scholar and critic. He was the architect of the crusade to establish linguistic standards, and his *A Welsh Grammar*, published in 1913, became the definitive account of the traditional literary language. In 1911, he launched a new literary periodical, *Y Beirniad* (The Critic), which set new critical standards for literary and linguistic studies.

T. Gwynn Jones epitomized the revival in poetry in these early years. He hailed from a humble background and, although having renounced a formal education at an early age, he became professor of Welsh literature at Aberystwyth in 1919. In 1902, he won the chair at the Bangor National Eisteddfod for his poem *Ymadawiad Arthur*, often considered the most important poem of the literary revival. W. J. Gruffydd was also emerging as a writer of immense capability, with a wide range of talents as a scholar, critic, essayist, poet, dramatist and editor of the influential literary journal *Y Llenor*, which he founded in 1922. His work embodied a reaction against the censorious and moralistic chapel culture which had evolved in nineteenth-century Wales. His early poetry was a celebration of sensual experience and his play, *Beddau'r Proffwydi* (1913), which represented a new movement in Welsh drama in the pre-war years, upbraided the chapels for their hypocrisy. In 1910, another product of rural Caernarfonshire, R. Williams Parry, proclaimed his arrival on the national poetic scene with his prize-winning *awdl*, *Yr Haf* (Summer), at the

Colwyn Bay eisteddfod. A humanist spirit and a poignant awareness of human transience pervaded his poetry.

The cultural revival was not confined to the Welsh-language
world of writing. The publication of Caradoc Evans's collection
of short stories, *My People*, in 1915 is often seen as the harbinger
of a new genre of Welsh writing through the medium of the
English language. This and *Capel Sion*, which appeared in 1916,
concentrate on the greed, lust and hypocrisy of his Cardiganshire
peasants. Like his Welsh-language contemporaries, he rejected
the Nonconformist establishment and attacked its oppressive and
hierarchical social order with ferocity. No other Anglo-Welsh
prose writer seems to have displayed such animosity towards
Wales or its inhabitants. Another work which is frequently
treated as a founding text of Anglo-Welsh literature is J. O.
Francis's play, *Change*, published in 1912. It was performed in
London and New York, and toured south Wales. The play
addressed a range of social, religious and political issues. Francis
recognized the new labour activism of the pre-war years with its
increased militancy and class consciousness, and saw moral
authority sliding away from the chapels to the new labour
organizations. Whereas Welsh-language writers tended to reject
industrialization and withdraw from the economic and social
challenges of the period, J. O. Francis and a coterie of Anglo-
Welsh authors who followed him accepted the industrial world of
south Wales and produced trenchant descriptions of its society.

The crisis of war severely tested the new generation of
dramatists, poets and prose writers. The overwhelming mass of
the Welsh people plunged into the war with unstinting enthusiasm. In the *Beirniad*, academics such as Sir John Morris-Jones
attacked Germany in the most belligerent terms. Nonconformist
ministers urged their congregations to fight the good fight on
behalf of liberal values. Largely because of the pervasive
influence of Nonconformity, it was almost impossible to produce
literature in Wales which would criticize the war effort. Poetry
columns appeared in local, denominational and literary periodicals, such as *Y Brython*, *Y Goleuad* and *Y Geninen*, which voiced pro-
war propaganda and anti-German invective. Even the National
Eisteddfod was commandeered for jingoistic purposes. At Bangor
in 1915, Lloyd George delivered a belligerent address from the
eisteddfod platform in praise of the Welsh military tradition. The

erstwhile sanctuaries of learning were tarnished by unseemly acts of persecution as scholars were harassed for their conscientious objections to war. At Aberystwyth, the elderly Professor Ethé, a linguist of international reputation, was forced to flee the town rabble and expelled from his professorial chair.

Amidst such militaristic euphoria it was scarcely surprising that Welsh prose failed to flourish during the war years. Various poets did respond to the war, and pre-eminent among these was the Merioneth shepherd, 'Hedd Wyn'. At the Birkenhead eisteddfod in 1917 he was awarded the chair posthumously for his poem, *Yr Arwr* (The Hero). Hedd Wyn had been killed in battle before the commencement of the eisteddfod and the chair was draped in black. He came to symbolize Wales and the First World War, a youthful and romantic sacrifice for Welsh national honour and liberal values. R. Williams Parry was more restrained in his response to the impact of war, and remained detached from the romanticism found in Hedd Wyn's poetry. The Revd T. E. Nicholas, the Independent minister and Christian Communist, composed several poems which were strongly critical of the war. His sermons were often politically provocative and his pronouncements were usually closely monitored by the police. Both T. Gwynn Jones and the gifted young poet, T. H. Parry-Williams produced poetry which condemned the military response and reflected on a higher scale of values. Parry-Williams's poems became far more despondent and his Christian beliefs slowly evaporated as he contemplated the horrors and bestiality engulfing European civilization.

At a different literary level, the writing of Welsh history had blossomed in the early years of the century. With the establishment of the federal university in the 1890s, the emphasis on teaching and researching Welsh history had been fortified. The pioneer in this field was John Edward Lloyd, born in Liverpool, and a history graduate of Aberystwyth and Lincoln College, Oxford. His *History of Wales from Earliest Times to the Edwardian Conquest*, published in two volumes in 1913, was an enormous achievement. Welsh history was established as a recognized field of study, and his emphasis on pre-conquest Wales, when the nation had remained independent of the English yoke, undoubtedly contributed to the growing sense of national identity in Liberal Wales.

Literary Output in the Inter-War Years

The literary world flourished in this period. The writing of poetry, essays, stories, literary criticism and history, was lively and creative. Although some of the founding fathers had disappeared, with O. M. Edwards's premature death in 1920 and John Morris-Jones' departure in 1929, many of the pre-war luminaries were still active. T. Gwynn Jones was a professor at Aberystwyth, W. J. Gruffydd held a chair at Cardiff, and Thomas Parry-Williams was professor of Welsh at Aberystwyth from 1920 to 1952. Throughout the inter-war period those poets whose work commanded attention were usually ensconced within the universities. Their work reflected a shift to a more individualistic, alienated and analytical form of poetry. One of the most successful poets of the period, whose work exemplified the subtle changes, was T. H. Parry-Williams. He gave expression to the complex self-dissection of psychological experience in *Cerddi* in 1931. His depiction of the brain as machinery reflected his espousal of the post-war scientific view of personality as a collection of conditioned, biological impulses. All the mainstream poets, R. Williams Parry, T. Gwynn Jones and W. J. Gruffydd, adopted a far more critical approach and a sharper tone in their literary output. There were formidable younger poets in the ascendant, like 'Gwenallt' (D. Gwenallt Jones), who hailed from Alltwen, in the Swansea Valley and had been imprisoned as a conscientious objector during the First World War. He emerged as a poet of great and unusual gifts: an instinctive egalitarian socialist, whose early poetry resembled that of his Anglo-Welsh contemporaries, with its setting in industrial, depressed and dispossessed south Wales, his first published tome, *Ysgubau'r Awen* (Sheaves of Poetry) (1939), drew a sharp contrast between the golden past and the contemporary squalor of Wales. Most of these writers found a new outlet for their work with the publication of *Y Llenor* in 1922. The brainchild of W. J. Gruffydd, this new quarterly was the semi-official journal of the University of Wales's Welsh departments. It provided a platform for creative talent and a vehicle for the transmission of literature of the highest quality. Under Gruffydd's redoubtable leadership, *Y Llenor* expressed trenchant views on all aspects of Welsh cultural life. It reserved especial criticism for the eisteddfod, which it regarded as an amateur festival with ill-equipped adjudicators. The rise of academic criticism triggered a corresponding decline in the status of the eisteddfod. When academics eventually co-operated with the eisteddfod authorities in the mid-1930s to revise its constitution and practices, they were concerned more for the eisteddfod's survival as a national institution than for its apparent role as an agent of cultural excellence.

The thirties also witnessed the appearance of the Welsh novel. With jingoism in retreat and pacifism in vogue, conscientious objectors, who had been assailed as traitors during the war years, were now regarded as the custodians of individual conscience and the defenders of Christian principles. Several talented writers tried to portray the war in novel form. Gwenallt's *Plasau'r Brenin*, published in 1934, was based on Gwenallt himself who had been immured as a conscientious objector in Wormwood Scrubs and Dartmoor between 1917 and 1919. Kate Roberts, the daughter of a Caernarfonshire quarryman, and another contributor to *Y Llenor*, was one of the most gifted authors. In *Traed mewn Cyffion*, which appeared in 1936, she portrayed the hardships of a closely knit Welsh slate-mining community in the Nantlle Valley in the period 1880–1916. The novel presented a critique of Victorian and Liberal Wales. Earlier, in *O Gors y Bryniau* (1925) and *Rhigolau Bywyd* (1929), she had depicted the poignant struggles against poverty and despair experienced in the north Wales slate communities. Possibly the first Welsh novel devoted entirely to the war, *Amser i Ryfel*, was penned by a war veteran, T. Hughes Jones, in 1944. Many of the novels which had appeared in the 1940s were short and experimental. With the publication of T. Rowland Hughes's first novel, *O Law i Law*, in 1943, it became clear that a very significant author had entered the field. He based his work on the closely knit world of Caernarfonshire quarrymen and their families; *Y Chwalfa* (1946) was a portrayal of the effect of the Bethesda quarry strike of 1900 on family and community life. He had turned to writing novels after contracting a crippling disease, and his five novels written between 1943 and 1947 were reflections on his childhood in Llanberis.

The intellectual challenges emerging from the university and its constituent colleges combined with the impact of depression and poverty in the coalfield rekindled the substance of Caradoc Evans's writings in a new, and far more compassionate, generation of authors. One of the first short-story writers to portray Welsh eccentricities was Rhys Davies, whose first book, *Withered Root*, studied an evangelist during the Welsh religious revival of 1904. The contribution made by Glamorgan to the development of a modern Welsh literature in English was immense. The Glamorgan writers exhibited a condition of separateness in many forms: there was the personal isolation of Alun Lewis and Rhys Davies; and the conviction of solidarity with a unique society in the works of Gwyn Thomas, Jack Jones and Lewis Jones. A theme which inspired these Anglo-Welsh writers was their common experience of belonging to a historical region which was not entirely assimilable to England, but which could not be integrated into the *buchedd* (way of life) of traditional, rural, Nonconformist, Welsh-speaking Wales. Jack Jones in *Rhondda Roundabout* and later volumes provided an outlet for the proletariat of the Valleys, celebrating the heroism of the ordinary people of the south Wales mining community. He described the fluidity of life in the industrial townships and searched restlessly for a meaningful political philosophy. Lewis Jones in his two novels, *Cwmardy* and *We Live*, set out to show how the consciousness of human beings was being re-formed by the devastating social and economic conditions of the period. The novels and short stories of Gwyn Thomas offered a portrait of a hostile world, in which his Rhondda appeared as a new kind of society demanding new social, economic and political remedies. What all of these Anglo-Welsh writers shared was an involvement with the cultural, social and political tensions of their native land in the 1920s and 1930s. Many were of working-class origin, and many had worked in the mines before turning to literature. Some, like Jack Jones, actually wrote their novels between visits to their local labour exchanges.

A whole new cluster of poets emerged from south Wales who made dazzling contributions to the Anglo-Welsh literature of the period. Idris Davies, born in Rhymney, lived in England through most of his creative years studying and teaching English. In *Gwalia Deserta* of 1938, and *The Angry Summer* of 1943, he painted a sombre picture of a culture's failure to survive and of the collapse of a whole way of life. Although he was never really at the centre of proletarian consciousness, he sensed the careless cruelty, the affliction and 'the blood upon the coal'. His was a sombre yet sophisticated picture, which inspired much praise from contemporary critics, including T. S. Eliot. Alun Lewis of Aberdare, and Alun Llywelyn-Williams, a native of Cardiff, discerned that they were victims of powers over which they had no control. They experienced recent history, with its military slaughter, and economic devastation, as a predatory monster. Alun Llywelyn-Williams often criticized Welsh-language writers for not engaging with the social and political experiences of the period. He made a similar point with specific reference to the failure of Welsh poets to respond to the impact of the Second World War. Perhaps the most colourful and celebrated of this new generation of poets was Dylan Thomas. A native of Swansea, he spent most of his creative period in Laugharne in the forties and early fifties. He was deeply aware of Welshness and often wrote warmly of the heartfelt values of chapel people. Though not a supporter of nationalism, he had an abiding concern for his native land. His poetry often displayed the internal differences and tensions of Wales, with its rural–urban, religious–secular, Welsh and English frontiers. The founders of a literary quarterly, *Wales*, in the summer of 1937 provided these young poets and novelists with (in the words of Keidrych Rhys) a 'sort of forum' where they could express their views and discuss their achievements. In 1939, the *Welsh Review* appeared under the editorial scrutiny of Gwyn Jones, a distinguished writer and English scholar. Both *Wales* and the *Welsh Review* provided encouragement and stimulation to these aspiring littérateurs.

Arts and Music

The years before 1914 saw momentous changes in European art. New ideas and movements sprang up in rapid succession – Cubism, Fauvism, Expressionism, Futurism and abstract art. Most Welsh artists withdrew from the mainstream of modern art, and Cardiff was isolated from the revolutionary fervour. The Welsh middle classes were too preoccupied with establishing more grandiose and classical monuments to civic pride. There were many artists in Wales, but they preferred to work as individuals, with no collective identity and no school of Welsh painting.

In 1913, it was an Impressionist painting by Manet which aroused the indignation of visitors to a loan exhibition in Cardiff, and not the modernist movements that were swirling through the galleries of Europe. The National Museum of Wales, though not formally opened until 1927, had begun to organize exhibitions in the early twenties. At Gregynog, in mid-Wales, two remarkable sisters, Gwendoline and Margaret Davies, had amassed a collection of about 200 works of art and made substantial contributions to the promotion of art. It had been their intention to establish an arts centre at Gregynog, with studios, pottery workshops, a printing press and facilities for musical recitals. Industrial depression in the inter-war period undermined their financial strength and they were forced to relinquish some of their ambitious plans. They did move into Gregynog in 1924, and they set up a printing press which produced rare volumes and employed artists as illustrators.

In 1924, Eric Gill, with his family and friends, arrived at Capel-y-Ffin in Breconshire. Supported by his entourage and his disciple, David Jones, he established Capel-y-Ffin as a self-sufficient community, dedicated to furthering the high ideals of Christianity and creativity. The cold and damp winter conditions gravely affected the community and, after four years of relentless toil, Gill and his family moved to Buckinghamshire. Augustus John, the portrait painter, had encountered Picasso in Paris, but he distanced himself from the revolutionary trends. Although he had retained his Welsh connections, he played no part in fostering a Welsh school of art. Of the emerging generation of painters in the twenties, Ceri Richards, of Dunvant, Swansea, was one of the most promising. He had attended Swansea Art School from 1920 to 1924, during its halcyon period. Throughout the 1930s, and especially after the Second World War, Richards made a powerful impression on the art world. The depression years were especially harsh for struggling young tyros in all countries. Artists in Wales must have enviously descried the impressive achievements of Ceri Richards, newly established in the London art world, and Augustus John, who had grown affluent through his association with international art. Other artists were attracted by the Welsh landscape: John Piper, Graham Sutherland and John Nash settled in the Principality for periods. Piper came to south-west Wales in 1937, while Sutherland's Welsh series extended from 1934 to 1980.

In the musical world, the male-voice choirs had been undermined by years of depression, mass emigration and the gradual weakening of the chapels and congregational singing. The Morriston Orpheus continued to flourish, as did the choral festivals in many of the Valleys. These were lean years for the eisteddfod, with little of creative worth emanating from its seasonal tabernacles. As in the field of Welsh literature, aspiring young musicians preferred not to expose themselves to the amateur adjudicators of the festival. The Welsh National Orchestra, supported by the BBC, at first survived for only three years from 1928 to 1931, though it was resurrected after 1935. By 1924, there were departments of music at three of the constituent colleges of the University of Wales. Also, in 1924 the National Council of Music was established under the directorship of Sir Walford Davies.

The music composed was almost entirely vocal. The eisteddfod and Nonconformity were influential in demanding choral pieces for their chapel concerts and competitions. Before the First World War, there were very few opportunities in Wales to hear an orchestra, and few played orchestral instruments unless they were members of a chapel orchestra. At the university colleges, students could learn about instrumental music, but they rarely heard orchestral instruments apart from the harp and the violin, and possibly a local brass band.

In the inter-war years, there was a gradual improvement in instrumental music and in other fields of interest. One gifted, enthusiastic and inspired musician was largely responsible for the gradual transformation in musical fortunes, Sir Walford Davies. Before the First World War, he had achieved fame in England, as an organist and choral director. He was appointed professor of music at Aberystwyth in 1919, and he assumed the directorship of the National Council of Music to promote musical education in Wales. During his tenure at the University College of Wales, Aberystwyth, he employed professional instrumentalists to give regular series of concerts and to teach their instruments. From 1919 onwards, he encouraged schools and towns throughout the Principality to establish music festivals and to promote musical education. He brought prestigious orchestras to Wales and established a prominent festival in his own seaside university town. Elgar, Vaughan Williams, Sir Henry Wood and Adrian Boult visited Wales in turn. From 1933 to 1938, major festivals of music and poetry were held at Gregynog; though the first generation of Welsh composers to show an understanding of the orchestra and to use it imaginatively, Daniel Jones, Mansel Thomas, Grace Williams and Arwel Hughes, were rarely invited to perform in the concert hall in mid-Wales. These talented Welsh composers, all born at the time of the First World War, and shunned by the Anglicized bastion at Gregynog, composed mainly for orchestras and chamber recitals. Indeed, in 1953, one critic complained that works by Daniel Jones were usually performed outside his native land.

The Press and the New Media

By 1940, the increased press activity that had characterized the period 1890–1920 had decelerated to such an extent that, in the major centres of publication, the number of titles had been reduced to their 1880 levels. In 1880, there had been four newspapers in Caernarfon (two in Welsh), five in Swansea and six in Cardiff. By 1930, there were seven in Caernarfon (five in Welsh), nine in Swansea and eight in Cardiff. In 1940, the number of newspapers in Caernarfon had fallen to four (three in Welsh), there were five in Swansea (two in Welsh) and six in Cardiff.

The First World War had stimulated newspaper production and enhanced the importance of the industry as an agent of propaganda. The *Western Mail* and the English-language press moved swiftly to respond to the call of patriotism. *Welsh Outlook* and O. M. Edwards's *Cymru*, along with the denominational weeklies, *Y Tyst* and *Y Goleuad*, supported the government's military policies. Thomas Rees's *Y Deyrnas*, commencing in 1916 at the behest of a coterie of Welsh intellectuals, that included T. Gwynn Jones and T. H. Parry-Williams, campaigned openly against the war. The war intensified public interest in news and transformed newspapers into essential commodities. The number of titles rose markedly during the years 1914–20:

Table 4.1

Year	English-language titles	Welsh-language titles
1914	119	20
1920	131	21

The inter-war concentration of ownership in Wales followed the British trend. By 1918, D. A. Thomas, Viscount Rhondda, had acquired control of the *Western Mail*. He had also procured the *South Wales Journal of Commerce*, *Y Faner*, *North Wales Times*, *Y Tyst*, *Y Darian*, the *Cambrian News* and the *Merthyr Express*. The take-overs of the 1920s heralded a period of intense competition for the large, industrial market of south Wales. Rothermere purchased two Swansea newspapers, the Liberal *Cambrian Daily Leader* and the Conservative *South Wales Daily Post* in 1929. There were alternative sources of news, many of which were produced by left-wing groups. The Communist *Daily Worker* circulated from 1930. The miners' union produced two official journals, the *Colliery Workers' Magazine* from 1923 to 1927, and *Miners' Monthly* from 1934 to 1939. The *South Wales Miner* appeared from 1933 to 1935, edited and produced by Arthur Horner. The Labour Party produced *Y Dinesydd Gymreig*, which circulated until 1929. A revived nationalist press also surfaced during the inter-war years. At Aberystwyth, the student paper *Y Wawr*, edited by Ambrose Bebb, was actually banned by the college authorities. *Y Genhinen* and *Y Faner* continued to serve as vehicles of mainstream nationalist thought. In June 1926, almost a year after the new nationalist party was founded, the new monthly, *Y Ddraig Goch*, was launched. An English-language version, *Welsh Nationalist*, commenced in 1932. In addition to the more politically orientated newspapers and periodicals, there was a significant presence of cultural journals in the 1930s: Keidrych Rhys edited *Wales* from 1937 to 1939; and Gwyn Jones edited *Welsh Review* from 1939 to 1948.

The major international companies, Pathé, Éclair and Eclipse had distributed newsreels during the Edwardian years. By the mid-1920s the new media were beginning to mount a challenge to the print industry, and especially when radio arrived to complement the cinema newsreels. The BBC began transmitting programmes to Wales from the early twenties. A station was founded at Cardiff in February 1923, while others followed at Swansea in 1924 and Bangor in 1934. The University of Wales Advisory Committee on broadcasting, which included Saunders Lewis, lobbied for a separate Welsh region of the BBC. In July 1937, separation was finally achieved and a Welsh home service came into operation. News and current affairs programmes were often incomplete and patchy in the inter-war period. Sporting events were broadcast, and a number of schemes attempted to reflect Welsh industry and work. In 1935, a twelve-part series, *Workday World*, explored the problems confronting Welsh industry. In 1937, T. Rowland Hughes launched his Industries of Wales series, and in the following year the first Welsh national lecture was broadcast. By the Second World War, perceptive observers had come to appreciate the importance of sound broadcasting in the public arena, and pressure began to mount for more Welsh programmes and the appointment of Welsh-speaking producers and assistants.

SUGGESTED READING

Trevor Herbert and Gareth Elwyn Jones (eds.), *Post-War Wales* (Cardiff, 1995).

D. Johnston (ed.), *A Guide to Welsh Literature, c. 1900–1996* (Cardiff, 1998).

Gareth Elwyn Jones, *Which Nation's Schools* (Cardiff, 1990).

Gareth Elwyn Jones (ed.), *Education, Culture and Society* (Cardiff, 1991).

Gareth Elwyn Jones, *The Education of a Nation* (Cardiff, 1997).

R. B. Jones (ed.), *Anatomy of Wales* (Cowbridge, 1972).

R. Mathias, *Anglo-Welsh Literature* (Bridgend, 1987).

Kenneth O. Morgan, *Rebirth of a Nation: Wales 1880–1980* (Oxford, 1981).

E. Rowan, *Art in Wales 1850–1980* (Cardiff, 1985).

J. G. Williams, *University of Wales, 1893–1939* (Cardiff, 1997).

Part II
1945–2000

5. Restructuring the Economy

THE depression of the 1930s had been so severe in Wales that there had often appeared to be no solution to the economic problems other than prolonged contraction and large-scale emigration. Because governments were unable or unwilling to intervene to alleviate the continuing human distress, the industrial regions of Wales were indeed crucified during this wretched period in Welsh history. It had required the challenges of war to bring about the necessary regeneration of the Welsh economy. The war of 1939–45 had four enduring effects upon the Welsh economy: first, it produced a substantial increase in the employment of women; secondly, it resulted in a greater diversification of industry in south Wales; thirdly, war led to a run-down in the numbers employed in the basic industries of coal, steel and tinplate, and this, in turn, begat the rationalization of the labour force in the post-war years; and finally, there occurred a substantial extension of government involvement in economic affairs from 1945 onwards.

In the following pages we shall examine the ways in which the Welsh economy responded to these and other challenges during the second half of the century. It may be helpful to consider these enormous changes in two chronological sections: the first period, from 1945 to 1970; and the second from 1970 to the end of the century.

The Period 1945–1970

Agriculture

The contribution of agriculture to the Welsh economy was not vastly different from that which it made to the UK economy. In 1951, agriculture accounted for about 5 per cent of the national product in Wales and in the UK. In Wales, however, the sector employed 7.4 per cent of the working population, whereas in England the corresponding figure was 4.7 per cent.

Between 1931 and 1951 there had been a 15 per cent fall in the numbers engaged in agriculture, from 91,000 to 77,000. The proportion of the working population in agriculture had also fallen from 10 per cent to 7 per cent. The rural hinterland of Wales experienced a steady drift and decline of population. Incomes per head in agriculture were nearly always lower than those in other sectors of the economy, and this resulted in a transfer of labour from farming to other occupations. The rate of transfer was rarely steady and usually increased dramatically at times of industrial buoyancy.

Since 1931, the total number of agricultural holdings in Wales had dropped 13 per cent, from 60,410 to 52,816; and the fall in the amount of land in agricultural use was just under 13 per cent in the same period. The drift from the land produced the inevitable consequences that some holdings were amalgamated into larger units, while farm land was abandoned or surrendered to alternative uses.

Perhaps the most striking feature of Welsh agriculture was the relative importance of grassland and livestock. The rainfall pattern and the topography of Wales had largely determined the greater dependence on grass and livestock. There was a much higher density of sheep on the land of Wales than in the rest of the UK, and the numbers of sheep and cattle multiplied in the years 1920–60.

Table 5.1 Sheep and cattle populations in Wales, 1920–1960

Year	Number of sheep ('000)	Number of cattle ('000)
1920	3331	774
1939	4648	856
1960	5196	1127

Economic changes greatly affected the pattern of Welsh agriculture. During the depressed years of the 1920s and 1930s, the proportion of arable land fell by almost a half. The Second World War, with its ploughing campaign and sustained high prices for agricultural products, resulted in a vast extension of the arable area. In the post-war period, the proportion of arable land reverted almost to its 1920 level.

Table 5.2 Changes in the use of agricultural land, 1920–1960
(% of total agricultural land)

Year	Total arable %	Permanent grass
1920	20.4	45.9
1939	11.9	47.9
1946	26.4	31.0
1960	21.8	45.7

The farms of Wales continued to be relatively small and precarious enterprises, compared with those of England or Scotland. In Wales, 55 per cent of the agricultural land was distributed among the 85 per cent of the holdings of under a hundred acres. In England, the 77 per cent of holdings of under a hundred acres covered only 27 per cent of the agricultural area. There was little change in the size of Welsh holdings in the post-war years. In 1939, 88.3 per cent of Welsh holdings were of less than a hundred acres, while in 1958 the figure was 85.4 per cent. The smaller average size of farms meant that there was less demand for hired labour in the Welsh sector. In 1951, there were around 41,000 farmers in Wales and 29,800 farm workers by contrast with England, where the corresponding figures were 249,400 farmers and 551,000 farm workers.

Increased mechanization also reduced the need for agricultural labourers. In 1959, Wales had one tractor for every 20 acres of arable area, compared with one for every 33 in England. Between 1942 and 1960 the number of tractors in Wales increased sixfold, compared with a fourfold rise in England. The Welsh farmers' investment in machinery, and their increasing tendency to apply fertilizers and improved methods of harvesting, had accounted for the considerable improvement in crop yields since the 1920s.

The small size of Welsh farms, together with the reliance on livestock farming and the poor quality of land, were factors which accounted for the relative poverty of the Welsh farmer during this period. It has been estimated that the average return for the Welsh farmer in 1951 was about £346, compared with £1,233 for the average farmer in the UK. Nevertheless, agriculture in Wales continued to advance from the mid-1930s. The establishment of the Milk Marketing Board in 1933, and the commencement of the collection of liquid milk from farms, which had previously depended on the rearing of cattle and sheep, launched a period of greater security for the Welsh farmer. Between 1934 and 1939 the number of registered milk producers had grown by 92.4 per cent, and by a further 47 per cent in the years to 1947. As in other parts of Britain, the security of the monthly milk cheque induced a concentration on milk production. The Welsh farmer also derived some benefit from the attempt of the Fatstock Marketing Corporation and the National Farmers' Union to provide the beef producer with an equivalent form of support. Agricultural legislation passed since 1945 further buttressed the security of the Welsh farmer. Under the Agriculture Act of 1947 minimum guaranteed prices were assured for most farm products; and subsidies were provided for hill farmers. Total payments to Welsh farmers in 1958–9 in the form of subsidies and production grants came to almost £14 million, or 6 per cent of the total of agricultural support in the United Kingdom. The Agriculture Act of 1957 provided grants to farmers to cover up to one-third of the cost of major permanent improvements. Between 1957 and 1960 the number of farm-improvement schemes approved in Wales rose from 281 to 5,492.

Welsh farmers participated in agricultural co-operative societies on a grand scale. In 1955, the co-operative societies had a total membership of over 54,000, or one-fifth of the membership in the whole of the United Kingdom. The total value of sales by all Welsh co-operative societies was nearly £12 million in 1955, at least six times their value in 1939. In 1955, Wales had forty-five general-purpose societies, twenty-seven specialized marketing societies, eleven service societies and five farming societies.

Notwithstanding these improvements in agriculture, and often on account of them, the movement out of farming continued unabated. There was also a progressive disappearance of industry in rural Wales. Forestry, however, provided one outlet for employment, with the Forestry Commission acquiring land at the rate of 10,000 acres per year in the 1950s. There was also some rural employment in the construction of capital projects, such as the reservoirs at Clywedog in Montgomeryshire and Tryweryn in Merioneth. Hydro-electric schemes provided limited sources of employment, and defence expenditure provided civilian jobs at RAF Valley in Anglesey. But the dominant impression of the rural heartlands of Wales was one of decay. This was often heightened by the implementation of government decisions concerning public transport. The Beeching Report of 1963 savagely reduced railway mileage from 637 to 363. Lines from Swansea to Aberystwyth, Barmouth to Ruabon, Bangor to Pwllheli, and dozens of other local lines in the south Wales Valleys, were terminated. Commentators soon noted that it was no longer possible to travel from north to south Wales by train.

Coal

Although coal, steel and tinplate had lost the predominant position which they had enjoyed before 1939, they still continued to play an integral role in the development of the economy after the Second World War. The coal industry in 1946 was in an enfeebled condition: the geological structure of the south Wales coalfield, with its high incidence of faulting, the prevalence of old workings and the failure of coalowners in the inter-war period to promote the necessary mechanization, all contributed to the parlous position of the industry. Yet, there was a positive side to this picture: the total reserves of the coalfield were second only to those of the Yorkshire coalfield; and there was a variety of coals in the coalfield, which gave it a special significance. In the western rim of the south Wales coalfield there existed the only extensive reserves of anthracite coal in Britain, while Glamorgan possessed rich reserves of coking coals. The wartime decline in production was soon arrested in the immediate post-war years, and, when the mines were nationalized in January 1947, it seemed as if a bright new dawn was about to illuminate the Valleys, auguring well for the Welsh miners and their families. The years following 1947 can be divided into two subsections, with a distinct turning-point around 1957. Until 1949 little reorganization had occurred in the industry, as the National Coal Board responded to a post-war fuel shortage by continuing the policy begun by the private coalowners of working coal at all costs. Although the first 'Plan for Coal', which began in 1950, was far too optimistic, a more realistic plan appeared in 1956, which acknowledged that the rate of investment needed to be doubled if production targets were to be met.

With the onset of an industrial recession in 1956, and especially as a result of the increased availability of alternative fuels, there occurred a drastic contraction in the demand for coal. In 1962, the 18 million tons output of the south Wales coalfield was 35 per cent less than had been forecast in 1956. The national picture was even less cheerful, which prompted the National Coal Board to draw up a third major plan in 1959. This heralded a decade of mechanization and rationalization.

The chronological division into pre- and post-1957 years is important for a clear analysis of the coal industry during this period. Until 1957, coal experienced very little competition from other fuels, and the essential task was mining as much coal as possible. After 1957, the position altered drastically as new fuels increased in importance, and the problem became one of adapting to a changed market position. Between the years 1957 and 1972 the industry had to accept that it was no longer the sole provider of fuel to the British economy.

The National Coal Board's policy of revitalization and rationalization was based on the following methods: the closure of the older, smaller mines, because of the exhaustion of workable reserves, or because of uneconomic production; the modernization of existing collieries with adequate reserves for further exploitation; the construction of new mines; and the large-scale introduction of mechanization. The closure of collieries progressed throughout the period after nationalization; in 1959 alone, eight mines were closed in Glamorgan. No sector of the British mining industry underwent such a massive contraction as Wales after 1945. In 1960, there were still 106,000 employed in the pits there, but by 1970 there had been a dramatic fall to only 60,000 employees. Under Lord Robens, the National Coal Board introduced a major policy of pit closures in 1957–9, when twenty-three collieries ceased production. As late as 1958, there were twelve major pits working in the Rhondda; but, by 1969, only Maerdy was still operational. An average of ten pits a year closed in the 1960s, leaving only twenty-one anthracite collieries in Wales in 1963, as compared with thirty-nine in 1948. In the Swansea region, only three anthracite collieries were still functioning in 1970.

To replace these collieries, the NCB often sank new mines, such as the showcase new anthracite colliery at Cynheidre near

Llanelli, opened in 1960, and Abernant in the Swansea Valley, neither of which proved to be as successful as the NCB had hoped. Though the new mines made a significant contribution to the industry's progress after 1947, the main plank of the NCB's policy was the reorganization and modernization of those existing collieries which had the best workable potential. Of £170 million capital invested in the south Wales coalfield between 1947 and 1970, approximately 80 per cent was spent on the modernization of existing collieries. The reconstruction of specially selected mines usually involved the sinking of new shafts, or the deepening of existing ones. From 1948 to 1953, nearly £32 million was invested in pits in the Cardiff region alone, where less than £4,500,000 was expended on the new mining project at Nantgarw.

A further development was the introduction of mechanization into many coal-mining processes. Though coal could be cut mechanically, the real need was to devise machines which could cut and load simultaneously. In 1950, there was only one power-loader in use in Glamorgan and, as late as 1960, 80 per cent of total output was still loaded by hand. During the 1960s, however, there occurred a real breakthrough in the use of power-loading machinery.

The net result of these various methods employed by the NCB was a substantial improvement in productivity, and especially after the critical year of 1956. From 1962, the average rate of increase in productivity in the south Wales coalfield was approximately 5 per cent per annum, which compared favourably with other British coalfields. These substantial improvements in productivity did not lead to an increase in total output over the long term, however. As the competition from other fuels emerged between the mid-1950s and early 1970s, the demand for coal ebbed and total output contracted. As overall demand for coal decreased, the coal industry became increasingly dependent upon a narrow range of customers. The major market was for coking coals, and approximately 50 per cent of the total output of Glamorgan's coal was supplied to coking ovens. Another source, which accounted for 25 per cent of Glamorgan's coals was the domestic heating market. Electricity generation was a third major outlet for south Wales coal, comprising 22 per cent of the total demand.

Notwithstanding these improvements, the clear, irreversible trend was the deliberate and consistent run-down of the Welsh coal industry. From 1947 to 1972, 150 collieries in south Wales were closed down, and 75,000 jobs disappeared with them. New fuels were slowly dislodging the once-mighty King Coal from his throne: cheap imports of oil flooded in from the Middle East; oil reserves were being discovered in the North Sea; new nuclear-based power stations were sited in north Wales; and hydroelectric schemes were thriving in mid-Wales and Merioneth. Despite an apparent reprieve in the early 1970s, the unmistakable pattern was one of contraction.

Steel and Tinplate

The history of steel and tinplate manufacture since 1945 was quite similar to that of the coal-mining industry. There followed a dramatic process of rationalization and modernization which involved the replacement of numerous obsolete units of production by a few, large and highly mechanized plants. The essential difference between the two mighty industries was that, whereas coal mining contracted over the long term, steel and tinplate manufacture experienced a substantial expansion.

In 1945, steel and tinplate production was in desperate need of modernization. The industry embraced two major sections: the manufacture of crude steel, and steel finishing, which included the production of tinplate. The steel-making plants were mainly cold-metal shops which bought scrap and cold pig-iron. Steel was then supplied to the finishing plants for further processing. Each section of the industry functioned separately and the individual units of production were small. Concentration of the ownership of steel and tinplate plants, which had begun before 1945, had hardly affected the location of the plants, and wasteful inter-plant transfers were still a regular feature. By 1946, there were twelve small crude-steel-manufacturing plants and fifty-six sheet-steel and tinplate hand-mills in Glamorgan alone.

The modern era of steel production in south Wales had begun at Ebbw Vale in 1936 with the construction of Britain's first fully integrated, hot strip-mill. In 1944, Richard Thomas and Co. and Baldwins Ltd had decided to combine their resources in order to proceed with the construction of a new strip-mill. Inflated costs of production soon scuppered this plan, but in 1947 they amalgamated with Guest, Keen, John Lysaght Ltd and the Llanelly Associated Tinplate Company to form the Steel Company of Wales. This amalgamation soon proceeded with the construction of a new integrated strip-mill. The Steel Company of Wales envisaged the complete modernization and integration of the steel-making and finishing processes. Construction of the new integrated plant, the Abbey Works, began in 1948 on a green-field site near the existing Port Talbot and Margam steel-works, and was completed in 1952. The whole complex included four blast furnaces, twenty-one open-hearth furnaces and an eighty-inch strip-mill. It was the largest steelworks in Britain with a productive capacity of nearly 3 million tons a year, and providing employment for over 17,000 men in 1963.

A cold-reduction plant to roll sheet steel was constructed at Margam, but the other two plants, which concentrated on the finishing process of tinplate manufacture, were located at Trostre, near Llanelli, and Velindre, near Swansea, both sites being chosen on the basis of local employment needs. The overall effect of the expansion was the eventual closure of the older cold-metal works and the tinplate hand-mills. Of the fourteen tinplate hand-mills operating in 1957 in Glamorgan, only one, the Pontardawe works, remained open at the end of 1959, and that closed in 1961. The effect of the new Llanwern Steelworks coming into production in 1961 was the closure of most of the remaining cold-metal shops in Glamorgan. With the Ebbw Vale works thriving, and the John Summers works at Shotton showing a steady increase in production, the rejuvenated steel and tinplate industry made an invaluable contribution to post-war economic growth. Output in Wales rose by 23 per cent between 1948 and 1954, compared with only 18 per cent for Britain as a whole.

The major cause of the growth in demand for steel and tinplate was the enormous boom in consumer-durable goods. The post-war years of high mass-consumption generated a massive increase in the market for steel products. The expansion of the motor-car industry was especially important, and by 1976 motor-car manufacturing was consuming 60 per cent of the output of sheet steel from Port Talbot. The major proportion of tinplate output was supplied to the metal-box and can-manu-facturing industries for food-canning and other packaging purposes. The expansion of steel production was also boosted by the emergence of new uses, such as the use of sheet steel in building, for the manufacture of heating and ventilating systems.

With the expansion of the economy in the 1950s and 1960s and the continuingly insatiable demand for steel, the prospects for the Welsh steel industry seemed very promising. But, as with the other staple heavy industry, a concatenation of factors gradually weakened the industry: the legacy of low productivity, managerial inefficiency and a falling rate of capital investment had adverse effects; the political tergiversations, with nationaliza-tion in 1951, denationalization in 1953, followed by renation-alization in 1967, deprived the industry of clear-sighted policies; and increasing competition from the more efficient and product-ive steel industries of West Germany, the USA and Japan com-pounded the difficulties for the Welsh industry. In 1950, Britain manufactured 8.5 per cent of the world's total output of steel, but by 1976 this figure had slumped to around 3 per cent. Japan's productive capacity increased at a phenomenal rate: in 1955, Japan produced only half as much steel as Britain, yet by 1968, the two leading Japanese companies produced almost as much as the combined output of all the British plants. In 1976, Japan produced 102 million tons of steel, five and a half times as much as Britain.

North Wales Slate Industry

The number of men employed in slate production in 1939 was 7,589. At the end of hostilities, their numbers had been depleted to 3,520. In 1972, barely 1,000 men worked in the industry. As a result of the exigencies of war, at least twenty-three of the forty-one firms operating in 1939 had ceased production by 1945. The need to repair war-damaged houses brought a glimmer of hope to the industry in the immediate post-war years, and the number of employees rose to 4,050 in 1946. Ironically, the difficulty facing the industry was the shortage of skilled labour, the reasons for which were varied: during the war some workmen had joined the forces while others had been directed to war work outside the area, and many of these experienced workers had never returned to the industry; the inherent dangers of slate mining effectively discouraged cohorts of the younger generation from following in their fathers' footsteps; another factor was the widespread fear of silicosis.

The years 1952–5 brought mixed fortunes for the industry as foreign roofing-slates were imported, and the export of slates from the United Kingdom declined. During the 1950s and 1960s many quarries invested in modern machinery as part of a drive to increase output. In 1953, diesel locomotives were introduced in some of the mines, while at the Dorothea Quarry newly constructed roads enabled heavy rock-excavating machines to reach the bottom of the quarry. In 1962, the Dinorwic Quarry developed slate as a flooring material, and the Dorothea Quarry ventured into the realm of tourism. The possibilities of the export market were successfully explored by the Dinorwic Company in 1965, and by 1968 the Dorothea Quarry was celebrating an increased French demand for its flooring slates. In 1972, Penrhyn Quarries Ltd were producing 11,000 tons of roofing slates annually, a substantial proportion of which was sent to Ireland, France, Holland, Denmark, Belgium, Australia, the USA, New Zealand and Austria.

The decline of slate quarrying as an economic enterprise was relentless. The Dinorwic Quarry was forced to close in 1969 with the loss of 300 jobs. In 1970, the Dorothea Quarry followed along the same sombre path. By 1972, there were only five quarries still working in north Wales, one of which was Penrhyn in Bethesda with a total workforce of 350 men. There was a brief revival in the slate industry in the 1970s, and by 1978 it was reported that there were 550 quarrymen employed in Gwynedd. A number of factors were responsible for the decline of the industry: the contraction in housebuilding since 1969; the failure of local authorities to use slate in their housing programmes; a lack of capital had prevented the small Welsh firms from participating successfully in new markets; and a dwindling export trade had taken its toll.

Industrial Diversification

One of the dominant features of the post-war years was the trend to diversify and to modernize the industrial structure of Wales. The whole of south Wales was designated as a development area and its administration was the responsibility of an increasingly interventionist Board of Trade. Manufacturing industry was discouraged from siting new plants in London, the south-east and the Midlands, and actively encouraged to move to the older industrial areas, with the result that by 1949 new factories had opened in various parts of south Wales. The demand for building space and factory sites in south Wales was almost insatiable until the early 1950s. In the Rhondda, twenty-five government-assisted factories had been set up by 1955, producing a wide range of products. The old wartime ordnance factories were also converted for peacetime industrial purposes. The factory at Bridgend became the centre of a large new trading estate, employing over 30,000 workers. The government also sponsored a programme of building advance factories, and this project enticed such firms as Imperial Metals to Gowerton, near Swansea, and Girlings car components to Cwmbran. By 1951, 64,000 jobs had been created for Wales, and unemployment was largely confined to small enclosures in eastern Glamorgan and western Monmouthshire.

The expansion of the petrochemical industry in Glamorgan boosted the economy of west Wales in the period after 1945. An oil refinery had been based at Llandarcy, near Skewen, since 1921. With an increasing demand for oil, refining at Llandarcy grew steadily, reaching a crude-oil-processing capacity of 8 million tons in 1970. Before 1960 crude oil was imported through Swansea docks, but in 1961 BP built an oil terminal at Milford Haven in Pembrokeshire to connect with its refinery. The petrochemical industry attracted a wide range of manufacturing activities to the area. In 1965, the Wales Gas Board completed a plant which manufactured gas from oil supplied from the nearby Llandarcy works. The economy of Pembrokeshire was transformed by the arrival of ocean tankers. In 1960, Esso opened a large new refinery in the Milford area; this was followed by the BP refinery in 1961, a Texaco refinery in 1964, a Gulf Oil refinery in 1968 and an Amoco refinery in 1973. Milford Haven soon became the leading oil port in Britain, with 30 million tons shipped each year.

The war effort, coupled with the strategic siting of industry, had led to a rapid expansion in the engineering and electrical-goods industries. Although the engineering plants were often small, there were some noteworthy developments in south Wales. A Hoover plant came to Merthyr Tydfil, AB Electronic Components was based at Abercynon, and a number of general engineering establishments settled around Cardiff. In the western part of the coalfield, Sony located at Bridgend, the Metal Box at Neath, and Smiths Industries at Ystradgynlais.

In the late 1950s and early 1960s the government persuaded vehicle manufacturers to invest in south Wales. The Ford Motor Company came to Swansea in 1964, and by 1968 almost 2,000 people were employed there in the assembly of sub-frames and axles. The Rover Company arrived at Cardiff in 1963, and Borg Warner established a plant at Margam in 1969.

The expansion of the public, personal and professional service industry further invigorated the economic life of Wales in this period. Government departments were dispersed from London, and Wales attracted 16,500 civil service posts between 1963 and 1975. A new passport office was set up at Newport, Companies House came to Cardiff, the Ministry of Transport car registration and licensing centre and the Land Registry were relocated to Swansea, and the Royal Mint transferred to Llantrisant. By 1968, there were over 345,000 people employed in service occupations. A dominant feature of this changing industrial structure from the 1940s was the concentration of economic activity and employment opportunities in a narrower geographical part of south Wales. The coastal strip of southern Glamorgan, especially the area from Barry to Llanwern, absorbed much of the new industry. In north-east Wales, economic growth focused around Deeside in eastern Flintshire. There followed a geographical redistribution of working population away from the heartland of Wales to the north- and south-eastern peripheries. The old industrial and mining centres were losing population to these expanding peripheral zones. Cardiff and Newport increased their population by 40 per cent in the 1950s and 1960s, at a time when industrial south Wales was expanding by only 5 per cent.

The changes in transport, which eventually effected a fundamental realignment of the main arteries from a north–south to an east–west direction, tended to reaffirm the strong impression that the new centres of economic activity and prosperity would be confined within increasingly narrow parts of Wales. The opening of the Severn Bridge in 1966, the 'Heads of the Valleys' road along the northern rim of the coalfield, and the extension of the M4 motorway from London to the eastern suburbs of Cardiff, were seen as clear manifestations of this growing trend by the early 1970s.

The Period 1970–2000

Agriculture

During the 1970s and 1980s agriculture remained an important industry in Wales, contributing about 4 per cent to Gross Domestic Product and employing about 57,000 people as farmers or employees. Of these, only 32,000 were engaged on a regular, full-time basis; others were seasonal or part-time employees. The overall figures masked considerable regional variations within the Principality: agriculture accounted for 23.5 per cent of employment in Powys, 15.3 per cent in Dyfed, and as little as 0.7 per cent in south Glamorgan.

About a third of all agricultural land in Wales lies above the 1,000-foot contour, and over a half endures annual rainfall in excess of 50 inches. Under the Ministry of Agriculture's soil assessment, at least 60 per cent of Wales's agricultural land was of poor quality. This was also confirmed by the proportion of land designated as being in Less Favoured Areas under the EEC guidelines. Topography, climate and soil type have largely dictated agricultural practices in Wales. The scarcity of quality soils has limited the possibilities for horticulture and arable farming. Crop-growing occurs mainly in the form of cereals, stock-feeding crops and potatoes in the milder climate of the west coast. Sheep and cattle were still by far the most important sectors, and this was reflected by the areas given over to grass.

Table 5.3 Areas under crops and grass (%)

Year	Arable	Permanent grass	Rough grazings
1974	17.0	45.3	36.1
1979	15.3	49.3	32.7
1984	15.1	51.2	31.1
1989	13.3	53.4	30.4
1995	12.4	54.5	29.4

Physical and climatic factors also largely determined the sizes and structures of Welsh holdings. Traditionally, a much smaller percentage of Welsh holdings has been of a large size. During the 1970s and 1980s, however, the contraction of the industry ensured that the number of holdings dropped from 48,000 in

Table 5.4 Number of sheep and lambs on agricultural holdings

Year	Total in thousands
1974	6736.8
1979	7571.0
1984	9000.8
1989	10754.4
1995	11190.7

1970 to 30,000 in 1990. There was a reduction in the number of holdings of all sizes, but especially in the number of farms of less than fifty acres. In 1970, there were 28,434 farms of this size in Wales which, by 1990, had dropped to fewer than 12,000.

In Wales, as in many industrialized countries, the agricultural sector received generous levels of public support. Public policy towards agriculture has affected farm outputs, the use of farming methods and the welfare of farmers and farm workers. Total payments of grants and subsidies to Welsh farmers from both British and EEC sources reached a peak in 1984–5.

Table 5.5 Agricultural grants and subsidies (£m at 1985 prices)

	1977	1980	1983/4	1984/5
Total grants and subsidies	45727	62762	96094	82320

Political pressure designed to control agricultural spending in the 1980s succeeded in reducing the real value of agricultural support. This resulted in restrictions on production and on the payment of EEC subsidies.

The massive price support and direct aid of recent decades has not only fuelled a general expansion in agricultural activity, but also determined the choice of farming techniques, and especially the degree of mechanization. The number and size of tractors in use has increased sharply since the 1970s.

Changes in mechanization brought alterations to the structure and pattern of employment. Although the total number of persons engaged in agriculture fluctuated slightly over the period, the aggregate figures conceal variations in the composition of the

Table 5.6 Changes in mechanization: numbers of tractors

1971	*1985*
(10–50 h.p.) 33340	(10–54 h.p.) 24073
(over 50 h.p.) 6870	(over 54 h.p.) 26932
(total) 40210	(total) 51005

Table 5.7 Persons engaged in work in agricultural holdings

Year	*Regular whole-time*	*Hired workers, regular whole-time*
1974	8021	5824
1979	3456	5169
1984	3103	4245
1989	2869	3243
1995	2296	2864

Table 5.8 Total persons engaged in agriculture

Year	*Whole-time*	*Part-time*	*Total persons*
1974	22365	4735	52483
1979	25566	9618	56344
1984	25359	10298	55609
1989	23794	11515	53625
1995	22020	13472	53011

workforce. The picture that emerges is of a reduction in regular full-time work in favour of a growth in part-time and casual employment.

Many of those who remained in agriculture during the 1970s and 1980s were in receipt of adequate incomes. Real net farm incomes rose, but the average 1985–6 figure of £7,476 was below the level of earnings in manufacturing. Lowland cattle and up-land sheep farmers attracted miserable rewards for their efforts, as subsidies continually exceeded their average net farm incomes. Throughout the late 1980s and 1990s agriculture in Wales appeared to be in a perpetual state of crisis. Output decreased and the number of people earning a living in agriculture slowly diminished. World trade negotiations and competing claims on the limited budget of the EC gradually squeezed the sector into becoming more efficient. Though agriculture had received generous support from national and supranational sources in the form of subsidies, tariff protection and intervention purchasing, it had been sufficient only to decelerate the trend of falling prices. Livestock prices fared badly, and the spread of the BSE infection undermined beef prices from 1989 onwards. Aggregate farm incomes in Wales fell from a peak in 1988, and costs mounted steadily to squeeze the residue available for farming incomes. The net farm income figures for all Welsh dairy and livestock farms in 1998–9 were predicted to fall by 41 per cent to just £6,854, while cash incomes were set to drop by 21 per cent. The Welsh Office estimated that decline was attributable to falling prices for most commodities in the context of market conditions, to economic difficulties in Russia and Asia, and to the continuing strength of sterling.

In the EC as a whole, and certainly in Wales, the methods of support for agriculture have failed abysmally to achieve their predetermined objectives. In recent years agencies have focused on alternative rural economic developments in an effort to enhance incomes and promote employment prospects. Agriculture still employs a sizeable portion of the rural workforce, while the numbers of people in the predominantly rural counties of Dyfed, Powys and Gwynedd aged from sixteen to sixty-four are projected to increase by 5 per cent between 1991 and 2001, with a further 2½ per cent projected for the years 2002–7. These projections would entail an increase of 32,000 people, of whom at least 16,000 would be of working age.

Proposals for reversing the declining trends in rural employment have often been imaginative and wide-ranging. Diversification in agricultural output and new food-processing activities have ranged from alpaca wool production to worm cultures. Large-scale forestry and wood-processing is the second major land use after agriculture. In Wales, the large scale of afforestation has promoted capital-intensive harvesting and processing techniques.

Planning, however, is a long-term problem, often stretching over a forty-year period; and there are implications for conservation and the environment. Tourism has also played a rather limited role in the provision of alternative employment; according to the Wales Tourist Board estimate of 1990, 10 per cent of all farms in the Principality were involved in some form of tourism-related activity. Although most provided land-based facilities for caravanning or camping, around 1,200 farms participated in seasonal self-catering accommodation, and a further 500 in the provision of guest houses or bed and breakfast facilities. In 1992, the Wales Tourist Board launched a Rural Tourist Development Initiative, with £0.43 million earmarked for further developments.

As a result of innovations in information technology, the application of modern microcomputers and the rapid and accurate transfer of data over the telecommunications network, it is widely anticipated that a greater number of people will work from home, an expectation that underlies the provision of training programmes in information technology. In Wales, the Scheme to Introduce Modern Technology into Rural Areas (SIMTRA) has provided workstation facilities and networking in rural areas. Two prominent examples are the Taf and Cleddau Rural Initiative in Narberth and Antur Teifi in Newcastle Emlyn and Tregaron.

Those statutory bodies entrusted with the responsibility for developing manufacturing enterprises in rural Wales have tended, on the whole, to rely on the provision of industrial space as the main instrument of regional policy for attracting branch plants to rural locations. Despite the injection of sizeable amounts of capital, with £109 million invested in Dyfed, Gwynedd and Powys alone in 1989, productivity in rural Welsh manufacturing has been relatively unimpressive. The most trenchant criticism usually levelled at this policy has been its failure to offset the overwhelming external dependency of the Welsh rural economy. Investment funds are derived from external locations, as are the sources of inputs, and the eventual destinations of sales are also usually external. Considerable sums of money have been expended on rural developments in recent years, and yet the problems of population outflow, the impoverishment of social life, and the lack of decent levels of public and private service provision remain as fundamental challenges for the new millennium.

Coal

Following the huge leap in oil prices after 1973 the prospects for the coal industry looked promising, as the price of coal relative to oil more than halved in the years 1973–4. The incoming Labour government responded swiftly by endorsing a National Coal Board plan for a massive investment programme of around £4.5 billion over a ten-year period. At the time when the British demand for coal was looking healthier, major changes were occurring on the supply side of the coal market. Following the oil shock of 1973, there was a rapid expansion of coal capacity throughout the world and a consequent depression of coal prices, which coincided with the British government's policy of opening up the home market to foreign coals. This relieved the British Steel Corporation and the Central Electricity Generating Board of their former obligations to purchase coal from domestic sources.

During the years 1973–9 the industry experienced a further decline in demand, and the output of south Wales coal fell from 11 million tons to 7.6 million tons. The position worsened with the collapse in steel production after 1973. Neither did the area benefit from the increased use of coal in power stations, which had certainly bolstered the fortunes of many other coalfields in Britain. Productivity increases were especially disappointing at a time when miners' wages rose from 97 per cent of the average for UK manufacturing in 1973 to 123 per cent in 1978.

From 1979–84 a series of factors coalesced to exacerbate the plight of the industry: a severe contraction in economic activity depressed the energy market; imports became more competitive as a result of the fall in the world price of coal; and the coalfields began to feel the impact of the new Conservative government's economic policies. In south Wales, the main effect of the slump was witnessed in the market for coking coal, where demand fell by over a third. With over one-half of south Wales pits producing coking coal, this contraction seriously undermined the strength of the coalfield.

The decline in demand for coal, at a time when output was increasing in response to the previous Labour government's *Plan for Coal*, compounded the difficulties facing the National Coal Board. By 1984, NCB stocks had risen to nearly 50 million tons, or 50 per cent of annual output, while its losses escalated from

£26 million in 1979–80 to £595 million in 1983–4. At least a third of all the NCB's losses of £1,367 million between 1979–80 and 1983–4 was attributable to south Wales. The Conservative government responded by speeding up its programme of pit closures: eight pits were closed in 1979–84, with five disappearing in 1983–4. Rumours of further cutbacks eventually triggered the explosive miners' dispute of 1984–5. When the strike collapsed in March 1985, the NCB was in an invincible position to proceed with further restructuring plans. By 1987, fourteen of the twenty-eight pits operating in south Wales at the beginning of the strike had closed, and the number of miners had fallen from 20,286 in 1984 to 10,200. British Coal (formerly the National Coal Board) justified this sweeping onslaught almost entirely on economic grounds. From 1987 onwards the slaughter of the coal industry continued unabated, so that by 1992 only four collieries remained in south Wales.

Despite the continuous and substantial decline of coal mining in south Wales since the First World War, the industry had retained a prominent position in the local employment market, even as late as 1984. But, in the years from 1978 to 1984, 21,908 jobs had disappeared in the central and eastern coal-mining valleys of south Wales, or a 20.8 per cent reduction in employment. After 1982, over 40 per cent of all unemployment claimants among former miners had been unemployed for over fifty-two weeks.

Although the process of pit closure was brutal and the economic and social consequences were devastating for the coal communities, British Coal launched a programme of investment in the few remaining pits. By March 1986, £55 million had been expended on heavy-duty coalface equipment, £4.5 million on the construction of a new ventilation shaft and the opening of a new drift at Betws, and a further £4.5 million was provided to open up reserves at Abernant. The post-strike period also witnessed an improvement in labour productivity in south Wales, which was accompanied by an equally dramatic improvement in the coalfield's financial performance. Within twelve months of the end of the strike, the coalfield was profitable for the first time since 1958.

By the completion of the transfer of British Coal to the private sector at the end of 1994, only three deep mines remained –

Table 5.9 Trends in coal production in south Wales, 1983–1997

Year	Output (million tons) (deep mine)	Employment (thousands) (deep mine)	Collieries (deep mine)
1983/4	6.6	20.2	28
1984/5	0.3 (strike)	19.3	28
1985/6	6.6	13.4	17
1986/7	6.5	10.2	14
1987/8	5.0	7.5	11
1988/9	5.0	5.5	9
1989/90	3.5	3.7	6
1990/1	3.2	1.9	4
1992	–	1.3	4
1994	–	495 (hundreds)	2
1997	–	384 (hundreds)	2

Point of Ayr, Betws and Tower, with Point of Ayr being eventually closed in 1996. Around 2,000 are currently employed in deep and drift mines, in opencast and other allied activities, producing in 1998 almost 3 million tons per annum. After decades of decline, the Welsh coal industry is showing some faint signs of revival. Companies such as Celtic Energy and Goetre Tower Anthracite are establishing vibrant new businesses, and a new pit may be sunk near Port Talbot to extract coking coal.

Steel
Steel was another staple heavy industry which declined in similar fashion. By the end of the 1960s, the worldwide demand for steel was falling, and Welsh steel was being priced out of many markets by more efficient and productive steel enterprises in West Germany, the USA and Japan. The position of the industry was reasonably stable up to 1973, with a fairly consistent output of just under 9 million tons and a workforce of 70,000 employees. The stunning collapse of steel between 1973 and 1975 was largely the result of the recession induced by deflationary policies following the first oil price increase. There was a weak recovery to the end of the decade, but the second oil crisis heralded a further collapse in 1980. The British Steel Corporation faced mounting financial losses after 1975 as growing foreign

competition caused a substantial reduction in demand, which cut Welsh steel production by a third.

After 1979, the BSC devised a plan to maintain steel production at Port Talbot and Llanwern in south Wales. Port Talbot was near to deep-water facilities for importing ore and coking coal, while crude steel would be transported to Llanwern for rolling. The BSC plan envisaged a total British production of 4.8 million tons, of which 2.7 million tons would be distributed among the two south Wales plants. The effect of the 'slimline' option was to reduce the combined employment at Port Talbot and Llanwern from 22,000 to 10,600. At Port Talbot the number of man-hours required to produce a ton of liquid steel eventually fell from 9.4 to 5.7, and at Llanwern from 6.0 to 4.7.

BSC attributed its lack of international competitiveness to poor labour productivity; and in the 1970s labour productivity in the British steel industry certainly compared unfavourably with that of its European counterparts. But this did not mean that British steel producers were enduring labour-cost disadvantages, since poor productivity levels were actually offset by lower wage rates, which resulted in lower labour costs in the UK than in most European countries. Many of BSC's troubles in the 1970s were in fact self-inflicted, with poor planning and management resulting in the loss of efficiency and quality. The Corporation was backward in exploiting new techniques and in refurbishing its plants: not until 1983 was approval finally granted to modernize the hot strip-mill at its Port Talbot works.

Since 1980, the profitability and productivity rates of the steel industry have improved markedly. Labour productivity doubled between 1977 and 1984, and in 1985–6 the British Steel Corporation announced a net profit for the first time in eleven years. In Wales, the closure of plants continued relentlessly: the Dowlais works ended its days in 1987, and Velindre followed in 1989, reducing the Welsh workforce to 17,000, with a total annual production of 4.5 million tons. By 1996, the turnover of British Steel was around £2 billion, and it was Wales's largest manufacturing employer. It employed 13,000 people and provided additional work for subcontractors. In 1998, British Steel announced further job losses for the industry largely as a result of the continuing strength of sterling, the falling demand for steel in Russia and eastern Europe, and the implosion of Asian economies. The loss of 850 jobs at the Port Talbot complex would reduce the workforce to barely 3,000 by the new millennium.

Manufacturing

One of the most significant developments in the Welsh economy since 1970 has been the decline of manufacturing. Between 1966 and 1986 around 125,000 jobs out of a total of 331,000 were lost in Wales, representing a decline of no less than 38 per cent. Quite sizeable reductions have occurred since 1974, but the real amputation came after 1979. In the 1970s the weakening of regional policy and a fall in industrial investment resulted in a rapid decline in the manufacturing arena. From 1979 to 1983 Wales lost more manufacturing jobs than any other area of Great Britain. There was also a change in the type of employment available, with a shift away from male-dominated industries to those enterprises employing far more women. Steel-manufacturing accounted for a major slice of the decline, along with man-made fibres and petrochemicals. A town such as Barry in South Glamorgan lost 80 per cent of its manufacturing jobs in a decade.

The bulk of Welsh manufacturing industry was located in south Wales, and it was this region which suffered yet another round of industrial dislocation and unemployment. From 1973 to 1981 male employment in manufacturing in south Wales fell by more than 60,000, or 32 per cent. The decline in female manufacturing employment in south Wales was even more pronounced: of the 69,000 women employed in this sector in 1973, only 49,400 were left in 1981 – a fall of 41 per cent.

Despite the decline in metal manufacture from 1970 to 1983, the importance of the sector should not be underestimated. In 1983, it still accounted for 18.8 per cent of total manufacturing output and ranked second only to engineering as the dominant industrial group in manufacturing. Engineering accounted for about 36 per cent of total output in 1983, as compared with 28 per cent in 1968. In 1983, the total net output of manufacturing industry in Wales was £3,454 million, or 4.3 per cent of the UK total.

Along with other parts of the UK, north Wales suffered a devastating loss of manufacturing employment in the early

Table 5.10 Industrial distribution of net output in Wales (%)

	1968	1983
Food, drink and tobacco	5.5	9.7
Textiles and clothing	8.4	3.9
Engineering and allied industries	27.7	35.8
Chemicals	7.9	9.2
Metal manufacturing	29.6	18.8
Other manufacturing	20.9	22.6

1980s. Thereafter, the region successfully reindustrialized, and the major reason for this was the level of inward investment. An estimated 290 inward investment projects, valued at £1.66 billion, were attracted into north Wales between 1985 and 1995, providing around 16,000 jobs. Firms such as Kimberley Clark, Toyota and Sharp established plants in the area. Much of the employment in manufacturing was located in specific geographical areas, and especially in those parts near to the border with north-west England. Since 1981, the former county of Clwyd increased its number of manufacturing jobs by 12 per cent, while in Gwynedd manufacturing employment fell by 23 per cent. The manufacturing miracle in north Wales from 1985 to 1995 must, however, be assessed cautiously: a slimming-down of the workforce to maintain competitiveness in Europe and the rest of the world; the loss of development-area status in north-east Wales; the threat of increased competition from adjoining areas, and especially Merseyside; the absence of significant numbers of service industries; and the vulnerability of key industries to external effects may well be important factors in determining the future prosperity of the area.

There is little doubt that manufacturing remains one of the strengths of the Welsh economy in the 1990s. It employs 21 per cent of the total civilian workforce (980,000 employees in employment, plus 160,000 self-employed), and generates around 28 per cent of Wales's GDP. Following the loss of 96,000 jobs in the coal-mining and steel industries in the 1970s and 1980s, the Welsh Development Agency and other bodies have attracted new investment into manufacturing. In 1994, manufacturing output in Wales was 41 per cent above its 1984 level, compared with 21 per cent in Scotland and the UK as a whole. The manufacturing sector in Wales is not a homogeneous entity, ranging as it does from the massive, capital-intensive steel-producing sector to the scattered labour-intensive clothing industry. Metals and metal products still account for around 20 per cent of Wales's manufacturing GDP and employ 39,000 people. In 1996, there were over 20,000 people employed in the automotive components industry, and 25,000 in the electronics sector in Wales, which now accounts for 16 per cent of total manufacturing output in the Principality. Manufacturing continues to play a crucial role in the industrial prosperity of modern Wales.

The Service Industries

One of the startling features of the post-war period has been the growth of the service sector. Its sheer size, and the wide range of activities it embraces, makes it almost impossible to discuss all aspects of its economic growth. The sector, which in 1965 accounted for 48 per cent of all employees in employment, had escalated by 1985 to 64 per cent. For the UK as a whole the comparative figures were 48 per cent and 65 per cent respectively. Over the period 1965–85 the number employed in the service sector increased by 93,000. The shift to services was most marked in the period after 1971, when a strong growth in service-sector employment was combined with an even stronger decline in industrial employment. Within the service sector all the major subsectors exhibited an increase in the number of employees, apart from transport and communications which relied heavily on the fortunes of the industrial sector of the economy. The service industries manifesting the largest gains in employment were education, health and other services, which in 1985 accounted for over a third of all service-sector employment.

It is generally recognized that the productivity of many parts of the service industry tends to lag behind that of the manufacturing and industrial enterprises, and this does have financial and social implications. Over the six-year period from 1977–8 to 1983–4 the net cost per pupil in maintained secondary schools in Wales increased by 113 per cent, as compared with an 80 per cent increase in the retail price index. In the health service, the cost per patient-week for acute illnesses increased sixfold over the thirteen-year period to 1984–5, compared with a fourfold increase in the retail price index. Governments and employers often responded by reducing the direct contact between customers and suppliers, and emphasized the importance of efficiency. Competitive tendering for local-authority contracts and hospital ancillary services, as well as the deregulation of bus services became the order of the day throughout the Thatcher era. One consequence of crippling financial burdens and government parsimony was the steady erosion of standards in the public-service sector. The growth of expenditure on the health service was not sufficient to keep waiting lists constant, let alone to reduce them. In education, revenue expenditure by local education authorities declined steadily by at least 10 per cent in the years 1975–85.

The transport sector experienced an appreciable decrease in employment in the 1970s and 1980s. Road haulage in Wales was affected by the decline of extractive and manufacturing industries, while road-passenger transport was battered by severe reductions in rural services and a retrenchment in urban carriage services. The Welsh railway network was butchered by the 'Beeching Plan' of 1963. In 1961, there were 1,889 miles of track in Wales and 538 stations in use, whereas by 1985, there were only 916 miles of track and 180 stations. Most freight traffic in Wales was carried on the roads by the 1980s. Although rail mileage and investment have fallen over the years, the provision of road track has expanded. The internal road system has improved, and especially the east–west links. In the south this was provided by Wales's only motorway, with seventy-five miles of the M4 stretching from Dyfed to the Severn Bridge, and the Heads of the Valley route to the West Midlands. During the 1980s the main investment was in the north Wales trunk road. Bus services have also declined since the 1970s. In 1980, the number of passenger journeys was 260 million, but by 1984 had fallen by 18 per cent to 213 million. The deterioration in bus services has resulted largely from the greater use of private motor cars.

Since the mid-1980s service industries have been the main provider of new jobs in Wales. The number of people employed in these industries rose from 64 per cent of the total numbers employed in 1985 to 70 per cent in 1995. This compared with an overall British figure of 75 per cent on the same year. Of the

160,000 self-employed people in Wales, 54 per cent work in the services sector. Of the inward investment projects in 1995–6, 20 per cent were in the service industry. In 1988, the secretary of state for Wales launched the Financial Services Initiative (FSI) in an attempt to establish south Wales as a recognized centre for the financial services industry. Banking and insurance companies had been steadily relocating their operations away from the south-east of England since the early 1970s, but most had moved to areas outside Wales. In 1993, the FSI was relaunched with some measure of success. At least 470 tele-banking jobs were created by the Midland Bank in Swansea and 300 jobs in tele-insurance by Legal and General in Cardiff. Cardiff Bay is also being connected by optic-fibre cables to serve as a potential international mecca for multi-media companies, telecommunications and information-technology businesses. Centres of legal and financial expertise are slowly emerging in Cardiff to compete with those in Bristol, Birmingham, Manchester and Edinburgh.

There is no sufficient presence of government-funded research and development institutions in Wales, and only a few companies, notably British Steel, have established thriving research plants. Research activities in the UK are concentrated around the M25 in London. The dearth of international private companies in Wales contributes to this shortage of research and development activity in the business sector. The south-east, with 31 per cent of the UK population, attracted 49 per cent of the research and development expenditure in 1994. Wales was almost bottom of the league table for research and development expenditure by region in that year. In 1996, the secretary of state expressed the hope that expenditure on research and development by the business sector in Wales would double over the next decade, but it is difficult to see how this can be achieved unless there is more effective promotion of the Principality as a suitable location for inwardly investing research and development companies.

Tourism

As a constituent member of the service sector, it was estimated in 1977 that tourism had created 27,479 full-time jobs in hotels and other centres of accommodation. By 1985, the Wales Tourist Board calculated that the tourist industry had created around

90,000 jobs in Wales, or 20 per cent of the total number employed in services. Unfortunately, earnings in many parts of the tourist industry are low, and much of the work is part-time and seasonal. In 1984, full-time employees had average earnings which were only 71 per cent of those for all industries and services. About 35 per cent of males and 70 per cent of females worked part-time in hotels and catering. Total expenditure by tourists in Wales in 1985 was around £600 million, and this included £500 million expended by the 11 million UK visitors and £100 million spent by 500,000 overseas visitors to Wales.

The Wales Tourist Board, the Welsh Development Agency and the Development Board for Rural Wales have often combined to promote various tourist ventures. Attractions as diverse as Rhyl Sun Centre, Blaenavon Big Pit and the Dan yr Ogof Cave Complex have received generous support from these various agencies. In order to develop the potential of ancient monuments and historic sites in Wales, the Welsh Office and the Welsh Tourist Board established Cadw (Welsh Historic Monuments) in 1984. There are also various sources of aid for tourism within the EEC, such as the European Regional Development Fund and the European Coal and Steel Community.

Throughout the 1970s the tourist trade was sluggish, and there was little or no growth in the 1980s. The number of overseas visitors to Wales represented only 4 per cent of the British total and, in real terms, the estimated revenue from tourism in the first half of the 1980s was at a lower level than in the early 1970s. Changing trends and increasing competition have affected the industry, and especially the coastal resorts. Tourist requirements in the 1980s differed from those of the immediate post-war years.

Tourism brought an estimated £1.6 billion to the Welsh economy in 1995, with £1,044 million from domestic UK visitors, £360 million from day visitors and £198 million from overseas visitors. Tourism in Wales has traditionally been regarded as a 'rural and resort' product. The seaside resorts of Wales, including Barry Island, Porthcawl, Tenby, Llandudno and Rhyl, accounted for around 60 per cent of total holiday expenditure, with only 20 per cent of expenditure generated in the countryside. City and urban tourism is still relatively under-developed; Cardiff attracted an estimated 600,000 visitors in 1995, as compared with the 2 million visitors a year attracted to

Glasgow, and over half of the 24 million overseas visitors to the UK in that year who went to London, Oxford, Cambridge, Bath and Stratford-upon-Avon. The tourist industry in Wales still employs an estimated 90,000 people, or 9 per cent of the working population, and generates around 6 per cent of GDP. The comparative figures for Scotland are 8 per cent of the workforce contributing 5 per cent to GDP.

In Wales, the tourist industry consists mainly of small, independent operators. There are over 6,000 private-sector enterprises, mostly small family units. There are forty country-house hotels in Wales, but fewer than ten four-star or five-crown hotels, and only 6 per cent of the hotels in Wales have more than forty bedrooms. Two-thirds of the available beds are in self-catering accommodation, and 70 per cent of these are in caravans or camping sites, concentrated near the west and north Wales coasts. The Wales Tourist Board, currently the principal agency in Wales for tourism, is the centre of a complex network of institutions whose activities are tourist-related. These include Cadw, Countryside Council for Wales, Arts Council of Wales, National Museums and Galleries of Wales, Museum of Welsh Life at St Fagans, the Environment Agency, Forestry Commission, Sports Council of Wales, local authorities, National Trust, National Eisteddfod of Wales, Llangollen International Eisteddfod and the Campaign for the Protection of Rural Wales.

In 1994, the Wales Tourist Board published a report, *The Year 2000: A Strategy for Wales*. It set targets for the growth of tourism in Wales, some of which have already been met. The income generated from tourism in Wales has increased, but at a much lower rate than that of the UK. The number of UK domestic visitors to Wales in 1995 had substantially exceeded the target set for the year 2000, but the growth of overseas visitors was paltry by comparison. The challenge for Wales is to compete more effectively with Scotland and Ireland for a greater share of the overseas visitors' market.

Inward Investment and New Businesses
Inward foreign investment to the United Kingdom showed a remarkable increase during the 1980s, and by 1990 net inward investment had soared to £18 billion. In Wales, the presence of foreign firms is not a recent phenomenon, the history of foreign

inward investment in the Welsh economy dating back to the last century. However, the economic importance of foreign investment to the Principality is of fairly recent origin. In 1950, Wales had eighteen foreign-owned companies (FOCs) employing 14,000 workers in manufacturing. By 1977, the number employed had grown to over 50,000, whilst in 1991 there were more than 67,000 employees in FOCs, representing 28 per cent of Welsh manufacturing employment. Nearly a quarter of the jobs created by these companies were in the electrical and electronics industries.

Traditionally, Wales has been a region of manufacturing and extractive activities. The early 1980s inaugurated a period of widespread structural change as recession undermined the ancient pillars of the Welsh economy. There was increased investment in the service industries of Wales as firms relocated from the centre of London to the peripheral regions. Chemical Bank moved to Cardiff in 1983, as did the National Provident Institute, the TSB's insurance division and AA Insurance. Aggregate employment in banking, insurance and finance increased by over 60 per cent from March 1984 to March 1992.

Much of the earlier investment originated from the USA. However, whilst it remains the main provider of foreign employment in Wales, its employment share has withered in the face of growing investment from the EC and Japan. In 1991, the EC and Japan's combined employment share equalled that of the USA at 41 per cent of foreign employment. Latterly, foreign investment has adopted a more cosmopolitan appearance, with Scandinavian and Far Eastern economic settlements in the Principality. The Robert Bosch investment near Bridgend and Toyota's engine factory in Deeside typify the pattern of inward investment in Wales, both with respect to their provenance and location. Increasingly, foreign investment has settled along the M4 corridor in south Wales, and in Alun and Deeside in the northeast. The former counties of South Glamorgan and Clwyd were the only two counties in Wales to have experienced growth in their share of foreign employment in the early 1990s. Clwyd was especially successful, more than doubling its proportion of employment from 1974 to 1991 to 18 per cent. The overall Welsh figure remained unchanged from 1981 to 1989.

Table 5.11 Foreign manufacturing employment in the UK regions ('000s)

Area	1981	1989	Change 1981–9
North	42.4	46.8	+ 4.4
Yorks/Humberside	49.9	51.4	+ 1.5
West Midlands	68.0	69.4	+ 1.4
Wales	45.4	45.4	0
Scotland	81.5	76.6	– 4.9
North West	115.0	86.7	– 28.3
Northern Ireland	24.8	13.6	– 11.2

Table 5.12 Proportion of new overseas projects and jobs for selected regions

| | % of UK new projects | | % of UK new jobs | |
	1981–3	1988–90	1981–3	1988–90
Scotland	20.9	12.8	28.8	23.5
Wales	13.6	15.9	11.3	14.4
North West	9.6	10.9	8.0	7.2
West Midlands	3.8	22.2	3.7	16.0
South East	18.4	6.9	12.6	5.8

Table 5.13 Employment in foreign-owned companies by country of origin (as a % of total overseas employment in Wales)

	1974	1981	1988	1991
USA	83.1	68.4	51.9	41.6
Canada	6.4	9.4	7.0	7.6
EC	7.8	8.7	14.8	23.6
Japan	–	–	13.4	17.5

Despite having secured only 4.4 per cent of total UK employment, Wales successfully attracted 15.9 per cent of all new inward investment projects and 14.4 per cent of associated new jobs in the period 1988–90. Although the USA retains its dominant position as provider of foreign direct investment in Wales, its relative importance has shrunk over the last two decades, with the EC and Japan gradually expanding their commitments. Japanese investment, which was not separately classified in 1974 and 1981, accounted for 13.4 per cent of total FOC employment by 1988. The EC's share more than tripled in the period 1974–91. By 1991, there were over 330 FOCs in Wales, including 150 from Europe, 140 from North America and 41 from Japan. Wales experienced an inward investment boom during the 1980s, but the distribution of the investment suggests that it was not uniformly dispersed. The south-eastern and north-eastern urban counties, in close proximity to England and the M4 and A55 corridors, attracted the lion's share of inward investment.

What attracted these foreign companies to Wales? The EC's common external tariff and trading agreements encouraged foreign firms to locate within the expanding market of Europe. The communications infrastructure of the host country was an important determinant of relative regional success in attracting foreign investment to the UK. Improvements to the M4 and A55, together with the construction of a second Severn crossing, had beneficial effects on inward investment flows. The availability of factors of production in the form of surplus labour, suitable land for development, and capital investment grants, was an inducement for FOCs. The Welsh Development Agency and the Development Board for Rural Wales were granted extended powers to invest in companies and to provide commercial and industrial support for new ventures. In addition, the relatively low level of wages in Wales was a contributory factor in the process of attracting foreign investment.

In recent years 'Team Wales' (WDA, Welsh Office, Land Authority for Wales, Local Training and Enterprise Councils, local authorities, FE colleges, the University of Wales and the private sector) has attracted companies from the so-called 'Asian Tigers' to search for bases in Wales. The Welsh Development Agency established its office in Seoul, South Korea, in 1990, and by 1995 it had secured a £16 million investment commitment at Merthyr Tydfil. A new factory for Ocean Technical Glass in Cardiff provides 750 jobs in the manufacturing industry. Ringtel Electronics, sited at Llantarnam Park, Cwmbran, represents Wales's first major investment from Taiwan. GSS Array Electronics is the first Thai company to be established in Wales, creating a further 300 jobs. In 1995, Shimizu was the first Japanese company to invest in mid-Wales. In 1996, 'Team

Wales' attracted the LG conglomerate to Imperial Park, Newport. LG is one of the four principal industrial organizations in South Korea, and it is hoped that the £1.7 billion investment, the largest single investment in Europe, will employ over 6,000 people and provide indirect employment for an estimated 15,000 others. In April 1999, south-west Wales received its second massive economic boost with the announcement that the £300 million Baglan Energy Park was proceeding. This announcement followed the declaration in March 1999 that this area and the Valleys would qualify for Objective One status with billions of pounds of European investment.

Of equal importance is the expansion of existing companies. In 1995–6, of the 477 foreign inward-investment projects, 271 were expansions of established operations. The Japanese electronics giants, Sony and Matsushita, have greatly extended their activities since coming to Wales in the 1970s. The Ford engine plant at Bridgend intends to expand its operations by a £340 million investment. In April 1996, the American GE Company announced a £27 million expansion of its Nantgarw enterprise.

The Welsh Economy on the Threshold of the New Millennium

Interested parties often argue that an economic miracle occurred in Wales during the 1980s, and they cite the reduction in unemployment rate disparities, employment growth, improved productivity growth and the diversification of Wales's industrial structure as evidence of this economic transformation. Yet recent research claimed that, in spite of the very significant changes that did occur, and the influx of new jobs through inward-investment programmes, Wales's relative economic position remains unchanged. Wales's economic position has improved, but other regions have also flourished, leaving Wales's relative economic status fixed. Wales is caught in the structural economic problems of the 1970s, and recent surveys of the Welsh economy point to a number of disturbing features. There has been further deterioration in terms of GDP per head in Wales relative to the rest of the UK. This was lower in 1995 than in 1984, and it was the second lowest of all regions in the UK. Wales also had the lowest level of personal income per head in the UK, and the gap with other regions continues to widen.

Employment figures reveal that female employees now outnumber males in Wales. In addition, the number of part-time male employees has increased in the 1990s. The unemployment rate fell to 8.2 per cent in 1996, but Wales had a rising percentage of very long-term unemployed (i.e. five years or more). This figure climbed from 4.8 per cent in 1995 to 6.8 per cent in 1997. Youth unemployment was particularly severe in Wales, accounting for 27.6 per cent of the total number of unemployed persons in Wales, as compared with the UK average of 25 per cent.

A national comparison of earnings levels in the UK shows that Wales appears at the bottom of the league table for all employees, at just 89 per cent of the British average. Welsh males have the lowest weekly earnings of any region, and Welsh earnings in non-manual and service activities are traditionally lower. Low pay was such a manifestly crucial issue that the new Labour government committed itself to introducing a national minimum wage, a gesture that may well be of little assistance to the poorer workers of Wales.

An assessment of economic performance must acknowledge the structural changes that have transformed the Welsh economy since the 1970s. In 1971, coal mining and metal manufacture accounted for 14 per cent of employees, but by 1997 barely supported 2.7 per cent of all employees. In 1995, FOCs employed over 73,000 employees, or 7.3 per cent of total employees in employment. Yet foreign direct investment has done little to improve Wales's performance in the GDP earnings league tables. In August 1993, significant changes were made by the government with regard to the designation of Development Areas, as a result of which, barely 15 per cent of the population of Wales lived in a Development Area. The reformed Development Areas in Wales were the northern ends of the south Wales Valleys and the two new designated areas of most of Anglesey and Pembrokeshire. These changes restricted the ability of the Welsh Development Agency to offer lucrative packages to potential investors in many parts of Wales.

What impact the single European currency will have upon the Welsh economy is one of the debatable questions for the new millennium. Equally important considerations will be the future success of the Welsh economy in promoting new inward investment, encouraging small and medium-sized enterprises in manufacturing, and in attracting international companies in rapidly growing business services sectors. *An Economic Strategy for Wales,* published in 1997 by the Welsh Office, identified existing weaknesses in the Welsh economy and presented an updated approach to economic development in Wales. It proposed an all-Wales strategy, action on establishing regional economic priorities and recommendations for economic activity at local levels.

SUGGESTED READING

K. D. George and Lynn Mainwaring (eds.), *The Welsh Economy* (Cardiff, 1988).

Trevor Herbert and Gareth Elwyn Jones (eds.), *Wales between the Wars* (Cardiff, 1988).

Philip Jenkins, *A History of Modern Wales, 1536–1990* (London, 1992).

A. H. John and G. Williams (eds.), *Glamorgan County History*, vol.V (Cardiff, 1980).

Gareth Elwyn Jones, *Modern Wales: A Concise History* (Cambridge, 1994).

Kenneth O. Morgan, *Rebirth of a Nation: Wales 1880–1980* (Oxford, 1981).

Prys Morgan (ed.), *Glamorgan County History*, vol.VI (Cardiff, 1988).

Brinley Thomas (ed.), *The Welsh Economy* (Cardiff, 1962).

6. Social Change and the Decline of Organized Religion

Religion

The Years 1945–1980

IN THE late 1940s a group based at the University of Wales, Swansea, conducted research into social and economic issues in an area which approximates the former county of West Glamorgan and industrial Carmarthenshire. Brennan's study of social life in this area showed that organized religion still fulfilled many functions in the late 1940s and early 1950s. The churches were the focus of spiritual life and a source of guidance for personal and social behaviour. They were meeting grounds for different social classes and for people who held divergent political convictions. Brennan and his colleagues believed that organized religion had contributed to social and economic stability during the period of severe economic dislocation in the inter-war years. They realized also that the role and influence of religion had been circumscribed by the chapels' inability to go beyond a very limited agenda of social comment.

Apart from references to domestic and internal affairs, denominational reports were normally confined to a narrow range of issues: Sunday observance; temperance; gambling; international peace; and the presentation of Welsh culture. The largest number of reports dealt with questions of Sunday observance and opposition to the use of public buildings for political meetings on Sundays. The issue of opening cinemas on Sundays in the borough of Swansea was a test case for the local churches in 1950. The borough council put the matter to the electors, and local churches conducted an intensive campaign to prevent Sunday opening. In the face of strong opposition, a majority of only 2,909 voted on behalf of opening Sunday cinemas. In Cardiff two years later the vote was 55,935 in favour of Sunday cinemas, and 21,542 against. The battle continued in town after town throughout the decade.

Churches also opposed proposals to extend the facilities for drinking. James Griffiths, Labour MP for Llanelli, was censured in 1947 by the Llanelli Free Church Council for voting in favour of the Labour government's Civic Restaurants bill, which would allow restaurants to apply for licences to sell alcoholic drinks. Gambling attracted a great deal of hostile attention at the assembly of the Baptist Union of Wales in May 1951, when speakers expressed disappointment with the report of the royal commission on gambling and appealed for a complete ban on the conduct of raffles in church halls. Resolutions opposing war and rearmament were proposed at the national and district conferences of the Baptists, Congregationalists and Free Church councils in 1941 and 1951.

A review of the contents of religious periodicals in Wales for the period 1949–51 illustrates that the subject matter was theological, institutional, domestic or historical. Discussion of social subjects was infrequent and rarely polemic, the churches seeming to be hardly aware of issues such as employment, poor living conditions or a sense of exploitation and oppression among the ordinary workers. Brennan and his co-researchers believed that some of the apparent indifference to social questions could be attributed to the individualism in Nonconformity, which saw morality solely in terms of personal relations. It was not until 1970, for example, that the Council of Churches for Wales established a Department for Social Responsibility. The researchers unearthed evidence which suggested another explanation for the dilatory and reserved approach to social matters. The Nonconformist denominations in West Glamorgan had manifestly not lost their working-class members, nor did a predominantly working-class Nonconformity confront a predominantly middle-class Anglican Church. They showed that the composition of Nonconformity was 50 per cent middle-class, while the Anglicans were 65 per cent middle-class, so that all denominations had sizeable proportions of both classes among their membership. This sociological report clearly indicated that Christianity could transcend secular divisions, but it displayed the limitations that were imposed on the social witness of the churches. The clergy were reluctant to raise topical, political or social issues which might be fissiparous, and usually confined their pronouncements to traditional theological or historical themes.

In 1949, nearly half of the population in the prescribed area had been members of a church or chapel. By 1960, a new survey, based mainly on Swansea, demonstrated that attendances had plummeted to 23 per cent of the population.

Table 6.1 Denominational Allegiance, West Industrial South Wales 1949 and Swansea 1960

WISW 1949		Swansea 1960	
Denomination	*%*	*Denomination*	*%*
Congregationalists	30.5	Welsh Nonconformists	15
Baptists	23.0	English Nonconformists	24
Welsh Presbyterians	21.4	Church in Wales	51
Wesleyan Methodists	3.7	Roman Catholics	7
Church in Wales	21.4	Others	3

It would seem that in the industrial areas there had been a more marked decline in the 1950s among Welsh Nonconformist than English churches. This movement was associated with several related phenomena: Anglicization; secularization; and a gradual decline in the traditional working-class groups. The decline in Welsh-speaking was especially marked in industrial south Wales and involved a drift of younger generations to English-speaking denominations. Secularization often entailed the abandonment of any significant commitment to religion; while changes in the occupational structure began to affect the composition and size of working-class groups. In 1967, the Blaendulais Ecumenical Centre commissioned a survey of religious denominations in a similar area to Brennan's. Its report, *The Church in a Mobile Society*, revealed that there were 740 places of worship in the area (or one place of worship for every 703 persons) and 427 Christian ministers (one for every 1,250 persons). There was a marked difference between the provision of places of worship for the Welsh and English populations – one Welsh-speaking place of worship for every 425 Welsh speakers, and one English-speaking place of worship for every 1,019 monoglot English persons. These figures revealed the extent of the decline in Welsh-speaking. The survey also exemplified the problems facing the Welsh-speaking denominations: they were saddled with the burden of maintaining buildings which were too large for the existing, ageing congregations; and the supply of Welsh-speaking ministers was steadily contracting. The findings further illustrated the importance of mobility, not only between the two cultures of Wales, but also between the classes, and especially between geographical areas. Within Glamorgan, in the post-1945 period, there had been a substantial redistribution of population from the industrial Valleys to the coastal plain. The Valleys and the industrial parts of Carmarthenshire had lost 3–4 per cent of their population, while the coastal plains had witnessed a population increase of around 11 per cent in the years 1951–67. This migration produced a geographical imbalance of religious provision with an overconcentration of ministers and buildings in declining areas. Whereas demographic and industrial changes had disadvantaged the established Church in the nineteenth century, they undermined Nonconformist denominations in the middle years of the twentieth. The Church in Wales, with its even distribution of parishes, places of worship and incumbents, was better adapted to meet the needs of settlers in the growth areas. Meanwhile, the Nonconformists were firmly entrenched in the declining, Welsh-speaking areas.

In the rural areas of Wales, a comparatively high proportion of people attended church or chapel even as late as the early 1970s. In 1971, 77 per cent of respondents to a survey had attended chapel or church in Cardiganshire, and the distinctive feature of religious life in the county was the continuing numerical strength of Nonconformity. The social outlook of the rural chapels rested firmly on their strong Welsh character. Temperance and Sabbatarian issues still dominated the social complexion of the Nonconformist phalanx in the rural heartlands. In the statutory referendum on the Sunday opening of licensed premises in 1968, 34.8 per cent of the Cardiganshire electorate voted against Sunday opening, as opposed to 19.2 per cent in favour. The remaining 'dry' counties – Merioneth, Caernarfon, Anglesey and Carmarthen – were all located in the rural, Welsh-speaking heartland areas of north and west Wales. Temperance and Sabbatarian attitudes were clearly linked to chapel membership, and two-thirds of Nonconformists in Cardiganshire claimed to have voted against Sunday opening in the referendum of 1968. Demographical surveys of the referenda in 1961 and 1968 have demonstrated the close links that existed between the proportion of the population voting dry and the degree of Welshness as measured by the proportions of Welsh-speakers at the 1961 census. In 1969 and 1975 the same basic pattern emerged of a Welsh-speaking, rural and Nonconformist complex recording high voting rates against the Sunday opening of public houses. The division between 'wet' and 'dry' encampments drifted relentlessly westwards with only 'fortress Wales' remaining.

Table 6.2 Percentage voting dry in comparable areas

	1961	1968	1975
Anglesey	76	66	54
Cardigan	74	64	59
Merioneth	76	66	57
Montgomery	57	41	29

Especially noteworthy was the sharp decline of 10 per cent in Anglesey between 1961 and 1968, which reflected the fall in the number of Welsh-speakers from 75 to 65 per cent during the period 1961–71.

As membership of the Nonconformist denominations spiralled steadily downwards, and especially after 1945, the Church in Wales remained reasonably buoyant. After the Second World War there was evidence of considerable activity in the Welsh dioceses. In 1944 *Cymry'r Groes* was launched as an organization to promote youth work. A Provincial Evangelistic Council followed in 1951, and a pilgrimage of young people to St David's in 1955. In 1957, the Church in Wales elected Alfred Edwin Morris, bishop of Monmouth, as the new archbishop. The election of an Englishman to the primacy of the Church in Wales, and of the non-Welsh-speaking Bishop John Thomas to the diocese of Swansea and Brecon, were interpreted as severe blows by many Welsh-speaking Anglicans. By 1964, the saintly Bishop Glyn Simon underlined the statistical weakness of the Church in Wales, with less than 10 per cent of the people of Wales recorded as Easter communicants. He noted that, whereas nearly 300 men had trained for the ministry in 1939, there were fewer than 100 candidates for ordination in 1964, a figure which had dropped to 51 in 1979. In the early 1970s the Church commissioned a survey on the diocese of Bangor. In his report, the eminent sociologist C. C. Harris concluded that there was an urgent need to adopt a more flexible and varied pattern of ministry and to regroup parishes in the rural parts of the Bangor diocese.

The Years 1980–2000

A report of a census of the Welsh churches conducted in 1982 put the membership of Christian churches in Wales at 24 per cent of the population, and attendance at 13 per cent. In terms of attendance, the split between the three main denominations was: Roman Catholics 20 per cent, Anglicans 29 per cent and Non-conformists 51 per cent. If the churches are compared, the Church in Wales emerged as the largest single denomination in every Welsh county except Gwynedd and Clwyd. Only the Roman Catholics, Anglicans and 'others' actually increased attendances from 1978 to 1982. All other denominations exhibited a significant decline.

Table 6.3 Census of the churches in 1982

Church	% change in adults attending 1978–82	% change in membership 1978–82
Church in Wales	+7	−3
Presbyterian Church in Wales	−6	−6
Baptists	−4	−7
Independents	−3	−7
Methodists	−4	−10
Roman Catholic Church	+1	+3

Although the Church in Wales lost, on average, 3 per cent of its members between 1978 and 1982, it registered quite significant increases of 7 per cent in south Glamorgan and 6 per cent in Clwyd. The Roman Catholic Church continued to augment its membership figures by an impressive 15 per cent in Gwent, 7 per cent in Mid Glamorgan, and by 5 per cent and 3 per cent respectively in the Welsh-speaking counties of Gwynedd and Dyfed. Nonconformist losses were unremitting and quite depressing in the old industrial regions. It has to be remembered that the established Church and the Roman Catholics are inclined to give figures for Easter attendance, and these are considerably higher than average. The Presbyterian Church in Wales had experienced a 10 per cent fall in membership in West Glamorgan, 15 per cent in Mid Glamorgan and 11 per cent in Gwent. The Welsh Baptists had lost a half of their members since 1950, with further losses of 12 per cent in Clwyd, 14 per cent in Gwynedd and 6 per cent in Dyfed between the years 1978 and 1982. In south Wales, the Independents lost 9 per cent of their members in West Glamorgan and 11 per cent in Mid Glamorgan. The 1982 census also revealed that one in seven of the churches in Wales was without a minister, and that three-quarters of the churches had fewer than fifty members.

In September 1993 thirty-four Trinitarian denominations, Independent churches and networks endorsed the idea of a year-long survey of the Welsh churches. The results of the survey, which were produced in 1995, revealed that an estimated 8.7 per cent of the population attended churches in Wales. The Church in Wales recorded the highest attendance with 28 per cent, followed by the Roman Catholics with 21 per cent and the Presbyterians with 10 per cent. All the other groups achieved single figures only:

Table 6.4 1995 survey of the churches in Wales

Denomination	% church attendance
Church in Wales	28.4
Roman Catholics	21.0
Presbyterian	10.4
Annibynwyr (Welsh Independents)	6.6
Baptist Union of Wales	6.2
Methodists	6.1

The less densely populated counties displayed more impressive rates of church-going than the industrial regions:

Table 6.5 Church attendances as a proportion of county population, 1995

County	% church attendance
Mid Glamorgan	6.3
Gwent	7.9
Clwyd	7.8
South Glamorgan	9.5
West Glamorgan	7.5
Dyfed	12.0
Gwynedd	11.9
Powys	10.3

Yet, over the fourteen-year period 1981–95, all the counties experienced a declining attendance rate as a proportion of their populations. Dyfed's rate dropped from 18.7 to 12.0 per cent, and Gwynedd's from 21.5 to 11.9 per cent. In the older, more established churches, 62 per cent of those attending were aged forty-five or over, and 35 per cent were aged sixty-five and over. The figures tended to reinforce the impression that church culture reflects the aspirations and attitudes of the age groups above forty-five. At least 67 per cent of those who attended churches were women. The 1995 survey also showed that 731 congregations had disappeared since the 1982 church survey. At least 24 per cent of churches in Wales had no minister, and 22 per cent shared a minister.

In this new secular world there were indications of burgeoning social and political concerns within the churches. Throughout the 1980s the Church in Wales had considered major social and ethical issues. A report on Christians and warfare was debated in 1981, on world poverty in 1982, and on housing and home-lessness in 1986. The study sector of the Division of Social Responsibility followed the lead of the Church of England in its controversial report, *Faith in the City*, by producing its own reports, *Faith in Wales*, which mapped areas of multiple depriva-tion in the Principality, and *Faith in the Countryside*. One of its more recent papers concerned *Wales in Europe* (1994). The Church in Wales has developed considerably beyond the position described by Brennan and others in the 1940s. It has evolved into a more self-consciously Welsh institution, and some of its leaders have sought to identify themselves with national aspirations. The churches appeared sympathetic to devolution when they were required to present evidence to the Royal Commission in 1970, and the archbishop of Wales, Gwilym Williams, called for a 'yes' vote in the devolution referendum.

On the eve of the new millennium, perhaps we can try to account for the declining fortunes of the churches in Wales. Victorian religion probably reached its apogee in the great tidal wave of revivalism that swept through Wales in 1904–5. Thereafter, the history of religion has been a chronicle of unremitting decline. Some of the factors that were to weaken the chapels were already operative shortly after the First World War: the burden of mounting debt; overexpansion in thinly populated rural areas; the difficulty of establishing links with the non-Welsh-speaking population; and the continuing inability of the chapels to retain their hold over the industrial and urban masses in the sprawling industrial communities of south Wales.

The persistent fall in the proportion of Welsh-speakers from nearly 55 per cent of the population in 1891 to 18.6 per cent in 1991 was a critical factor in the process of decline. In the industrial communities, the evaporation of the Welsh language has left generations unaware of the medium of communication in the chapels. The redistribution of population away from rural areas into urban centres has left many congregations struggling to preserve their religious heritage. Inward migration of non-Welsh-speakers has further eroded the pillars of Nonconformity in the erstwhile Welsh communities. The outward shift of population from rural areas, from the former industrial Valleys, and from town and city centres to outlying suburbs and picturesque villages has left many churches stranded in oases of desolation and despair. The remaining skeletal congregations struggle to sustain a burden of upkeep that augments each year.

Economic and structural changes have penetrated deeply into the old industrial regions. The collapse of the traditional industries of coal and steel have severed the connecting social and economic strands in these former industrial heartlands, leaving the chapels isolated and rudderless in a torrent of economic change. The chapel was once the focus and expression of communities that lived, worked, worshipped and died in tightly knit communities. The fragmentation and dispersal of those communities has undermined the ethos of Welsh Non-conformity.

Scientific and intellectual factors have challenged the theological certainties of the churches since the middle of the nineteenth century. The development of new forms of biblical criticism and the demythologizing of religious texts have severely impaired the confidence of generations of Welsh people. The expansion of scientific thought and the speed of technological transformation have compounded the intellectual challenges facing the churches in the so-called post-Christian era. The growing influence of Liberal theology with its anti-dogmatic stance has favoured a more open-minded and tolerant approach towards a variety of different beliefs. Other non-Christian religions have slowly flowed into the territorial bastions of Welsh Nonconformity. The Jewish community, which has been established in south Wales since the early part of the nineteenth century, now has deep roots in parts of Wales, and especially in urban centres. There are synagogues in Cardiff, Newport and Swansea. The Muslim community has grown in recent times and spread to various corners of Wales. There are five mosques in Cardiff, one in Newport, two in Swansea, as well as prayer rooms and mosques in Bangor, Chepstow and Lampeter. The advent of overseas students to the colleges of the University of Wales has brought many Muslims into the university, and endowments from the Middle East have supported the introduction of Islamic Studies at the University of Wales, Lampeter, a former citadel of Welsh Anglicanism. Small communities of Hindus and Sikhs have settled in Cardiff, Newport and Swansea. Buddhism has often attracted Welsh people to its ranks, and especially in the rural areas of the Principality. The growth of religious pluralism and the dissemination of alternative lifestyles have fractured the influence and appeal of the Christian churches.

The collapse of the Church as an instrument of social control has eroded a cornerstone of organized religion. Education and cultural activities are no longer the preserves of the Christian churches. The growth of a collectivist state, the increasing tendency to control education from the centre of government, and the explosive development of mass-media communication are immensely powerful forces in the disintegration of religious influence.

The devastating impact of two world wars in the century has further weakened the churches. The First World War ended the jejune optimism of the nineteenth century and destroyed the widespread belief in inevitable and unlimited human progress. The Second World War intensified the process and disrupted the long-familiar practices of attendance and worship. The threat of nuclear destruction and the creeping paralysis of intellectual anxiety and meaninglessness shattered many religious hopes and annihilated individual beliefs.

Substantial social changes since 1945 have made the appeal of religion far more peripheral. Improvements in the material conditions of society, the emergence of materialism as a dominant feature in modern Western civilization, and the rampant individualism of the Thatcher years have transformed social and religious attitudes. The consolations and reassurances of belief seem far less necessary and more rebarbative in an age of material expectations and comforts. The Sunday Trading Act of 1994 removed the last vestiges of the traditional Welsh 'Sabbath', the legacy of Puritan influence on Welsh society. Working, shopping and holidaying have become regular weekend features.

Increased mobility and the dominating influence of the media have probably made Wales far less distinctive in recent years, and caused it to be more like one of the regions of England. All over the Principality there is a tendency for people to think and behave like the English. In political terms, a large swathe of Wales now seems to conform to national voting patterns. Writers have commented on the gradual assimilation of monochrome Western ways of thought and north Atlantic patterns of social behaviour.

The churches and chapels have long since ceased to be the religious, social or intellectual cynosure of the country. Clergy have lost their status and influence and are compelled to devote much of their time and energy to thankless routine financial and organizational tasks. There appears to be a collective crisis of belief among the leaders of religion as they endeavour to steer a course between the Scylla and Charybdis of doubt and simplistic declarations.

Social Changes

Population and Language Trends in Modern Wales
Population: The rate of growth of the Welsh population has been far more erratic than that of the United Kingdom since 1891. In the years up to 1921, the population of Wales grew at a faster rate than that of the UK. After 1921, the Welsh population declined sharply until 1939, whereas the UK figure increased. Since 1945, the Welsh population has increased, but at a slower rate than the UK population. After 1971, population growth slowed down, and in the early 1980s the population of Wales and the UK was declining. The overall picture conceals different stories within the counties of Wales. Almost all of the increase in the population of Wales occurred in the industrial counties. South Glamorgan's population grew rapidly between 1891 and 1981, while the most spectacular leap was recorded in Mid Glamorgan. In contrast, the rural counties of Dyfed, Gwynedd and Powys experienced much slower rates of growth. In recent decades, and particularly from 1971 to 1981, this position was reversed, with much faster rates of growth occurring in rural areas.

The most important component of population growth in Wales has been migration. In the 1920s the extent of emigration from Wales was sufficient to outweigh substantial natural increase, and the population of Wales fell accordingly. During the 1970s there was very little natural increase in the Welsh population, but net immigration into Wales enabled its population to grow at a faster rate than that of the UK. In the 1980s the gains made by continued immigration were balanced by the recession-induced out-migration. The age distribution in the 1980s showed that Wales had a greater proportion of its population in the age range between fifty-five and seventy-five, and a lower proportion in the twenty-to-thirty-five range. Distribution figures also revealed that the female population was older than the male. Further analysis unveils a pattern of considerable variation between the Welsh counties. The former county of Mid Glamorgan had the highest proportion of children (33.3 per hundred population), while Powys and Dyfed had the lowest. Gwynedd contained the highest proportions of retired people (36.5 per hundred adults), with the two districts of Aberconwy and Dwyfor registering the highest ratios of retired people (45.8 and 45.6 per hundred respectively) in the 1980s.

Welsh society has received four tidal waves of English and other foreign settlers since medieval times – first, in the early Middle Ages; secondly, from the late eleventh to the thirteenth centuries; the greatest influx of immigration began after 1750 and accelerated to a peak between 1870 and 1911; and a fourth flow which started after 1945 and remains unabated – and most of the recent settlers have gravitated to the attractive rural parts of the country. Retirement migrants, somewhat unkindly labelled 'the geriatric infill', totalled over 2,300 in 1985. Key workers are often induced to take up employment positions which local people cannot fill. Ex-urban dwellers come in search of a rural retreat and scenic alternatives to the modern urban sprawl. In demographic terms, Wales has become the most cosmopolitan society among the four home countries. In 1981, only 79.4 per cent of the population were born in Wales, with English immigrants as the largest minority, representing 17 per cent of all residents. In England 89.8 per cent of residents were English-born in 1981. In the same year, a mere 48 of the 483 local government districts in the UK had a proportion of foreign-born minorities greater than 20 per cent of their resident population. Of the 364 districts in England, only twenty-eight had foreign-born rates in excess of 20 per cent, and twenty-three of those were in Greater London. In Wales, however, eighteen of the thirty-seven districts had foreign-born rates in excess of 20 per cent. This fact alone tends to suggest that an ethnic cleavage exists in modern Wales.

The population of Wales grew by 2.8 per cent between 1981 and 1991, compared with 3 per cent in England. Over the decade the natural change (i.e. births over deaths) and migration were positive, producing a growing population. In the former counties of Clwyd, Dyfed, Gwynedd and Powys, a small decrease in population through natural change was more than offset by net migration from other areas. This pattern of population growth, negative natural change and positive growth through migration is consistent with an ageing population. Retirement migration has ensured that Dyfed, Clwyd, Gwynedd and Powys had the highest proportion of migrants over the age of fifty-five. The Welsh Office has produced forecasts for population growth up to the year 2006, which predict population increases in the counties of Wales, and project that Clwyd, Dyfed, Gwynedd and Powys will have the highest proportions of their populations over retirement age. It is envisaged that Wales, as elsewhere, will experience a very significant increase in the number of people over the age of seventy-five.

The population in 1986 comprised 1,035,300 households, the average size of which was 2.7, just fractionally ahead of the figure of 2.6 for Great Britain. A fifth of all households comprised only one person, and a third contained two persons. Wales has experienced a fall in the number of households of three or more persons and a rise in the cohort of small households. In recent years, the number of single-person households has augmented from 5 per cent in 1931 to 9 per cent in 1951, and to 21 per cent in 1986. This latter figure may be attributed to a number of factors: an increase in the number of elderly or widowed; rising divorce rates; and the tendency of young people to live independently of their parents.

In 1986, 57 per cent of all households had an economically active head, of whom 36 per cent were in skilled manual occupations, 21 per cent in semi-skilled or unskilled occupations, and 43 per cent in non-manual occupations. The variations between subregions in the social status of households were quite pronounced. Powys and South Glamorgan had the highest-status household heads, followed by Gwynedd and Dyfed. Mid and West Glamorgan households contained the lowest-status household heads. Household income in Wales was 10 per cent lower than in Great Britain.

Language: In the nineteenth century the growth of population had resulted in the expansion of the Welsh-speaking population. Until the end of the century most of the migrants to the coalfields of north and south Wales came from the rural Welsh-speaking areas of Wales. In the five decades of the latter half of the century, natural population increase produced percentage gains of 12.3, 13.52, 14.73, 13.73 and 14.06 respectively. A natural increase of mainly Welsh families resulted in a growth of Welsh-speaking numbers.

In the twentieth century, depression and the collapse of the old industrial economy have undermined the strength of the Welsh language. The proportion of Welsh-speakers in the population of Wales fell relentlessly from 1901 onwards.

Table 6.6 Percentage of the population able to speak Welsh 1901–1951

	1901	*1911*	*1921*	*1931*	*1951*
Wales	49.9	43.5	37.1	36.8	28.9

Despite gargantuan efforts to promote the use and status of the language since 1945, the position deteriorated in the 1960s and 1970s: the out-migration of the young continued unabated, while the in-migration of non-Welsh-speakers overwhelmed many communities in the Welsh heartlands; the impact of rural depopulation on the fate of the Welsh language was critical; de-industrialization, symbolized by the decimation of the coal industry, led to significant population losses; the Anglicization of core 'Welsh-Wales' areas in Anglesey, Caernarfonshire, Denbighshire, Merioneth and Cardiganshire was particularly intense in the 1960s and 1970s. In 1961, the total number of Welsh-speakers stood at 656,002 and had fallen further to only 542,425 in 1971. The losses were greatest in the industrial Valleys of south Wales: by 1971, the Rhondda had 11,938 fewer Welsh-speakers, Merthyr 5,224, and Aberdare 5,039. Further west, the Welsh-speaking population of Swansea fell by 6,517 and Llanelli's by 5,035. Most of these losses were attributable to major restructuring programmes in the heavy staple industries. The pattern of industrial contraction and out-migration repeated itself in the coal-mining areas of north-east Wales. There were even reductions along the north Wales coast, as Bangor recorded a decrease of 1,328 in the 1960s.

From 1971 to 1981 the total number of Welsh-speakers continued to fall, but at a much reduced rate. The old industrial regions of south and north-east Wales accounted for the lion's share of the national loss. There was a sizeable reduction in the number of communities where 80 per cent of the population was able to speak Welsh. In 1961, there were 279 of these communities in existence, compared with only 66 in 1981. From 1961 to 1971 the number of Welsh-speakers had fallen by a massive 17.3 per cent. The pace of decline had decelerated between the years

1971 and 1981 to 6.3 per cent, giving some measure of hope to enthusiastic supporters of the Welsh language.

Table 6.7 Percentage of the population able to speak Welsh 1961–1981

	1961	*1971*	*1981*
Wales	26.0	20.8	18.9

The 1991 census showed that 18.6 per cent of the total resident population were Welsh-speakers. The former counties of Dyfed and Gwynedd remained the strongholds of the language, accounting for over a half of the Welsh-speakers, with a combined total of 283,411, out of a total of 508,098. At the other extreme were the counties of Gwent, Powys and South Glamorgan. The majority of the Welsh-speakers were located in two main areas: the urban and old industrial heartland of southwest Wales; and along the coast of north Wales, from Caernarfonshire in the west to Flint in the east. There were also concentrations of Welsh-speakers along the coast of west Wales and in selected inland market towns, such as Carmarthen, Llandeilo, Lampeter and Llandysul.

Table 6.8 Percentage of county population able to speak Welsh 1991

County	*% of Welsh-speakers*
Clwyd	18.2
Dyfed	43.7
Gwent	2.4
Gwynedd	61.0
Mid Glamorgan	8.4
Powys	20.2
South Glamorgan	6.5
West Glamorgan	15.0
Wales	18.6

The 1991 census confirmed the gradual fragmentation of the core areas and the steady erosion of Welsh-speaking in *Y Fro Gymraeg*. While the overall decline in the number of Welsh-speakers was 1.4 per cent between 1981 and 1991, compared with 6.3 per cent in the previous intercensal period, fluctuations within the Welsh counties varied greatly. In South Glamorgan there was an increase of 14 per cent in the number of Welsh-speakers recorded in the intercensal period. This hardly compensated for the losses of 11.2 per cent in West Glamorgan and 2.7 per cent in the heartland of Dyfed. There were encouraging signs in Gwent, Mid Glamorgan and South Glamorgan, where more than 30 per cent of Welsh-speakers were under fifteen years of age. The intercensal analysis also revealed a quite remarkable increase of 22.8 per cent in the numbers of young Welsh-speakers. It was noteworthy that only Gwynedd, in the heartland of Wales, witnessed a decrease of 3.1 per cent in the numbers of young Welsh-speakers.

Although the results of the 1991 census were generally encouraging, scholars have suggested that they need to be interpreted cautiously. Various pieces of evidence would tend to indicate that prospects for the language are not quite as healthy as originally assumed. The Committee for the Development of Welsh Education produced figures for 1988–9 which exposed a far less promising picture throughout the primary schools of Wales.

Table 6.9 Primary school children (5–11 years) by ability to speak Welsh, 1988–9

County	1	2	3	4
Clwyd	4.3	5.9	24.0	65.8
Dyfed	19.5	9.0	22.7	48.8
Gwent	0.5	1.3	0.2	98.0
Gwynedd	39.2	19.5	32.0	9.3
Mid Glamorgan	1.0	9.0	5.5	84.3
Powys	5.5	4.2	21.3	59.0
South Glamorgan	1.3	2.6	10.6	85.5
West Glamorgan	2.8	3.3	4.1	89.8
Wales	7.0	6.4	12.6	74.0

Key:
Column 1 = Speak Welsh at home
Column 2 = Fluent, but do not speak Welsh at home
Column 3 = Speak Welsh, but not fluently
Column 4 = Do not speak Welsh

One of the dominant issues in contemporary Wales has been the steady erosion of the territorial heartland of north and west Wales. Although the pace of absolute decline in the number of Welsh-speakers has moderated, and the appearance of Welsh-medium schools represents a major development in the creation of a new generation of Welsh-speakers, Welsh-speaking in the traditional heartlands is in slow retreat. The bilingual community is also fragmented, and the Welsh-medium schools often represent the only significant domain within which a predominantly Welsh-medium experience can be gained outside the heartland areas. Wales is now a plural society, with a unilingual majority and a bilingual minority. The dominant tendency is for the social and cultural life of the Principality to become increasingly similar to that of other constituent regions of the UK. For many Welsh people, their diurnal routines and pastimes are hardly distinguishable from those of their fellow citizens in British communities.

An array of unresolved issues dominates modern society. The increasing internationalization of language imposes a massive and pervasive centripetal force upon the languages of the smaller nations. The revolution in telecommunications, the extension of digital technology, the appearance of mini-satellite televisions and interactive computing systems, and the proliferation of mass migrations have liberated language from the traditional bonds of time and space. World languages such as English, French and Spanish, have derived enormous power from this process of internationalization. With the conquest of the 'tyranny of distance' it remains to be seen whether Welsh and other smaller languages can survive into the twenty-first century.

A second factor of fundamental importance is that Welsh is now a predominantly urban language. As the traditional rural heartlands exhibit symptoms of decay and Welsh-speakers slowly retreat into kraal-like communities, a key question is whether a viable Welsh culture can survive without its own heartland as a resource. The old images of Wales seem to be in need of up-dating and remodelling for the modern world. The rural, Non-conformist, coal-mining, steelworking and quarrying identities appear increasingly troglodytic in a contemporary setting. The general drift away from a rural, agricultural-based social and economic order has altered the character of conventional

Welsh-speaking society. A set of urban Welsh identities, which correspond to contemporary concerns, would seem to be a priority for the new century.

The Impact of Economic Changes

Unemployment Patterns

Unemployment, which had stood at 5.2 per cent of the adult working population in 1947, and was the highest of any region in Britain, fell steadily thereafter. The British economy was stimulated to a high level of activity, with three recognizable periods of economic growth from 1945 to 1970. Unemployment dropped from 4.6 per cent in 1948 to 2.0 per cent in 1956. From 1954 the growth in the economic performance of south Wales was at best comparable with the rest of the UK. In 1957–8, recession produced a higher level of unemployment to around 4.1 per cent in December 1958. This was far less severe than that of the 1930s, and the Conservative government responded with a fillip to the development-area policy. New advanced industries such as chemicals, engineering and artificial fabrics were brought to various parts of Wales. A third surge of economic activity in south Wales came in the later 1960s. In 1966, the whole of south Wales was given development-area status, and new companies flowed into the areas.

From 1966 to 1986 unemployment rates veered upwards and remained consistently above the British average. The most dominant feature of this pattern was the massive increase in unemployment after 1978, from about 75,000 people to over 170,000 by the end of 1984. There was also a significant increase in the numbers of long-term unemployed in both Wales and Britain. In Wales, the long-term unemployed (i.e. those unemployed for a year or more) accounted for 27 per cent of the jobless in 1979, while by 1986 42.5 per cent were categorized as long-term unemployed.

Job losses during the recession of the early 1990s were less severe in Wales than elsewhere in the UK. This was largely attributable to the strength of the service sector, which accounted for 71 per cent of total employment in 1993. There was a 44 per cent increase in the number of female part-time workers in Wales between 1981 and 1994; a figure well above the UK average of 25 per cent.

Table 6.10 Annual average unemployment rates, Wales and the UK, 1984–1993

	1984	1985	1986	1987	1988	1989	1990	1991	1992	1993
Wales	13.2	13.7	13.7	12.1	9.9	7.3	6.7	9.0	10.0	10.3
UK	10.6	10.9	11.1	10.0	8.0	6.2	5.8	8.0	9.7	10.3

By 1997, female employees actually outnumbered males, and the number of male part-time employees had also surged ahead. The remarkable growth in female part-time employment occurred largely as a result of the demand for low-cost labour by multinational firms. Since part-time positions are overwhelmingly low-skilled, the expansion of this sector was symptomatic of a deskilling of the workforce.

Housing and Material Comforts
After the Second World War, Wales had a poor housing stock, and one of the major tasks confronting public and private bodies was the clearance of unfit dwellings. Some slum clearance had been undertaken by the Luftwaffe, especially during the wartime blitz in Swansea. The major problem was the availability of durable stone-built houses, a great number of which dated from the nineteenth century; in 1962, at least 52 per cent of existing Welsh houses dated from before the First World War. The problem was not so much one of unfit dwellings as that of large numbers of houses lacking basic modern amenities. In the years after 1945, considerable efforts were made to construct subsidized council houses by local authorities. In Swansea, there was a concentrated programme of public housing from 1946 to 1952, and 6,000 were built in all. In Cardiff, the older communities of Butetown and Tiger Bay were largely demolished, and Merthyr's 'Chinatown' also disappeared. In the 1950s, there was a boom in private housebuilding and in the activities of housing associations and co-operatives. Building societies, which loaned money to prospective home-owners, spread to most of the towns and cities of Wales. In 1965, a record number of 19,524 new houses were built.

One of the causes of the improvement in the housing stock has been the increase in owner occupation, which has risen from

49 per cent in 1961 to 69 per cent in 1988. Although the incidence of owner occupation varied little among the Welsh regions, what was significant was the balance between the public- and private- rented sectors. The proportion in the public sector in 1989 was highest in West Glamorgan and Gwent, and lowest in rural Wales and South Glamorgan. Substandard housing was a far bigger problem in Mid Glamorgan than elsewhere, and homelessness was quite severe in West Glamorgan and Gwent. Even greater variations surfaced within the administrative districts of Wales. The proportion of dwellings without an inside toilet was nearly 18 per cent in the Rhondda, and homelessness was more than twice the national average in Neath, Monmouth, Newport and the Cynon Valley in 1986.

From 1950 to 1980, the average number of houses built spiralled by 40 per cent per annum, with the proportion being erected by the private sector increasing from just over a quarter in the 1950s to just under two-thirds in the 1970s. The private sector extended its share of housebuilding between 1981 and 1986 from 60 to 70 per cent. The average number of houses completed each year in this period fell sharply by more than 50 per cent. Conservative governments' policies since 1979, which have included privatization, strict control of the Public Sector Borrowing Requirement and fewer statutory restrictions on market transactions, have greatly affected the housing market. The sales of council houses in Wales soared to 15,926 in 1982, reaching a cumulative total of over 45,000 by 1985. The overall effect of governments' new financial provisions was a heavy cutback in local-authority housing programmes. Total net public expenditure on housing programmes in Wales, which had exceeded £200 million in 1979–80, fell to £140 million by 1984–5. Housing expenditure, which represented 12.2 per cent of the Welsh Office budget in 1978–9, had dropped to around 4.9 per cent by 1986–7. The implications of these cuts were graphically illustrated in a report of the South Wales Chief Officers' Group in 1984: councils were forced to abandon modernization programmes; grants for renovation were severely curtailed; and improvements to poor dwellings were stymied. Expenditure cuts also produced a marked reduction in the completion of new houses.

An additional problem in Wales was a surge in the number of second or holiday homes. It was estimated that there were 11,000

such dwellings in Wales in 1977–8, or 15.9 per cent of all those
registered in England and Wales. More significant were the concentrations of these homes in the scenic and sparsely populated
areas, with Gwynedd and Dyfed having the highest concentrations in the early 1980s. Whatever the effect of second homes on
local house prices and employment, their opponents viewed them
as a threat to the language and culture of Wales. The increasing
hostility to non-Welsh residents in some parts of rural Wales was
the result of a particular form of immigration which threatened
to weaken a Welsh way of life.

Better housing and wider distribution of home ownership were
part of a more general trend towards a materially more comfortable and affluent society. There was a sharp rise in the private
ownership of cars in the post-war years: between 1960 and 1970,
the 266,000 licensed cars in Wales rose to more than 576,000. The
use of telephones also expanded, with 70,000 domestic phones in
1960 and 297,000 in 1970. Affluence also brought a growth in the
sale of consumer durables from the mid-1950s with the dissemination of refrigerators, television sets and washing machines. In 1960,
5 per cent of Welsh homes had a refrigerator, and in 1970, 60 per
cent of homes had a television. By the early 1980s Wales's relatively
low expenditure per head on durable goods (92 per cent of the UK
level in 1984–5) seemed to suggest that Welsh households had
fewer consumer durables than their British counterparts. In fact, as
table 6.11 indicates, the level of such ownership in Wales was not
significantly different from that of the UK.

Table 6.11 Ownership of durables in Wales and UK 1969–1970 and
1984–1985

		1969–70			1984–5	
	Wales	(Rank in UK)	UK	Wales	(Rank in UK)	UK
Central heating	18.1	10	27.2	70.4	5	67.7
Washing machine	67.3	5	63.8	87.2	4	82.4
Refrigerator	53.9	8	62.8	97.9	3	97.2
Television	92.2	3	91.3	97.4	4	97.4
Telephone	22.7	11	33.5	77.2	6	79.4
Car/van	53.8	5	51.6	67.5	4	62.1
Video recorder	–	–	–	27.3	8	30.1
Home computer	–	–	–	14.1	3	12.6

The percentage of households owning a car, a washing machine or a freezer was above the national average, while the ownership of telephones was marginally lower in Wales.

Women in Society

The war of 1939–45 encouraged women to find work in factories and in industrial occupations, a trend which continued in the newer industries and trading estates after 1945. In Merthyr Tydfil, women comprised one-third of the entire labour force in the town by 1965. In factories and other workplaces they found opportunities for securing an independent income and lifestyle outside the home. Since 1921, and especially after 1951, the absolute number of men in the Welsh workforce has actually fallen, whilst that of women has risen substantially. If it were not for the greater participation by women, the total Welsh work-force today would be smaller than it was fifty years ago.

Female occupational structure changed much less than its male counterpart in the period from 1921 to 1971. The four leading male occupational groups accounted for two-thirds of the total occupied males in 1921, and 46.5 per cent in 1971. For employed women, however, the four leading occupational groups accounted for 79.3 per cent in 1921, and 73.2 per cent in 1971. One of the significant changes occurred in the location of female employment, as women moved in large numbers into offices, hospitals, hotels and other public institutions.

The 1980s brought economic retrenchment and unemployment to women in Wales. Before 1979, the number of women in the workforce had increased on average by 2 per cent per annum, as approximately 94,000 women entered the workforce after 1965. Between 1979 and 1986, almost 40 per cent of these new entrants were lost from the workforce as the number of women in employment fell by 36,000, with 42,000 full-time female positions being lost in the period, and by 1987 there were actually fewer full-time females in the workforce than at any time since the 1950s.

The two principal sectors which had attracted female labour in the period before 1987 were manufacturing and the services. Between 1965 and 1974 an additional 15,000 women entered the manufacturing workforce, an expansion which accounted for only 29 per cent of the total increase in female employment. The most significant developments in the late 1960s and early 1970s were in the service sector. By 1981 the participation of women in manufacturing had steadily diminished to its 1950s level, with only 16.6 per cent of women workers in the manufacturing industries. The service sector was much more successful in attracting women workers in the period between 1972 and 1987. From 1965 to 1974, 39,000 women entered the service sector, and a further 43,000 from 1974 to 1981. The greatest increase occurred in the public sector, and especially in the state-dominated education and health services, and public administration, which accounted for half of the expansion in female employment in Wales between 1971 and 1981. The concentration of female employment in the services has never been greater. In 1987, a massive 80 per cent of women worked in services, with at least a half of those in the four major public services of education, health, national and local government. In 1993, the total number of employees in Wales was 936,000, of whom approximately one-half were women, and by 1997 female employees clearly outnumbered the employed males in Wales.

Women's domestic role has remained largely unchanged despite the vast expansion of female employment. More women than men remain outside the workforce, with a third of the women of working age in Wales being economically inactive in 1991. At almost every stage of their lives, domestic responsibilities have taken priority over other activities. Two major sources of female employment, part-time and domestic positions, developed precisely because they accommodated women's domestic responsibilities. Women's domestic role has also persisted in spite of changes in family structure. The number of households headed by women has escalated as marital breakdown and single parenthood have proliferated in modern society. In 1987, one-fifth of the households with children in South Glamorgan was supervised by a single parent; one of the highest rates existing outside the London boroughs.

Women in Wales have clearly benefited from a new sense of personal and occupational freedom which has pervaded the social landscape since the Second World War. Since the late 1970s, a remarkable trend in the labour market has been the unprecedented increase in self-employment. During this period part-time female employment has increased faster in Wales than in the rest of the UK. In 1971, 31.2 per cent of employed females were engaged in part-time employment, whereas by 1993, 48.1 per cent were so engaged, compared with 10.7 per cent of employed males. In 1987, almost one-quarter of Welsh jobs were held by women working in part-time positions. They have entered a wide range of occupations even though the traditional outlets, such as schoolteaching, have retained their appeal. Although emancipation has spread slowly, and in a far less aggressive form than in many parts of Europe, it is now possible for women to participate in much more rewarding and challenging lifestyles than hitherto.

Recreation

Sport in Wales
The end of war inaugurated a new period of interest in mass sporting events. In 1951, 48,000 spectators watched one rugby match between Cardiff and Newport, and in the following year a local derby between Cardiff and Swansea attracted 40,000 passionate supporters. In the immediate post-war years there were few outstanding players, and the international results were quite modest, with the home side playing thirteen and winning six games in 1947–9. The Northern League clubs continued to hunt for new players and mounted an offensive in 1949. Wales, however, won the Triple Crown and Grand Slam in 1950 and 1952 under John Gwilliam's highly disciplined regime, in which Lewis Jones and Cliff Morgan emerged as superb entertainers and match-winners. From 1950 to 1956 Wales won the championship outright on three occasions and shared it twice. Throughout the 1950s Welsh rugby's responses to the rising tide of economic affluence proved to be ambivalent. The increase in material prospects diverted many away from the traditional Welsh pursuits of football, the cinemas and the churches. From the mid-1950s the televising of rugby internationals often produced falling gates; for example, when the 1955 Scotland v. Wales match was broadcast from Murrayfield, the local game between Aberavon and Abertillery attracted only 400 spectators and produced £9 for the clubs. On the other hand, media attention did generate a new interest in the game, and many

clubs expanded in response to local initiatives. Grounds were leased, stands erected and clubhouses refurbished in a period of growing national optimism. Even in rural Cardiganshire, clubs such as Lampeter and Aberystwyth entered on a period of expansion, the latter climbing from its foundation in 1947 to membership of the Welsh Rugby Union in 1954. Wealthier clubs in south Wales were expanding their activities into Europe, and in 1957 Llanelli became the first British side to play Moscow.

From the mid-sixties Welsh rugby reached new peaks of excellence after a period of introspection and an embarrassing overseas tour to South Africa in the early part of the decade. A number of factors promoted a new enthusiasm in the game: regular televising of internationals coincided with a more overtly nationalistic mood; in 1967, Wales became the first country to adopt a national coaching and squad system; the WRU sought to rebuild the foundations with an increasing emphasis on the Schools Union and Youth Union; and a cluster of bright new stars emerged to improve the fortunes of Welsh rugby.

The seventies were the halcyon years of Welsh rugby: Ireland failed to register a win against Wales; Scotland won two games out of nine against Wales in 1971–9; England, without a win at Cardiff since 1963, managed one win at Twickenham in 1974. In the five-nations championship, only France presented a token challenge to Welsh dominance with three away victories in the nine games played. In 1971, the Lions were conquering heroes, with thirteen Welsh players, captained by John Dawes, the first Welshman to captain a British Lions side, and coached by the Celtic brilliance of Carwyn James. A pantheon of coruscating players emerged to dazzle international spectators with the brilliance, speed and skill of their performances. The names of Barry John, Mervyn Davies, Gareth Edwards, Gerald Davies, J. P. R. Williams, John Dawes, Delme Thomas, Arthur Lewis and Phil Bennett have been idolized and immortalized throughout the land.

The confidence and buoyancy of the 1970s contrasted sharply with what was to follow in the 1980s and early 1990s as Welsh rugby plunged into a pit of despair, self-doubt and defeat. In 1995, rugby union seemed to accept the inevitable and turned professional. As premier clubs battled for superiority on the pitch, an alternative war was waged to compete in the lucrative corporate-hospitality market. The new era of the businessman's hospitality box is now as much a part of rugby union as the towering goalposts. At Cardiff, there are a staggering thirty-eight hospitality boxes, thirty-five of which are available on a seasonal basis and cost a new customer £10,500 or more. Cardiff, which has temporarily opted out of domestic Welsh rugby, attracts business sponsorship for home games against English opposing sides. At the new Millennium Stadium, premium space has been allocated for prestigious hospitality suites, and much of the WRU's strategy for meeting the building and running costs of the £121 million structure is based around corporate hospitality.

Cricket became increasingly popular in the post-war years, and especially after the Glamorgan cricket team, under Wilfred Wooller, captured the county championship in 1948, which brought the title out of England for the first time. The feat was repeated in 1969 under Tony Lewis's captaincy, and again in 1997 under Mathew Maynard. Sophia Gardens, Cardiff, and the Elysian fields of St Helen's, Swansea, were splendid locations for this relaxing summer pastime.

In athletics Ken Jones, an artistic rugby player, captured the Welsh imagination with his track performance and medal in the 1948 Olympic Games in London. In 1964, the long-jumper from Nant-y-moel, Lynn Davies, reached an apogee in Welsh athletics when he took the gold medal at the Tokyo Olympics. Other heroic feats have illuminated the post-war decades. The achievements of Ray Reardon, who won six world snooker titles in the 1970s, inspired amateur champions, such as Doug Mountjoy in 1976, Cliff Wilson in 1978 and Terry Griffiths who took the world professional title in 1979 at his first attempt. Harry Llewellyn, on the horse Foxhunter, carried off an Olympic gold medal at Helsinki in 1952. Golfers, such as Dai Rees and David Thomas, played an important international role, and in 1987 Ian Woosnam spearheaded the successful Welsh bid for the World Cup.

New sports have also infiltrated the Principality. Cardiff has acquired an ice-rink, and the Cardiff Devils glided effortlessly to the top of Britain's Heineken Premier Division in the early 1990s. British rally-driving events have penetrated Wales's heartland in the last quarter of the century; and maritime adventures have proved just as alluring. Tracy Edwards, enthusiastic skipper of an all-woman crew in the Whitbread Round the World yacht race, became the first female to be named 'Yachtsman of the Year' in 1989.

Welsh aptitude for sport remains enthusiastic and undimmed. Latest statistics suggest that about one and a quarter million people participate in some form of sport each year. There are 112,000 who play soccer, 46,000 rugby adherents, 630,000 walkers, 325,000 swimmers, 133,000 cyclists and 20,000 ice skaters. Leisure facilities abound and sponsorship schemes continue to spread to most parts of the Principality.

Films and Cinemas
In 1945, it seemed that British cinema was perched on the threshold of an era of expansion. Critics believed that, as Hollywood appeared to be floundering, the British film industry would revive. Unfortunately, there was no renaissance in Britain: commercial restraints hampered the British industry; Hollywood still bestrode the industry like a colossus; and British studios were unable to produce sufficient films for the vast film audiences of the period. Features based on Wales or the Welsh by British studios in the 1940s and 1950s tended to be simple, genre films, many of which focused on idiosyncratic and humorous Welsh people. *A Run for Your Money*, produced by Ealing Studios in 1949, was a lively study of Welsh miners at an international rugby clash in London who fall prey to alcoholic and sexual diversions. Splendid performances by Meredith Edwards, Donald Houston and Hugh Griffith made the film a memorable Welsh comedy. Ealing had effectively produced a picture which defined the way in which the Welsh would be depicted in so many films throughout the 1950s.

Films set in Wales in the immediate post-war years portrayed mining communities and industrial or national conflicts. In the 1950s, industrial and cultural issues were abandoned in favour of more comfortable and less demanding images. Features set in Wales tended to be simple, humorous diversions, which avoided unsettling or challenging topics. *Valley of Song*, produced in 1953, was a distinctive Welsh comedy, with Rachel Thomas as the archetypal Welsh 'mam'. The film presented a happy, homogeneous community with no impression of post-war austerity. Perhaps the most important contribution to realism came in the late 1950s with the production of television documentaries. Two outstanding directors emerged, John Ormond and Jack Howells. From the 1950s to the 1970s they generated personal films, biographies and character studies, many of which celebrated the work of artists such as Dylan Thomas, R. S. Thomas and Graham Sutherland.

Despite the closure of many cinemas and studios in the 1950s, film was increasingly recognized as an art form and an instrument of social change. The film-society movement burgeoned soon after the end of military hostilities. Cardiff Film Society was established in 1948, and the Newport Film School was centred on the Newport College of Art. The latter produced a coterie of talented film-makers, such as Richard Watkins and Geoffrey Thomas, who focused on social conditions in the Valleys. Notable documentaries were prepared for the Medical Research Council based on studies of thoracic complaints in the Rhondda.

In the 1970s, few influential film-makers graced the studios of Wales, and production levels were disappointing. The reluctance of arts groups to sponsor films was one reason for the un-impressive output of these decades. Film-making grants augmented slowly from £14,500 in 1978–9 to £41,554 in 1980–1. In the 1980s and 1990s Colin Thomas, a native of Carmarthen, collaborated with the charismatic historian Gwyn Alf Williams to produce a series of entertaining and searching documentaries. Their first success, with Gwyn Alf Williams and Wynford Vaughan Thomas as co-narrators, was an effervescent and stimulating view of Welsh history entitled, *The Dragon Has Two Tongues* (1985). In 1988, they dramatized events in the lives of heroic revolutionary figures, and followed this with *Back to Barcelona* for S4C, a record of south Wales miners revisiting the Basque capital on a reunion mission. The zenith of their achievements came in 1992–3 with an ingenious drama-documentary on Saunders Lewis.

The birth of the workshop movement in Wales was an important feature of these years. Film workshops, such as those at Cardiff's Chapter Arts Centre, emerged in response to demands for educational and creative centres of collaboration. Throughout the 1980s women film-makers, trained through Chapter, generated works on social injustices, the plight of distressed pit communities, and on aspects of women's battle against sexism.

Since the early 1970s Karl Francis has been one of the most powerful and combative voices in Welsh film-making. His films have ranged across many controversial issues including local-government corruption, class cleavages, national and cultural divisions. He has focused on life in the Valleys and deliberately sought to provide a mode of expression for English-speakers in these communities. In the early 1990s Francis was influential in campaigning for a fifth television channel which would promote the interests of the English-speaking population of urban south Wales. He protested against the alleged élitism of the Welsh language's proponents.

In the 1990s, film-makers have demonstrated that output with a distinctively Welsh flavour can appeal to an audience beyond the British shores. *Hedd Wyn* (1992) became the first Welsh-language film to be nominated for Hollywood's foreign-language Oscar in its thirty-eight-year history, and captured the Royal Television Society's best drama award. *Leaving Lenin* (1993) was adjudged the best British film at the 1993 London Film Festival, an honour which *Hedd Wyn* had only narrowly missed a year earlier.

For those operating almost exclusively in Wales, the scarcity and uneven geographical distribution of cinema provision continue to beset the independent film industry. Because the large conglomerates concentrated on the cities, most south Wales Valleys had no cinemas in the 1980s. AMC opened its ten-screen cinema in Swansea in 1989, and Rank a five-screen Capital-Odeon in Cardiff in 1991. The Welsh Arts Council played a pivotal role in the early 1990s in attempting to revive cinemas in Wales. The Welsh Office and local authorities provided grants to establish cinemas in less obvious population centres. The Municipal Cinema in Pontypridd was one of the first to open under the Valleys initiative. Subsequently, more multi-screen cinemas opened in the 1990s, notably at Cardiff Bay and Nantgarw. By 1993, the Welsh Arts Council, Ffilm Cymru and S4C had collaborated to create a Welsh Film Council, whose task was to co-ordinate screen interests. An independent Welsh branch of the British Academy of Film and Television Arts was also established in 1989.

Crime in Wales

Since 1945 there has been an alarming increase in the rates of
crime. By the 1960s the first signs of a national neurosis concerning criminal statistics emerged from a range of professional
reports and newspaper articles. Political responses were largely
organizational, as governments proceeded to amalgamate police
forces and establish inter-regional agencies in a determined
campaign to reduce criminal activity. In the 1970s the dangers of
drug abuse, violence and vandalism surfaced in newspapers and
public meetings. It was estimated that 60 per cent of these and
other crimes in south Wales were committed by young people
under twenty-one. In the late 1980s and 1990s south Wales had
the unenviable distinction of being near the top of the British
crime league table, with a reputation for drunken behaviour,
violence against the police, criminal damage, car thefts and
hooliganism.

Table 6.12 1989 National comparisons: notifiable offences recorded in
England and Wales in 1989, per 100,000 of the population

Category of Crime	England	Wales	South Wales
Violent crimes	352	358	348
Burglaries	1660	1366	1925
Theft and handling of stolen goods	4035	3804	4760
Criminal damage	1252	1284	1737
Sexual offences	59	57	39
Robberies	69	14	18
Fraud and forgery	270	235	209
Other offences	56	41	44

Rising crime levels have prompted diverse explanations from
several quarters. Social reformers have tended to concentrate on
the influence of the domestic scene. Studies of children in
juvenile courts in south Wales in the 1950s and 1960s highlighted
the fact that delinquency began at an early age; and that many of
the offenders were from 'deprived' or 'broken homes'. Some
theorists considered possible links between economic depression
and social delinquency, while others postulated a much simpler
explanation for the soaring crime rate and emphasized the

importance of temptation and opportunity. Since the 1960s police forces have campaigned vigorously for crime prevention schemes throughout most parts of the Principality.

As we saw in an earlier chapter on social patterns, the character of criminals seems to have changed little during the century. It was estimated that in Glamorgan during the period 1938–68 between a quarter and a half of detected indictable offences were carried out by juveniles. In 1971, of 26,793 people reported or arrested for crimes like break-ins and criminal damage in south Wales, 16.4 per cent were aged ten to thirteen years, 26.2 per cent were fourteen to sixteen years, 22.6 per cent were seventeen to twenty, and 34.8 per cent were twenty-one or over, so crime was predominantly a young person's activity. The concern about delinquency, which increased from the 1950s, would seem to have emerged from a pellucid appraisal of the facts. By 1989, only eight police forces in Britain returned worse figures of recorded indictable crime. More people now experienced crime, attended court and received fixed penalties than at any time in the century. Surveys in south Wales during the 1980s, indicated that people were convinced that violence was escalating relentlessly. Although a superficial reading of the statistics can create the impression that people in 1989 faced the same kind of dangers as their forefathers in 1900, the level of reporting crimes has changed considerably. Improved communications have enabled people to contact the police, and the authorities have taken a much more serious view of certain categories of offences.

The incidence of crimes depends largely upon the geographical locality. In the early 1980s, violence was a feature of certain types of communities in town centres, poor inner-city areas, impoverished housing estates and declining industrial zones. In 1999, the new Labour government targeted these deprived communities and released additional funds for the provision of neighbourhood schemes and CCTV (closed-circuit television) cameras. Industrial collisions were rare in the post-1945 period, with the exceptions of the miners' strikes in 1972 and 1974, and the most bitter conflict of all in 1984–5, when there were 479 arrests in 1984, and numerous acts of intimidation, violence and criminal damage were recorded. The death of a taxi driver, as the result of a brick thrown through his windscreen by strikers on the Heads of the Valleys road, was the most poignant moment of the strike. Governments introduced a new Public Order Act in 1963 in response to clashes over a number of issues: the apartheid system in South Africa; the threat of nuclear warfare; college campus demonstrations; and campaigns concerning the status of the Welsh language. Police forces were granted a further extension of powers in the 1986 Public Order Act.

The rate of property crime multiplied after the end of the war. By 1969 the rate of property offences was three times higher than in 1957, and from 1969 to 1989 it more than doubled again. In 1989, one indictable property crime was recorded for every twelve people in south Wales, which gave the region the unenviable distinction of recording one of the highest rates in Britain. Victimless offences also increased as a result of various social and government campaigns: the attempts to impose stricter controls on the use of motor vehicles was one such example. By 1963, almost three-quarters of the cases heard in the magistrates' courts of Glamorgan were proceedings under the Road Traffic Acts. By 1990, the vast majority of victimless offences were concerned with motoring, the licensing of television sets and radios, and the sale and use of drink and drugs. A tentative conclusion would seem to be that, although Welsh society has become more civilized throughout the century, it has also plunged into more criminal forms of activity. Criminal behaviour has mounted since the late 1930s, with sharp rises in recorded property offences after 1957, and ascending trends in recorded violent crimes over the last thirty years.

SUGGESTED READING

J. Aitchison and H. Carter, *A Geography of the Welsh Language 1961–1991* (Cardiff, 1994).

D. Berry, *Wales and Cinema* (Cardiff, 1994).

T. Brennan et al. (eds.), *Social Change in South West Wales* (London, 1954).

D. P. Davies, *Against the Tide* (Llandysul, 1995).

Trevor Herbert and Gareth Elwyn Jones (eds.), *Post-war Wales* (Cardiff, 1995).

R. Jenkins and Arwel Edwards, *One Step Forward* (Swansea, 1990).

D. J. V. Jones, *Crime and Policing in the Twentieth Century* (Cardiff, 1996).

Kenneth O. Morgan, *Rebirth of a Nation: Wales 1880–1980* (Oxford, 1981).

D. Smith and G. Williams, *Fields of Praise* (Cardiff, 1980).

Gareth Williams, *1905 and All That* (Llandysul, 1991).

Glanmor Williams, *The Welsh and their Religion* (Cardiff, 1991).

7. Politics in Wales

The Post-War Decades

Labour Ascendancy

IN MAY 1945, the Labour and Liberal members of Churchill's government resigned from their posts on the ending of war in Europe. After a brief intermission of 'caretaker' Conservative government, Churchill called a general election. The results were declared on 26 July, and the outcome was a Labour landslide, which represented a massive shift of public opinion, comparable with the elections of 1906 or 1997. Labour won 393 seats, compared with 210 for the Conservatives and twelve for the Liberals. In Wales, Labour captured twenty-five seats and took 58.5 per cent of the votes cast. The electoral victory reflected the mood of social solidarity generated by years of military conflict, industrial stagnation and economic depression. The Conservatives retained only four seats in Wales – Monmouthshire, Flintshire, Denbighshire and Caernarfon Boroughs. The fall of the latter to the Conservatives marked the end of an era, as Lloyd George's old constituency slipped gently out of the Liberal fold. The Liberals held seven seats, which were essentially rural in complexion. Nearly all the Plaid candidates sacrificed their deposits.

The Labour advances were impressive, with seven seats captured from other parties. The three Cardiff seats secured by Labour produced some colourful new members such as George Thomas, in Cardiff Central, later to become the redoubtable 'Mr Speaker' and Lord Tonypandy; Professor Hilary Marquand in Cardiff East; and James Callaghan, a young naval officer with a strong background in white-collar trade unionism, in Cardiff South. There were other Labour gains in Caernarfonshire, Llandaff and Barry, with near-successes at Anglesey, Merioneth and Pembrokeshire. Huge majorities of 20,000 votes and over were recorded in Caerphilly, Neath, Pontypridd, Ogmore, Abertillery, Ebbw Vale and Aberdare, James Griffiths's majority of 34,000 in Llanelli being the largest in the British Isles. The sweeping victories provided an appropriate dénouement to the tragedy that had unfolded in Wales since the 1920s. The new government reflected the progressive and reformist mood that had emerged during the bleakest years of war, expressing enthusiasm for national planning, social transformation and egalitarianism. The local government elections that ensued in 1945–6 merely confirmed the advance of reformism.

After 1945, Welsh politicians held prominent positions in the party and the administration. Aneurin Bevan, as minister of health, launched the National Health Service; James Griffiths passed the National Insurance Act of 1946; and Ness Edwards and Morgan Phillips served in government and Transport House respectively. The Attlee government's achievements were greeted with passionate enthusiasm in Wales: the establishment of the welfare state, support for full employment, and nationalization of the major industries were seen as beacons of the new society. The nationalization of the coal mines on 1 January 1947 epitomized the radical and communal mood of Labour in Wales. In the election of February 1950, when Labour's majority nationally dropped to a mere six seats overall, the party's strength in Wales hardly faltered, with Labour holding twenty-seven of the thirty-six Welsh seats. Even in the general election of October 1951, when the Attlee government finally succumbed, Labour still retained twenty-seven seats and secured a 60 per cent share of the poll. Losses to the Conservatives in Conwy and Barry were balanced by Labour gains from the Liberals in Anglesey and Merioneth.

Throughout the 1950s, political life in Wales, as elsewhere, was dominated by the spread of affluence, as unemployment almost disappeared and wages rose significantly. By 1950 even farm workers were enjoying a minimum of almost £5 per week. Car ownership was steadily increasing, and Welsh people were reaping the growing benefits of owning their own homes. After 1945, under the government's new housing priority, Pembroke Rural District Council became one of the first councils to receive approval for 180 new houses for farm workers. Advance factories were created to improve employment prospects, while in 1959–60 the car industry experienced a new surge of activity. In this new climate of optimism and economic buoyancy, Labour still clung to its electoral position in Wales. In the 1955 general election, Labour retained its twenty-seven seats and registered a 57.6 per cent share of the poll. At the 1959 general election, with Labour nationally in apparent disarray, the party in Wales again held on to twenty-seven seats.

Conservative rule from 1951 to 1964 witnessed some limited concessions to Welsh distinctiveness. R. A. Butler had suggested that some kind of watchdog, or 'Ambassador for Wales', should be established, and in 1951 the first minister for Welsh affairs was created by the Conservative government. Although the holders of the post in the 1950s were often vilified, the existence of a Cabinet minister with responsibility for Welsh affairs was a first tentative step in the long march to separate governmental treatment for Wales. The Labour government of 1945–51, by contrast, had made few concessions to Welsh national sentiment. There had been some recognition of Wales as a distinct entity in the nationalized industries. Demands from the Welsh Labour members that a secretary of state should be created were conveniently sidelined. Attlee had declared that a Welsh Office would be an 'unnecessary duplication' of administration.

In 1964, Labour returned to office once more and demonstrated its impregnable position in Wales. Swansea West was recaptured for Labour, and Michael Foot entered Parliament as member for Ebbw Vale, in succession to his friend and mentor, Aneurin Bevan. In the general election of March 1966, Labour reached the zenith of its power in Wales, capturing thirty-two of the thirty-six Welsh seats. Conwy, Cardiff North and Monmouth were seized from the Conservatives, while Elystan Morgan wrested Cardiganshire from the Liberals. The election of 1966, and the capture of Cardiganshire in particular, seemed to proclaim the apparently relentless march of Labour in Wales since the end of the First World War.

In the new Labour governments, Welshmen or Welsh MPs secured prominent positions. James Callaghan (MP for Cardiff South East) became Chancellor of the Exchequer in 1964 and Home Secretary in 1967; John Morris (Aberavon) was appointed to the Ministry of Power; Cledwyn Hughes (Anglesey) to the Commonwealth Office; and James Griffiths (Llanelli), became the first secretary of state for Wales. Local authorities such as

Glamorgan, Monmouthshire, Wrexham and Swansea were dominated by the ebullient Labour Party. Trade-union bosses of immense influence and patronage emerged to control their local parties and local government. Lord Heycock, a former engine-driver from Port Talbot, became a leading figure on the Glamorgan County Council and a recognized authority on education. Alderman Tom Evans, Ynysymeudwy, an outspoken member of the Glamorgan County Council, became a party doyen in the Swansea Valley. By the late 1950s, however, there were increasing indications that the old guard of trade-union activists were yielding their power bases to ascending middle-class party workers such as teachers, lawyers, journalists and university lecturers. By 1970, only two Labour MPs were direct nominees of the National Union of Mineworkers. Llanelli had been won by a London barrister, Rhondda West by a former schoolmaster, and Abertillery had fallen to a lawyer. The whole complexion of the Labour Party in Wales was changing, as middle-class values and centralist tendencies gradually eroded the zeal of erstwhile socialist activists.

Following the death of Lady Megan Lloyd George, the Welsh Nationalist Party, Plaid Cymru, captured Carmarthen from Labour in July 1966. In two by-elections, in Rhondda West in March 1967 and in Caerphilly in July 1968, Labour experienced further setbacks with the collapse of its majorities in traditional Labour strongholds. In Rhondda West, there was a 30 per cent swing to Plaid Cymru and Labour's majority fell from over 17,000 to 2,306, while in Caerphilly, the swing to Plaid was nearly 40 per cent and Labour's majority was reduced to a breathtaking 1,874. The Labour Party was deeply shocked by the erosion of its vote and the malaise in organization and morale in the industrial heartlands. In the June 1970 general election, Plaid Cymru fought all thirty-six seats for the first time. Its candidates polled a total of 175,016 votes, or 11.5 per cent of the Welsh total. They gained over 30 per cent of the vote in Aberdare, Carmarthen and Caernarfon, and over 25 per cent in four others. Although Plaid Cymru failed to secure any parliamentary seats, Gwynfor Evans had lost at Carmarthen, and there were twenty-five lost deposits, the party had made an indelible impression on the national political scene. Labour did cede territory in the 1970 election, but mainly to the Conservatives, when four seats were sacrificed by narrow margins. Even allowing for these territorial concessions and the sudden upsurge in nationalist fortunes, Labour controlled twenty-seven seats out of thirty-six, with the Conservatives holding seven and the Liberals one. Labour was still firmly in control of Welsh politics.

The two general elections of 1974, fought against a backdrop of growing economic crisis, union troubles and long-standing industrial unrest, produced further shocks for Labour in Wales. In February 1974, its share of the poll at 46.8 per cent, fell to under 50 per cent for the first time since the Second World War. It held twenty-four Welsh seats, while the Conservatives' tally rose to eight. Labour lost three seats at this election: Cardiganshire rejoined the Liberal fold, while Anglesey and Merioneth fell to Plaid Cymru, and Gwynfor Evans failed by the narrowest of margins, only three votes, to regain Carmarthen for Plaid. In October 1974, Labour suffered further shocks with its tally of seats falling to twenty-three. The Conservatives held on to their eight seats, while the Liberals retained Cardiganshire with an almost identical majority of 2,400. Plaid Cymru recaptured Caernarfon, Merioneth, and Carmarthen with a majority of over 3,300 for the veteran Plaid leader, Gwynfor Evans. Throughout the 1970s it seemed as if Labour's position in north, central and rural Wales was being undermined by Plaid Cymru and the steady advance of the Conservatives. At the 1979 general election, Labour held only twenty-one Welsh seats, as against eleven for the Conservatives, two for Plaid Cymru, one for the Liberals, and the Speaker. There was a swing of 4.8 per cent to the Conservatives in the Welsh vote, as they captured Brecon and Radnor, and Anglesey from Labour. The Conservatives also won Montgomeryshire, a Liberal stronghold since 1880.

After 1979 Welsh politics were dominated by the redoubtable new prime minister, Margaret Thatcher, and her devoted followers. Unemployment was permitted to rise rapidly, coal mines were ruthlessly eliminated, public expenditure was cut savagely after 1981, monetarist tenets were preached and the virtues of privatization were trumpeted in the four corners of the land. The 1979 general election seemed to be a watershed in Welsh political history with the collapse of the devolution issue, the weakening of Labour and the reawakening and revitalization of a 'new right' Conservative government.

The Death of Liberal Wales

In the 1945 Parliament the seven Liberal members were a disparate group, led by the veteran Clement Davies, MP for Montgomeryshire since 1929. In 1950, Liberals had hoped for a renaissance in Wales, with the party's manifesto extolling the virtues of parliaments in Scotland and Wales. Only five Liberal members, however, retained their seats, with Roderic Bowen recording a majority of 8,038 in Cardiganshire. The 1951 general election saw six Liberals returned nationally, and only three in Wales, all three elected without a Conservative challenge. Lady Megan Lloyd George was defeated in Anglesey by the able young solicitor, Cledwyn Hughes, and the three Liberal MPs elected in Wales tended to be on the right of the party.

During the 1950s the Liberal Party had changed significantly, with professional people on the political left slowly gravitating towards Labour ranks. The Tories had extended a number of olive branches to the Liberals, and electoral agreements were often sealed in Britain. Although no formal pacts were agreed in Wales, Clement Davies's hold on Montgomeryshire was rendered more secure by the absence of Conservative opposition in 1951 and 1955. Roderic Bowen, relieved of Tory opposition in Cardiganshire on three occasions in the 1950s, was eventually defeated when a four-cornered contest emerged in 1966. Similarly, no Conservative stood in Carmarthen in four parliamentary contests in the 1950s.

Devolution continued to occupy the attention of the Liberal Party throughout the 1950s. Clement Davies and Lady Megan Lloyd George had consistently supported devolution proposals in the 1930s and 1940s. Davies's first speech to the 1951 Parliament was devoted to regional devolution and electoral reform. In 1955, five Liberal MPs retained their seats, including three in Wales. When Sir Rhys Hopkin Morris died in November 1956, Lady Megan Lloyd George won the by-election in Carmarthen for Labour, and reduced the Liberal cohort at Westminster. In 1959, six Liberals were again returned and, with Clement Davies's death in 1962, Emlyn Hooson was elected for Montgomeryshire. In south Wales, the Liberal Party's position was precarious on the eve of the 1964 general election, but in north Wales party organization remained vibrant in Anglesey, Merioneth, Denbigh, East and West Flintshire and Montgomery. Hopes of a revival were soon dashed, however, as the Liberal Party candidates polled only

7.3 per cent of the vote, and Roderic Bowen and Emlyn Hooson were returned with sharply reduced majorities.

From 1964 to 1966 Hooson concentrated on preparing a Liberal economic plan for Wales, with proposals for a rural development corporation and an overhaul of rural transport facilities. At the 1966 general election, Cardiganshire was lost to Labour, reducing the number of Welsh Liberal seats to one, in Montgomeryshire. The Liberal position in local government had similarly withered since 1945. Well-known Liberals were obliged to stand as Independent candidates in local county council elections during the 1960s, and in the heartlands of rural Wales Liberals were facing a formidable Plaid Cymru challenge. Their initial response was twofold: first, a Welsh Liberal Party was formed in September 1966; secondly, the Welsh Liberals introduced Home Rule bills in Parliament. On St David's Day 1967, Emlyn Hooson introduced a Government of Wales bill in the House of Commons, and in 1968 a Government of Wales bill was introduced into the House of Lords by Lord Ogmore, with only seventeen peers actively supporting the measure.

Financial and organizational problems persisted in the late 1960s. The 1970 general election was a national disaster for the Liberals, with only six British Liberals returned to Parliament. In Wales, Liberal fortunes waned, as candidates sacrificed deposits and party organization fell into desuetude. At the Merthyr by-election in April 1972 the Liberal candidate polled a mere 765 votes. Even so, Emlyn Hooson provided inspirational leadership and worked for a revival of Liberal fortunes. Dramatic Liberal achievements at the February 1974 election, with fourteen seats nationally, augured well for Wales. Thirty-one candidates stood in Wales, and Cardiganshire was restored to the Liberal fold by a local farmer, Geraint Howells. In October 1974, too, the Liberal performance was not unimpressive in Wales, as the party contested all thirty-six seats and seized about 16 per cent of the vote, well ahead of Plaid Cymru's static share.

Despite their commitment to devolution, the Liberals fared badly in the historic general election of 1979. The total Liberal vote declined, and they were left with Cardiganshire as their only Welsh seat. Patriotic Liberals had defected to Plaid Cymru, while aspiring young radicals had affiliated to the Labour Party. Welsh Liberalism seemed anachronistic, outdated and antediluvian.

Welsh Nationalism and the Rise of Plaid Cymru

Although by 1944, membership of Plaid Cymru had increased to 2,500, with 140 local branches, the party emerged from the Second World War with little hope of success in the 1945 general election. Eight candidates stood at the election, most of whom were academics or intellectuals. Seven of these forfeited their deposits, and only in the university did Plaid secure a reasonable share of the vote. In all, Plaid collected 16,447 votes, or 1.1 per cent of the total vote, seemingly incapable of making an impression on any aspect of political life in this immediate post-war period.

In the early 1950s, in conjunction with the Liberals, some Labour leaders and the Communist Party, Plaid Cymru campaigned to launch a petition to Parliament for a 'Parliament for Wales'. Between 1950 and 1956 the campaign made a considerable impact on Welsh opinion. In 1955 S. O. Davies, Labour MP for Merthyr, introduced a private member's bill in support of Welsh home rule. In 1956 Goronwy Roberts, Labour MP for Caernarfon, presented a petition to Parliament which contained 250,000 signatures endorsing the campaign.

In 1950, Plaid Cymru fielded only seven candidates, all of whom lost their deposits. In 1951, the party contested only four seats, and again candidates fared badly. At the 1955 general election, there were signs of improvement with eleven candidates securing 45,119 votes. The later 1950s brought further advances for the party, as Plaid fielded twenty candidates in the 1959 election and polled 77,000 votes. Deposits were saved at Caernarfon, Merioneth, Anglesey and Llanelli. Throughout the 1950s Plaid Cymru became involved in various movements and extended the range of its activities. In 1951, a group of nationalists led by the young and politically astute new party president, Gwynfor Evans, sat down in front of an army camp at Trawsfynydd, in protest against the proposed extension of land held by the War Office. In 1957, Plaid became involved in the Campaign for Nuclear Disarmament. By the 1950s a more flexible and pragmatic style of leadership enabled Plaid to widen the basis of its support. A number of factors promoted this increased level of support for Plaid Cymru from the early 1950s: first, there was growing disillusionment with the post-war Labour government's centralist and anti-devolution stance; secondly, unemployment levels were often consistently higher in Wales than in the rest of

the UK; the pace of decolonization undermined imperial pretensions and fortified the claims of small nations; the continuing
decline of Welsh-speakers and of values deemed essential to the
Welsh tradition added a sense of urgency to nationalist protests;
the support of some Labour and Liberal MPs in the 'Parliament
for Wales' campaign greatly encouraged Plaid; and finally, the
party began to formulate a serious economic plan from 1970,
which appealed to the older industrial areas.

Although Plaid contested twenty seats in 1959, sixteen of its
candidates were university graduates. Twelve of the latter were
graduates of the University of Wales, and ten of the candidates
were lecturers or schoolmasters. The Welsh Nationalist Party remained a predominantly small, rural-orientated movement, based
on a declining constituency of Welsh-speakers. It made little
appeal to the mass of the Welsh electorate in industrial, urban and
working-class centres. In the period 1959–66, the party again
displayed a loss of confidence and a gloomy Celtic introspection.
Party leaders stoutly defended constitutional methods in pressing
the nationalist cause, and eschewed more militant methods,
remaining a fringe movement, with a literary and cultural
identity, as opposed to a more vigorous political presence.

A broadcast on the fate of the language – *Tynged yr Iaith* – by the
veteran scholar, Saunders Lewis, on 13 February 1962 heralded
a new era in nationalist politics. In his radio lecture he called
for more militant methods to defend and preserve the Welsh
language. He argued that the fate of the language was of greater
significance than Welsh self-government. His prophetic style
engendered a new mood of activism among young people, which
led ultimately to the founding of the Welsh Language Society at
Plaid's summer school and conference held at Pontarddulais in
1962. Its aims were to secure official status for the Welsh language,
equal with that of English, and to ensure that Welsh was used by
public bodies in Wales. Between 1962 and 1970 the society was
largely based on the university colleges in Wales. Its non-violent
and largely democratic methods aped those adopted by student
protest movements in Europe and the USA in the 1960s. The
society agitated for bilingual road signs, official forms and road
licences, and for bilingual signs on Welsh post offices. The passage
of the Welsh Language Act in 1967, following the Hughes-Parry
Report in 1965, had given Welsh equal validity with English. At

the end of the 1960s the society expressed the frustrations of the rising generations of Welsh-speaking youth, whose political imagination had been awakened by the historic victory in the 1966 Carmarthen by-election. Membership of the society grew from 300 in 1963 to about 1,500 in 1970. The Language Society emerged as the principal protest movement for the youth of Wales after 1966 in response to a number of factors: first, there was Saunders Lewis's portentous radio message; secondly, young people were disillusioned with Plaid Cymru's abortive constitutional methods; there was a widespread feeling of disappointment with the Labour governments of the 1960s; young people responded to the transcontinental disillusionment with parliamentary democracies; language-society protests were part of a wider student protest movement within Europe and the USA; finally, language protesters reacted against the infiltration of mass culture and the impact of the television age.

Table 7.1 Votes cast at general elections for Plaid Cymru, 1945–1979 (%) (seats in brackets)

	1945	1950	1951	1955	1959	1964	1966	1970	1974 (Feb)	1974 (Oct)	1979
Plaid Cymru	1.1	1.2	0.8	3.2	5.2	4.8	4.3	11.5	10.7 (2)	10.8 (3)	8.1 (2)

Gwynfor Evans's by-election victory in Carmarthen seemed to presage a new dawn for Plaid Cymru. Two further by-election shocks in Rhondda West in March 1967 and in Caerphilly in July 1968 confirmed that Labour's massive majorities in the industrial heartlands were fracturing. At the June 1970 general election, Plaid Cymru fought all thirty-six Welsh seats for the first time, and polled 11.5 per cent of the Welsh vote. Professor K. O. Morgan has described 1970 as a turning-point at which Welsh politics refused to turn. Despite capturing two seats in the February 1974 election, and three in the October 1974 election, Plaid's serious challenge to Labour had been withstood. In the Rhondda, Labour's majority had climbed back to over 34,000. After 1970, Plaid's share of the poll steadily declined to 7.3 per cent in 1987. Plaid's electoral performances can be divided into three periods: in the early years, from 1926 to 1945, Plaid was incapable of fighting parliamentary seats and contesting elections to any great degree; from 1945 to the 1960s, it entered its growth phase and committed itself to fighting as many parliamentary seats as possible; from the 1960s onwards, Plaid Cymru began to develop into a significant political organization, with increases in membership and an expansion of organizational capabilities.

From 1945 onwards Plaid Cymru also began to respond to the burgeoning European community. Plaid had become involved with the International Congress of European Communities and Regions as early as 1947, and had attended meetings of the Congress from 1949 to 1954. As the 1960s progressed, Plaid became more hostile to the reality of European union and to the practices of the European Community. After the Plaid Cymru conference of 1969, the party adopted an unequivocal position of opposition to UK membership of the European Community. The issue of Welsh representation was a stumbling-block, as was the possible threat to Welsh economic interests, and especially to Welsh agriculture.

Throughout the 1960s and early 1970s, the party sought to stress its commitment to European union and its dissatisfaction with the European Community. Once the UK joined the European Community in 1973, Plaid Cymru shifted the focus of its attacks on to the Community and sought to promote Welsh interests within the European arena. The continuing political ambiguity of Plaid's policy on Europe, after changes of emphasis at party conferences in 1969, 1973 and 1975, was reflected in the main theme that the party promoted in its 1975 referendum campaign. The party slogan urged: 'Europe, Yes. EEC, No.' One of the party's MPs, Dafydd Wigley, abstained from the referendum campaign on the grounds that he supported independence in Europe, and not opposition to the European Community. The results of the referendum campaign were a further disappointment to Plaid Cymru, when Wales voted solidly in favour of continued membership of the European Community. Not one of the Welsh counties cast a majority in favour of Plaid's 'No' campaign; even the heartland of Gwynedd supported continued membership with a 'Yes' vote of 70.6 per cent. Although Plaid's efforts had failed, its policy remained formally opposed to EC membership.

Devolution

In the immediate post-war period, the Labour government of 1945–51, with its emphasis on centralization in economic and social planning, paid little heed to national sentiment in Wales. Demands from Welsh Labour members, such as D. R. Grenfell and W. H. Mainwaring, that a secretary of state be created were dismissed peremptorily by the Attlee government. Growing pressure from a group of Welsh Labour MPs and the Welsh Regional Council of Labour for a wider recognition of the needs of Wales led eventually to a discussion of a secretary of state for Wales, or of some form of devolution, by the cabinet's Home Services Committee in 1948. The committee, despite Aneurin Bevan's staunch opposition, agreed that an advisory council should be created from the local authorities and both sides of industry. The Welsh Advisory Council, which dealt with cultural and minor economic questions, was ineffective from the outset and trudged along for eighteen inglorious years.

The Conservatives, who were no less committed to the unionist principle, did establish in 1951 a Ministry of Welsh Affairs, to be held jointly with the home secretaryship. The new ministry attracted few supporters from the Principality, and the incumbents provoked hostility and rebuke from various quarters. It was Henry Brooke, Home Secretary and minister for Welsh affairs, who approved the acquisition of water from the Tryweryn Valley in Merioneth by Liverpool and allowed the flooding of the small community, despite passionate opposition in Wales. Every Welsh Labour MP voted against the infamous Tryweryn bill in 1957.

Between 1950 and 1956 the Parliament for Wales campaign rekindled the issue of self-government for the Principality. Charismatic characters such as S. O. Davies, Labour MP for Merthyr, introduced a private member's bill in support of Welsh home rule in 1955, endorsed by several Welsh Labour members, including Cledwyn Hughes from Gwynedd and Tudor Watkins, Brecon and Radnor. The campaign was too badly organized to make much of an impression on the parliamentary scene, and, by 1956, it was struggling for survival. After thirteen years of Conservative rule, the 1964 election brought Labour to power, followed by a detectable new direction in government policy and propitious changes in Welsh society. A concatenation of circumstances proved conducive to the emergence of a new devolution movement from the early 1960s: the resurgence of nationalist feeling and the revival of Plaid Cymru threatened Labour Party strongholds in Wales; the appearance of the Welsh Language Society from 1962 triggered new radical approaches to language and culture; political parties sensed an urgent need for fresh local government proposals, and this put devolution firmly on the agenda of the Labour Party in Wales; the contributions of James Griffiths and Gwilym Prys Davies to Labour Party deliberations on the subject were very influential; the establishment of a Welsh Office in 1964 acted as a further catalyst; the unfortunate arrival of the fervent anti-devolutionist George Thomas at the Welsh Office in 1968 actually fortified the devolutionists; the appointment of the Crowther/Kilbrandon Commission on the constitution spurred the devolutionist movement; and finally, the electoral and constitutional uncertainty that existed in the early 1970s gave minority parties and pressure groups the opportunity to transform a dream into a tangible political issue.

The sixties were an exciting time for nationalists and devolutionists alike. By 1968 the Welsh-language movement was at its apogee, and the Welsh Language Act of 1967 had given Welsh equal validity with English. There was a booming Welsh pop culture, with unprecedented sales of Welsh records. Plaid Cymru had captured the Carmarthen seat in 1966, and had unsettled Labour in further by-elections. The Welsh Office had been established in 1964, with a reasonable range of powers, including housing, local government, road transport and aspects of local planning. By 1969, it also controlled health and agriculture, with education soon to follow. Yet the new Welsh Office was not a powerful department, having no global budget, little executive influence and no power over key decisions of economic planning, which were still controlled by Whitehall. In the words of one eminent historian, 'it was really a co-ordinating department in Wales for policies conceived elsewhere' (K. O. Morgan). With the arrival of George Thomas at the Welsh Office in 1968 a new attempt to conciliate Welsh opinion was devised. It was decided that the investiture of Prince Charles as Prince of Wales would appeal to the royalist Welsh people and thereby reduce the political influence of Plaid Cymru.

In 1969, Prime Minister Harold Wilson set up the Crowther (later Kilbrandon) Royal Commission on the constitution as a counter to nationalist sentiment in Wales and Scotland. Its main brief was to consider the prospects for governmental devolution in Scotland and Wales. Its members included two Welshmen, Sir Ben Bowen Thomas and Alun (later Sir) Talfan Davies. When the commission reported in October 1973, eleven of the thirteen members of the Kilbrandon Commission declared in favour of a Scottish legislative assembly, along with a more modest Welsh assembly with prescribed powers. Six of the eleven members called for a Welsh legislative assembly, a parliament with its own budget, tax-raising powers, and authority over a wide range of subjects. All thirteen commissioners strongly rejected separatism and insisted on the unity of the United Kingdom.

The major parties responded swiftly to the recommendations of the commission. The Conservatives continued their unionist stance towards Wales. Labour regained office in March 1974, with James Callaghan and Michael Foot playing leading roles in the cabinet, and Merlyn Rees, David Owen and Lord Elwyn-Jones serving in the new administration. The new Welsh secretary was John Morris, a committed devolutionist. The precise intentions of the incoming Labour government with regard to devolution were still uncertain, but broad views were outlined in a white paper, *Democracy and Devolution*, published in September 1974. This stipulated that there would be directly elected assemblies for Wales and Scotland, with the Welsh one having only executive powers instead of the legislative role granted the Scottish Assembly. Although the Cabinet had come reluctantly to accept devolution as a way of placating the political separatists, there were forceful and strident anti-devolution voices within the Labour movement. A group of south Wales Labour MPs, including Leo Abse, Neil Kinnock, Donald Anderson, Fred Evans, Ioan Evans and Ifor Davies, argued that devolution would lead to separatism.

In December 1976 the new prime minister, James Callaghan, introduced a joint Devolution bill for Wales and Scotland. The Welsh Assembly would be a less powerful body than that in Scotland, and a derelict coal exchange in the Cardiff docks area was earmarked as its future home. The government was forced to concede on the second reading of the bill that an advisory referendum should precede the implementation of the Act. Labour backbenchers had also forced an amendment which required 40 per cent of the electorate to vote 'yes' for the devolution measure to take effect. The anti-devolutionists seemed to have won the first phase of this devolution campaign. The progress of the devolution legislation through Parliament constituted the second phase of the campaign, and extended from late 1976 through to June 1978. It was played out against a unique parliamentary and political background, with the worst economic crisis since the 1930s, a 'Lib–Lab' pact and a succession of damaging defeats inflicted on the government. The Labour government was faced with an unprecedented problem of trying to carry through legislation it had been forced to introduce for reasons of political expediency, which was strongly opposed by a substantial number of its own backbenchers, but which had rapidly become a symbol of its own ability to survive.

The Wales Devolution bill was introduced as a separate measure in November 1977, and it passed its second reading by 295 votes to 264 on 15 November 1977. The Scottish and Welsh bills proceeded through the committee stage between February and April 1978. Devolution eventually reached the statute book partly because of the Lib–Lab pact, partly because many Labour dissidents were supporting their government on a matter of confidence, and partly because the anti-devolutionist Labour MPs were satisfied that the 40 per cent rule would test the electorate. With the safeguard of a referendum to come, the Wales bill passed its third reading by 292 votes to 264 on 9 May 1978. The referenda on Welsh and Scottish devolution were timed for 1 March 1979.

In the referendum campaign that ensued from 8 February to 1 March 1979, the opponents of devolution concentrated their attack on several issues: the costs of the new assembly; the bureaucratization of government that would be likely to follow; the fact that devolution might lead to complete separation for Wales; while Leo Abse and others played on the sociolinguistic aspect, that the assembly would be dominated by a Welsh-speaking élite. These arguments largely undermined the pro-devolutionist emphasis on the extension of democracy. The opponents of the assembly dominated the debate throughout the referendum campaign. Nearly all the Conservatives in Wales and the six dissident south Wales Labour MPs assailed the government's proposals for executive devolution. When the results of the referendum were announced, the 'yes' campaign was seen to be an abysmal failure. Only 11.8 per cent of the Welsh electorate had voted in favour of devolution, while 46.5 per cent had voted against. Each one of the Welsh counties voted strongly against; even in Gwynedd, with a Welsh-speaking population and two Plaid Cymru MPs, there was an almost two-to-one vote against Welsh devolution; and in the Anglicized south-east only 7.7 per cent of the electors in South Glamorgan and 6.7 per cent in Gwent had voted in favour. The devolution episode appeared as a fiasco and a complete humiliation for the tottering Labour government.

What explains the defeat of the devolution proposals in 1979? There was fear that governmental economic assistance would be obstructed by the creation of an intermediate executive body. The cost factor was employed to great effect by the critics of additional layers of local government. The anti-assembly co-alition concentrated their attacks on the Wales Act itself, and especially on its projected negative effects. Leo Abse and other opponents astutely exploited the north–south divide and alarmed the electorate with fears of increasing corruption and Welsh élitism in local government. The Labour Party had clearly mis-calculated the depth and extent of national feeling in Wales. The process of 'acculturation', with the acquisition of the politico-cultural characteristics of the wider English political and social system, had probably affected the attitudes and institutions of Wales. Wales was also subjected to a bombardment of unionist and centralist views from the London-based daily newspapers which penetrated the homes of most Welsh people. There was no single indigenous daily newspaper that covered the whole of Wales. Finally, devolution was clearly undermined by the grow-ing unpopularity of the Labour government after the winter of bitter industrial discontent in 1978.

Devolution seemed to have been obliterated, and nationalism was in retreat. In May 1979, James Callaghan's government was defeated at the polls, with a 4.8 per cent swing to the Conservat-ives in Wales. Labour held twenty-two seats, the Conservatives captured eleven, Plaid Cymru had two and the Liberals one seat. Labour had retreated in north and mid-Wales: its local authorit-ies were sometimes subjected to charges of alleged corruption; its pronouncements were sounding increasingly antediluvian; and its leaders appeared senescent and outdated.

Welsh Politics in the 1980s

From 1979 onwards Welsh politics entered a new epoch under the Thatcher hegemony. The old shibboleths of centralized economic and social planning, nationalization and welfarism were to be swept aside by an incoming tidal wave of right-wing orthodoxy. Monetarism, privatization, enterprise and individual profit-making were to be the catchwords of the new political culture. For almost two decades Wales would be submerged in Thatcherite rhetoric, and the political, economic and social landscape was exposed to relentless forces of change.

Following the 1979 general election, Welsh political society was greatly affected by the consequences of the devolution referendum of St David's Day. Almost 79 per cent of the voters had rejected the Labour government's proposals for executive devolution. The enormous impact of this political fact would soon weaken and undermine the political and cultural establishment of Wales. With the exception of the Conservatives, all the political parties in Wales had supported devolution, along with most of the religious denominations and the leading figures in the Welsh cultural community. The Conservatives appeared to have gauged the mood of the Welsh people, and this was reflected at the general election, when the Conservative vote climbed from 23.9 per cent in October 1974 to 32.2. per cent in May 1979. The Conservative argument that Wales did not require devolved government, nor separate treatment from the rest of the UK, appeared to have been vindicated. The Labour and Liberal parties, startled by the scale of the referendum defeat and threatened by the electoral advance of the Conservatives, adopted lower profiles on Welsh issues and quietly shelved their devolution policies.

The Conservatives had also consistently argued that problems of public accountability in Wales could be resolved within the framework of the Westminster Parliament. On 26 June 1979 the Wales Act was repealed by 191 votes to 8, and the Welsh secretary of state announced the government's intention to establish a Select Committee on Welsh Affairs to examine the expenditure, administration and policy of the Welsh Office and related public bodies. The committee began its work in January 1980 and, from the outset, a majority of its members sought to inflate the importance of the Select Committee in the hope that this would obviate the need for an elected assembly. The committee concentrated on nationalist issues, such as Welsh-language broadcasting and water in Wales, so as to prevent Plaid Cymru from presenting itself as the sole custodian of national interest.

The decline of Wales's traditional basic industries and the Conservative government's determination to cut public expenditure further influenced the pattern of Welsh politics in the aftermath of the 1979 general election. In 1979, 43 per cent of the working population of Wales was employed in the public sector, with the British Steel Corporation alone employing 63,000 steel workers. By May 1983 only 19,000 were employed in the steel sector. Manufacturing industries shed around 90,000 workers, and the service sector lost around 41,000 employees. Unemployment had increased rapidly from 5.3 per cent in 1979 to 13.2 per cent of the workforce in 1984. In February 1981, the National Coal Board published plans to close seven Welsh pits, which produced an all-out strike in the south Wales coalfield, which spread to other coalfields in Britain. The government conceded and promised to curb imported coal, to sustain investment and to provide additional subsidies to the coalfield in excess of £30 million. This was, however, only a brief interlude in a chronicle of contraction and decline; plans to reduce the south Wales coalfield by a third had only been temporarily deferred.

Meanwhile, the political parties were unusually reticent as the Welsh economy plunged into depression. The Conservative Party in Wales argued forcefully that government policies were clearly vindicated by the party's electoral successes. The devolution debate and the election defeat had left the Labour Party in a sombre mood, and it had proceeded to distance itself from its erstwhile devolution policy, and the issue was not even debated in Welsh Labour conferences. The party was not, however, infiltrated by the militant tendency of the period. The new left-wing activists made little impression on the traditionally working-class and socially conservative party, the vast majority of whose Welsh Labour MPs were entrenched on the right of the party. Welsh Liberals had lost their leader, Emlyn Hooson, in the 1979 election, and they were in no position to mount a serious challenge to the Conservative creed of the day. Plaid Cymru was also seriously weakened by the referendum debacle and the general election. A left–right cleavage emerged in the party between the traditionalists, who were committed to a decentralized community socialism, and the aspiring left-wing group led by the ebullient Dafydd Elis Thomas, who pressed for the establishment of a Welsh socialist state by means of a popular-front movement, embracing nationalists and the Labour movement. The political scene was complicated still further by the emergence of a splinter group, the Welsh Socialist Republicans. The appearance of unconstitutional activities in the years following the 1979 general election confirmed that Plaid Cymru was in danger of losing the initiative within the nationalist movement. By December 1980, there had been forty-two arson attacks on second homes and holiday cottages owned by English people, and during 1981 a series of thirteen bomb attacks led to the arrest of seven men on conspiracy charges.

With the Falklands War concluded, Prime Minister Thatcher called an election in 1983. The campaign, by comparison with those of the 1970s, was largely concerned with 'British' issues. The demise of devolution, the dominant role of the media and public opinion polls, the impact of the Falklands factor and a surge in unemployment all helped produce a distinctly metropolitan orientation to the 1983 general election. The three major British political parties made one concession to Welsh public opinion and produced separate Welsh manifestos. Denzil Davies, the shadow Welsh secretary, unveiled Labour's manifesto for Wales, *New Hope for Wales*, which promised a new organization to examine the Welsh economy and to proffer advice to the secretary of state. Labour promised investment in the traditional industries, a plan for jobs which would target severely depressed areas, and a massive expansion of public spending on housing, transport and the welfare services. The Conservatives started their campaign defensively, preferring to cling to their acknowledged lead in the opinion polls. Throughout the election period they attacked the unions and local government, and attributed economic problems to a world recession and to inflationary practices in the UK. Mrs Thatcher visited Cardiff on the evening of 23 May 1983 and enjoyed raising the terrors that would follow from any Labour administration. The Labour and Conservative manifestos, from which devolution was conspicuous by its absence, specifically emphasized the essential political and

economic unity of the UK. Plaid Cymru completely ignored
devolution and restored national independence to its pride of
place.

The election results confirmed the onward march of Conservatism and the steady erosion of Labour support. The
Conservatives captured fourteen seats, their highest number of
the century, Labour were reduced to twenty seats, their lowest for
many decades, while Plaid Cymru and the Liberal–SDP Alliance
took two seats each.

Table 7.2 General election results, 9 June 1983

Party	% of votes	MPs
Conservative	31.0	14
Labour	37.5	20
Alliance	23.2	2
Plaid Cymru	7.8	2

As Labour's share of the poll sank to a sixty-year low, the
immediate conclusion drawn from the electoral results was the
overwhelming association of Labour voting with areas of
industrial decline, outside which Labour failed to make any
significant impact. Psephologists detected a strong correlation of
'modernizing' tendencies with Conservative voting patterns.
Conservatives polled well in suburban and urban areas along the
M4 corridor in the south and the A55 in north Wales. The
Conservatives also attracted rural votes and the support of the
retired who had recently migrated to the north and south Wales
coasts.

In the aftermath of the 1983 general election, scholars began
to conclude that a 'three-Wales model' of voting had emerged in
the Principality: there was 'Y Fro Gymraeg' – a Welsh-speaking,
Welsh-identifying group based in north and north-west Wales;
'Welsh Wales', a Welsh-identifying, non-Welsh-speaking group
prevalent in the traditional industrial Valleys of the south; and
'British Wales' – a British-identifying, non-Welsh-speaking group
dominating eastern Wales, the border lands, south Pembrokeshire and the Anglicized coastal plains. Plaid Cymru was firmly
entrenched in 'Y Fro Gymraeg', Labour's electoral stronghold
was traditionally in the industrial Valleys of 'Welsh Wales', but

the Conservatives seemed to be appealing to the emerging Welsh middle-class groups. In 'British Wales', the British electoral pattern of Conservatives v. Labour v. Alliance (Liberals and Social Democrats) was replicated, and Welsh linguistic and cultural issues had made little impact.

After the massive Conservative victory in 1983, an air of recrimination soon engulfed Labour in Wales. Party officials attacked the power of the left, and identified defence and the Common Market as crucial policies which had resulted in catastrophic defeat. The Alliance was now the greatest challenger to Labour in Wales, having come second in nineteen seats, while the Conservatives had come second in eleven. Meanwhile, the Conservatives proceeded with their policies of privatization and de-industrialization. Unemployment in Wales had already increased from 5.3 per cent of the workforce in 1979 to 10.4 per cent in 1981. The figure climbed to 13.2 per cent in 1984, and thence to 13.7 per cent in 1986. Throughout the 1980s the unemployment rate was consistently higher in Wales than in the UK. Total industrial stoppages of work had fallen since 1977, and working days lost had slumped dramatically since 1980. Conservative policies seemed to be emasculating the unions and draining the workforce of its political energies.

The miners' strike of 1984–5 marked a turning-point both for the British coal industry and for the trade-union movement. Since the 1950s coal mining in south Wales had steadily declined in importance. The numbers employed in the industry had fallen from 99,000 in 1958 to 20,347 in 1984, while output had plunged from 22,822,000 tons to 6,720,000 in the same period. Severe recession in the late 1970s and early 1980s had undermined the old staple industries of the Valleys. The British Steel Corporation's 'rationalization' programme had exacerbated the position and resulted in the loss of 15,000 jobs from the region. The south Wales Valleys in the mid-1980s were senescent and declining communities. Two factors made the south Wales area exceptional. First, it had been deprived of investment, especially in high-quality coals. In 1982, a paltry sum of £7.63 million had been allocated to construct new capacity, compared with £453.5 million for North Yorkshire and £75.7 million for the Western Area. Secondly, the south Wales area of the National Union of Mineworkers had adopted a combative strategy in defence of pits and coalfield communities following the closures of the 1960s. The battle for Deep Duffryn Colliery in 1978–9 had been a watershed in the movement to preserve the industry. Saving a pit was associated henceforth with the fate of its dependent community. A spontaneous action in 1983, which had begun with a stay-in strike in defence of Lewis Merthyr colliery, had resulted in thousands of south Wales activists lobbying every pit in Britain.

The 1984–5 strike began amidst some confusion in south Wales. Oakdale and Betws collieries, located at opposite ends of the coalfield, and with no tradition of militancy, voted in favour of strike action, while many of those collieries which voted against industrial action were actually threatened with closure. By 14 March 1984, although the stoppage was complete in south Wales, there were still some lodges which had not officially voted for strike action. By the end of the long bitter struggle, mining communities felt that they had endured four different strikes: the industrial dispute which lasted from March to July 1984; followed by an accepted 'way of life' from August to November 1984; and a third stage saw the defence of the coalfield from November 1984 to January 1985; with a fourth, and final, stage during the last months of the industrial action bent on saving the union.

By April 1984 the strike had lasted longer than those of 1972 and 1974. The first National Women's Rally was held on 12 May 1984, and in June the South Wales Women's Support Group was formed. Food-gathering and fund-raising activities gathered momentum in April and May 1984. By the middle of May every mining village and town in south Wales had its own community-based or women's support group. The collective optimism of the coalfield was shattered on 1 August 1984 when all the south Wales area NUM bank accounts and food funds were frozen because of the area's refusal to comply with a court order banning its secondary picketing of Port Talbot Steelworks. By 5 November 1984 only nineteen men had returned to work, and sixteen of these were at the Cynheidre colliery in south-west Wales. By early January 1985 there were 119 men back at work, and 90 per cent of these were at Cynheidre. By February 1985 only 478 men had returned to work, but the position of the union was becoming precarious. In the New Year it was loyalty alone which was sustaining the fragile unity of the committed miners.

On 1 March 1985 the south Wales area conference took the momentous decision, by an overwhelming majority, to call for a national return to work.

On 5 March 1985 the long-suffering miners returned to work. In May, two Rhymney miners were accused of murdering David Wilkie, the Cardiff taxi-driver. Within ten months of the strike, nine collieries had disappeared in south Wales, and employment had been cut by nearly a half by the end of 1986. The process of disintegration and contraction continued unabated for the remainder of the eighties and early nineties. The strike had been an embarrassment for the opposition parties, but for the miners and their families it had been a period of the most grievous struggle and suffering. At the end they had been totally defeated and the government completely victorious. The union movement had been seriously damaged: the number of TUC-affiliated unions fell from seventy-five in 1980 to forty-eight in 1995; membership of trade unions in Wales dropped from 659,466 to 509,618 in the same period. Membership of individual unions plunged in much the same way:

Table 7.3 Membership of individual unions in Wales

	NUM	NUR	TGWU
1980	30410	11488	118000
1984	29260	6478	88333
1989	12500	5119	80034
1995	12500	4416	65000

With unemployment reaching a peak in 1986, industrial stoppages having dropped to eighty-six in 1985, and the number of working days lost at an all-time low of seventy-eight in 1986, the Conservatives entered the 1987 election in a reasonably confident mood. They promised more of the same to the electorate: privatization of water and electricity, a cut in income tax to 25p, further trade-union reforms, a tougher approach to crime, and radical changes in education. The Thatcher government emphasized the continuing fight to keep inflation under control and tax incentives for business and enterprise. Such was British Coal's confidence in the resilience of the government and the compliance of the miners that it imposed a two-year unilateral pay deal on all the NUM members in the middle of the election campaign. The Labour Party, promising to spend £6 billion on jobs and £3 billion on state borrowing, concentrated on unemployment, pensions, health and housing. Mrs Thatcher and the new Labour leader, Neil Kinnock, painted different pictures of the Welsh economy, the one buoyant and optimistic, the other disheartening and grim. Neither leader mentioned devolution, although Kinnock suggested increased support for local authorities. Plaid Cymru also seemed to have diluted its demands for independence for Wales, in favour of a Welsh senate which would work under the aegis of Westminster.

On the eve of the election in June 1987, political commentators were pondering the future of Labour in Wales. Since 1966, Labour's position had been increasingly undermined, not by Plaid Cymru, which had failed to overturn Labour in the late 1960s, and early 1970s, but by the progressive advance of the Conservative party in Wales. Conservatives had always claimed a quarter to a third of the electoral vote in Wales. The immense transformation had come in recent years as the proportion of support had been translated into parliamentary seats. In 1959, 32.6 per cent of the vote had given the Conservatives seven MPs; in 1983, a 31 per cent share of the vote had returned fourteen MPs. The electoral map of Wales appeared to have been redrawn since the late 1970s, enabling a junior minister at the Welsh Office to claim in 1979 that he could drive from the Severn Bridge to Holyhead without leaving Conservative-held territory. At the 1983 election, Conservatives, with their 31 per cent share of the vote, had come close to matching Labour's 37 per cent. It was noted that political patterns were changing in Wales, largely as a result of the growing homogeneity between much of Wales and England. The solidarity displayed by south Wales miners during the 1984–5 strike had provided remarkable testimony to the enormous strength of traditional values in the communities of south Wales. But the economic structure that supported these communities was in irreversible decline. In 1983, the Alliance party had claimed nearly one-fifth of the vote in Mid Glamorgan, and one-quarter of the vote in Gwent. Labour's ability to capture seats in rural Wales had declined dramatically. Outside the industrial areas of south and north-east Wales, only

Carmarthen, a notoriously volatile constituency, remained in Labour hands. New job opportunities and changing occupational structures in north-east Wales and along the M4 corridor in the south were reinforcing the marginal status of many erstwhile Labour constituencies. In addition, Plaid Cymru was taking the credit for many of the outstanding developments that had occurred in Welsh public life since the mid-1960s. Plaid had long set the agenda of Welsh politics and acted as a catalyst for processes of political change.

When the results of the 1987 general election were declared, despite the gloomy predictions of Labour's imminent collapse, the party had gained four seats from the Conservatives to take its tally to twenty-four. Its share of the vote had also augmented to 45.1 per cent, almost equal to its February 1974 figure. Meanwhile, the Conservatives, though still retaining 29.5 per cent of the vote, saw their tally of seats fall to eight. The Alliance and Plaid Cymru took two seats each. It seemed as if Labour was re-emerging phoenix-like to take its rightful place as the radical voice of anti-Tory protest.

Welsh Politics in the 1990s

Despite the embarrassing and overwhelming failure of the devolution referendum in 1979, the collapse of Labour throughout the 1980s and the presiding Conservative hegemony from 1979 onwards, the devolution debate resurfaced in the early 1990s and support for regional devolution sprouted in many quarters. Political changes in Wales since 1979 were partly responsible for this shift. The political establishment, which had once been hostile to devolution, was in disarray by the early 1990s. In 1979, the majority of the Labour Party had supported a centrally planned economy, and any concessions to decentralization were seen as detrimental to that long-standing objective. By 1992, and certainly after the election defeats of the 1980s, the Labour Party had begun to jettison its commitment to a centrally planned economy. Two days after the election defeat of 1987, the Labour leader, Neil Kinnock, one of the original 'gang of six' who had opposed Labour's 1979 devolution proposals, was reported to be pondering the advantages of supporting a Welsh assembly. The Conservatives were also having to face new political realities. Many realized that membership of the European Union had undermined the sovereignty of the British Parliament. Since the departure of Thatcher in 1990, Conservatives had become increasingly divided over issues of sovereignty, subsidiarity and devolved government. The Liberals, revived by the SDP Alliance, had restructured themselves into a more serious party and were posing a real threat to the Conservatives in areas such as south-east England.

In the late 1980s, with the demise of the SDP challenge, and the failure of Plaid Cymru to capture the Valleys, Labour had become more secure in its industrial heartlands. Observers had argued that the Valley constituencies were changing rapidly: the old working-class acolytes were disappearing; the economic structure was being eroded; and sociological changes were transforming the old Valley communities. It was widely believed that Labour would suffer as a result of these economic and social vicissitudes. In the 1970s, however, Labour had successfully withstood the challenge of Ratepayers' parties in Ebbw Vale, Swansea and Port Talbot. Plaid Cymru had won control of Merthyr districts and the Rhymney Valley until 1979. In 1983, the Social Democrat and Liberal Alliance had swept to second place in twelve Valley constituencies. Yet, the Labour Party had survived the onslaught of each party, and had manifested an enviable ability to renew itself. Its choice of new parliamentary candidates in the late 1980s and early 1990s, with Peter Hain in Neath and Alun Michael in Penarth, had displayed a willingness to embrace Liberal traditions.

During the Thatcher years, Welsh nationalism presented less of a threat to the political establishment in Wales than its counterpart in Scotland. Paradoxically, the emotive force of the language produced more significant concessions from government than one might have expected. The danger of inflaming nationalist sentiments on issues relating to the status of the Welsh language always produced sensitive responses from the political authorities. The early electoral successes of the 1960s and 1970s were not extended into the Thatcher years. Plaid Cymru tended to remain as a regional pressure group within 'Y Fro Gymraeg'. In the 1992 general election, in only five seats did Plaid's vote rise above 30 per cent of the poll, and they won four of those. In the next seat, Llanelli, Plaid polled barely 16 per cent of the vote. Its political rump was concentrated in the country's Welsh-speaking areas; beyond Llanelli, Plaid Cymru's 1992 general election vote hardly existed. In twenty-two seats Plaid Cymru had recorded little success, and the candidates lost their deposits. Despite Dafydd Elis Thomas's support of the miners in 1984–5 and his espousal of a form of Bennite democratic socialism, attempts to penetrate the Valleys were largely abortive. Plaid's socialism tried to link with a past that was on the verge of vanishing. In the late 1980s and in the 1992 general election, Plaid did emerge as a more credible political force. It came to regard its identification with 'Y Fro Gymraeg' as a positive electoral bonus. It adopted a more pragmatic approach, agreeing a joint parliamentary candidate with the Greens in Ceredigion for the 1992 general election. It exploited the government's slim majority in the House of Commons during the Maastricht debate to force concessions on committee representation. Notwithstanding these more pragmatic approaches, nationalism in Wales remained far more peripheral and less powerful a force than its Scottish counterpart. One cannot explain the changes in Welsh politics by the 1990s simply in terms of developments in Welsh nationalism.

The transformation of Wales's economic base recast Welsh politics and furthered the cause of devolution from the late 1980s onwards. At the time of the 1979 referendum, the Welsh economy had still been dependent on heavy industries, and had been dominated by the public sector, which employed 43 per cent of the workforce. During the campaign, business and commercial groups, concerned about Welsh economic interests in a British context, had voted 'No' to devolution. In the 1980s governmental policies of privatization and reduced regional aid transformed the political landscape. The Welsh steel industry shed over 50,000 workers, and coal was almost eliminated after the damaging miners' strike. As these staple industries collapsed, the central pillars of the traditional Welsh working-class movement had been virtually removed. Government pronouncements on the emerging global economy, the free market and the virtues of increased competition detracted from older beliefs in centralized planning and interventionist economics. Welsh industrial interests were encouraged to adopt a more proactive role in attracting inward investment. The Welsh economy, which attracted over 300 overseas companies in the 1980s and 1990s, developed a more balanced industrial base, and Welsh industrialists became more aware of Europe and the wider global economy. These economic factors had positive effects on support for devolution: the so-called new entrepreneurial classes were concerned that Wales should have political structures to match its developing economic interests in Europe and the wider world.

Meanwhile, changes in public administration since 1979 fortified the case for devolution. Although the Thatcher and Major governments remained implacably hostile to political devolution, their incremental changes to the system of public administration in Wales unwittingly strengthened the case of the supporters of devolution. Conservative governments increased the powers of the Welsh Office, enabling it to become responsible for health services, agriculture and secondary, further and higher education. By 1995, 2,500 civil servants were responsible for over £7 billion of expenditure. As the Welsh Office expanded, local authorities saw their functions being steadily eroded. New quangos and quasi-privatized groups emerged to control most aspects of Welsh life. The Welsh Development Agency and Tai Cymru were amongst the top forty quangos in the UK. The creation of hospital trusts, training and enterprise councils, funding councils for the various levels of education, and regional administrative entities resulted in a weaker sense of local responsibility and accountability. There was a growing confusion as to who was responsible for what. In the mid-1990s, approximately eighty Welsh quangos, with 1,400 nominated, unelected, members controlled over £2.4 billion of expenditure. In Wales, the arguments regarding quangos focused on two specific areas: first, there was a particular concentration of quangos in Wales, and a high proportion of public expenditure controlled by unelected bodies; secondly, Wales was not a Conservative heartland – only six Welsh Conservative MPs were elected to the House of Commons in 1992, while at a local level there were thirty-two Conservative county councillors out of a total of 494 in 1992 (in the old counties). A huge 'democratic deficit' emerged in the final decades of the century as the Westminster government established regional administrative bodies, which were largely unaccountable to the people of Wales.

A final factor of importance in the revived devolution debate was the impact of Europe. Since 1980 Wales has developed a consultative network within the European Union; a network operating at an institutional and an informal level. At the institutional level, it included the Welsh Office, the European Commission office in Wales, the WDA, the Welsh MEPs, local government and other agencies. At the informal level, it involved consultation and identifying Welsh interests. Various Welsh organizations participated in such Europe-wide structures as the Assembly of European Regions. Wales began to lobby in Brussels, and a Wales–European Centre was officially opened there in 1992. Even Plaid began to reconsider its European policy in the years after the 1983 general election. At the European elections, it adopted a more pro-European approach and performed reasonably well, gaining more support than at the previous general elections. In the 1989 European elections, Plaid Cymru presented a dual policy of independence for Wales in the European Community and a Europe of the regions. At the 1994 European elections, Plaid Cymru came second to Labour with 17.1 per cent of the votes, but it failed to capture a seat. Although Plaid's European policies remained ambiguous, its clear involvement with Europe had provided the party with an escape from traditional nationalist asseverations and a new mechanism for achieving an appropriate level of Welsh self-determination. Europe was proving to be a catalyst for the parties and for Welsh political society.

In April 1992, under their new prime minister, John Major, the Conservatives lost more ground in Wales. The results saw Labour winning twenty-seven seats with 49.5 per cent of the Welsh vote, as against six seats and 28.6 per cent for the Conservatives, four seats and 9 per cent of the vote for Plaid Cymru and just one seat for the Liberal Democrats. The election was fought mainly on British national issues, such as recession, the crisis of the economy and the plight of the NHS. Devolution made relatively little impact, despite serious attempts by sections of the Welsh media to raise the profile of Welsh issues. The *Western Mail* held a 'Great Debate' on devolution before the election, and published a letter in support of devolution on 2 April 1992 with the signatures of 900 Welsh dignitaries. Plaid Cymru demanded equal devolution of power to Wales and Scotland in exchange for supporting a minority government in the next Parliament.

The 1992 election confirmed the regeneration of the Labour Party and its dominance of the Welsh scene. With twenty-seven of the thirty-eight Welsh parliamentary seats, Labour appeared to have exorcized the ghost of the SDP Alliance and its dismal 1983 electoral performance. It had registered large majorities in the former mining seats of south Wales, and re-established itself in some of the more rural areas of Wales. Clwyd South West and Pembroke fell to Labour in 1992, as well as Delyn and Cardiff Central. Plaid Cymru's share of the vote had increased to 9 per cent, its best electoral performance since the 1970s, though the distribution of its vote was still skewed towards the north and west of Wales. In Dyfed and Gwynedd, Plaid Cymru competed well with the major British parties, securing 26 per cent of the total vote, compared with 28 per cent for the Conservatives and 32 per cent for Labour. In the remaining six counties of Wales, Plaid Cymru polled a mere 4 per cent of the vote, in contrast to 29 per cent for the Tories, 12 per cent for the Liberal Democrats and a massive 54 per cent for Labour.

The new Parliament was dominated by passage of the Maastricht treaty, but there were distinct Welsh issues on the political horizon. The Welsh Language Act of 1993 was a landmark in the long battle to secure equal status for the language, and the Cardiff Bay Barrage bill finally reached the statute book. In 1994, the Welsh legislative year was dominated by the passage of the Local Government Act, which reorganized local government on the basis of twenty-two unitary authorities. The new unitary authorities operated in Wales from April 1996. 'Shadow' local elections were held in May 1995 in preparation for the new unitary councils. Labour won outright control in fourteen of the twenty-two councils, and formed the largest party in several others. The Conservatives lost heavily almost everywhere in Wales, and especially in Cardiff, where only one councillor remained. In 1995–6 the Labour Party held hearings throughout Wales and considered views regarding a proposed national assembly. The Labour Party Wales conference accepted the recommendations to create a Welsh assembly.

The political year 1997 was an *annus mirabilis* for Wales and the UK. After eighteen years of unbroken Conservative rule, the Conservatives disintegrated at the general election. Nationally, Tony Blair's 'New Labour' secured its largest tally of MPs (418) and its largest majority (178). In Wales, Labour recaptured thirty-four of the forty parliamentary seats and took 54.7 per cent of the vote. The Conservatives failed to capture a single seat and saw their share of the vote slump to 19.6 per cent. Plaid Cymru secured 9.9 per cent of the vote and four seats, their best performance since October 1974. This was a memorable victory for Labour, with their highest share of the vote since 1970. The election results confirmed that the pattern of electoral trends for Wales since 1970 had shown remarkable stability. Plaid Cymru had yet to display at a general election the share of party support they had achieved in 1970. The Liberal Party had undergone considerable cosmetic changes between 1970 and 1997, fighting with the SDP as the Alliance in 1983 and 1987, before merging with the SDP as the Liberal Democrats. As an Alliance, they had polled over 20 per cent of the Welsh votes, but they had never seriously challenged the Conservatives as the second party of Wales. In 1997, the Conservatives failed to capture a single seat for the first time in a century. More seriously, perhaps, their share of the vote had plunged to below 20 per cent, and possibly as a result of a combination of factors: first, there was the increasing unpopularity of the Major government in the aftermath of 'Black Wednesday' and the revelations of the administration's economic mismanagement; secondly, the appearance of a Referendum Party candidate in nearly every constituency undermined the natural Conservative vote; thirdly, the relatively low turnout at the 1997 general election probably had a detrimental effect on the Conservatives' performance.

The year 1997 was a historic landmark in Welsh political history, for it brought a referendum on a Welsh assembly. The Labour Party was elected in 1997 having pledged in its manifesto to hold a referendum on the principle of establishing an elected assembly for Wales. The referendum was to be pre-legislative, to be held following publication of the government's proposals in a white paper, but before the drafting of a bill. The referendum, which was held on 18 September 1997, was a national referendum, with only the total number of votes cast being of importance. There was no qualified majority rule, such as the 40 per cent which was operated in 1979. The referendum campaign was conducted by the Welsh Office ministerial team under the direction of the secretary of state for Wales. It was assisted by an all-party umbrella group, the 'Yes for Wales' campaign. Opposing forces assembled under the 'Just Say No' banner, led by the Cardiff financier, Robert Hodge. The group was also an all-party affair, and it provided an outlet for dissident Labour voters to campaign against their party.

When the results were declared, there was a 50.3 per cent electoral turnout, and 50.3 per cent of these had voted in favour of an assembly, with 49.7 per cent in opposition to the scheme. The immediate response to the devolution referendum was to focus on its divisive nature. Of the twenty-two unitary councils, eleven had declared in favour, and eleven had voted against the proposed assembly. The nature of the 'Yes' vote was significant, for the referendum had manifested an almost unique alliance between Welsh-speaking Wales and the traditional industrial heartland of south Wales. The linguistic cleavage had been bridged by a common sense of purpose and identity. The patterns revealed by the referendum results seemed to suggest that a sense of Welsh identity remained an important feature in contemporary Wales.

The eventual passage of the Government of Wales Act introduced a new electoral system for the newly named National Assembly for Wales. The system combines a simple plurality election in each of the present forty parliamentary constituencies, with an additional member electoral system (AMS) employing party lists in the five former European parliamentary constituencies. Each region will return four members, giving the National Assembly a total membership of sixty. The first National Assembly election was held on 6 May 1999, which was also a remarkable and historic occasion. Labour was shocked and humiliated, while Plaid Cymru was euphoric after the declaration of results. With only twenty-eight out of a possible sixty Assembly seats, Labour was forced to operate a minority administration. The election seems to have transformed Plaid Cymru from a sectional party of north and west Wales into a genuinely national force. Plaid captured seventeen seats, including sensational gains in Labour industrial heartlands. The most astonishing successes were recorded in Rhondda, which had been considered the second safest Labour parliamentary seat in Britain, in Islwyn, Neil Kinnock's former parliamentary seat, and in James Griffiths's former citadel, Llanelli. The Conservatives managed to regain a foothold in Welsh politics, with nine

Assembly seats, and the Liberal Democrats secured six Welsh seats.

The final electoral turnout of 46 per cent in Wales, compared with 58 per cent in the Scottish election, was distinctly embarrassing for the Labour government. In the aftermath of the election, the disappointing turnout was attributed to a number of factors: that 75 per cent of electors had either abstained or voted against devolution in the 1997 referendum, and many of these had been Labour voters; many believed that the Assembly had no real legislative power; thirdly, the politics of contentment and sloth may have contributed to the low turnout, with many Labour supporters feeling that they had no need to vote after achieving a majority Labour government; fourthly, many Old Labour voters, especially in the industrial Valleys, may have been protesting against Blairism and its apparent indifference to the problems of south Wales; fifthly, a large number of voters may have found the whole concept of an Assembly simply incomprehensible; the Assembly election campaign proved to be uninspiring, lacklustre and sluggish; and finally, Labour seemed to be paying the price for the chaos which had engulfed the Welsh party since the 1997 general election. The unseemly row over the Assembly's location, the initial leadership contest between Ron Davies and Rhodri Morgan, Ron Davies's sudden departure as Welsh secretary, and the divisive second leadership battle between Rhodri Morgan and Alun Michael had sapped Labour strength and alienated many erstwhile supporters.

Plaid Cymru's performance had been impressive in many parts of the Principality. There were swings of 20 per cent or more from Labour to Plaid in Caerphilly, Cynon Valley, Islwyn, Llanelli, Merthyr Tydfil, Neath, Ogmore, Pontypridd, Rhondda, Swansea East and Swansea West. Swings of 10 per cent or more from Labour to Plaid were recorded in the additional seats of Aberavon (18.28), Blaenau Gwent (16.79), Caernarfon (10.75), Carmarthen East (14.82), Carmarthen West (15.59), Clwyd South (17.45), Conwy (14.31), Gower (18.62) and Preseli (16.27). Plaid Cymru presented itself as the voice of protest and challenged New Labour as the rightful inheritor of the radical tradition in Wales.

The National Assembly will contain a balance of power between the executive committee (cabinet) and the subject committees. The success of the Assembly will depend upon the working relationship between the cabinet and the subject committees. The executive committee, or cabinet, will have a first secretary, elected by the Assembly, and the assembly secretaries, appointed by the first secretary. The Government of Wales Act (1998) lists eighteen policy fields which will be transferred to the Assembly: these include agriculture, health, housing, industry, local government, education, social services, transport, economic development and the Welsh Language. It is impossible to foresee the future course of the National Assembly, but its progress will depend upon various factors: the nature of the relationship between the first secretary and the secretary of state in the British cabinet; the balance of power between the political executive and the policy subject committees; and the relationship that develops between the National Assembly and Whitehall departments, especially with regard to the secondary legislative powers invested in the new Assembly.

SUGGESTED READING

C. A. Davies, *Welsh Nationalism in the Twentieth Century* (New York, 1989).

D. Foulkes et al. (eds.), *The Welsh Veto* (Cardiff, 1983).

D. Griffiths, *Thatcherism and Territorial Politics: A Welsh Case Study* (Aldershot, 1996).

Trevor Herbert and Gareth Elwyn Jones, *Post-war Wales* (Cardiff, 1995).

I. Hume and W. T. R. Pryce (eds.), *The Welsh and their Country* (Llandysul, 1986).

Kenneth O. Morgan, *Rebirth of a Nation: Wales 1880–1980* (Oxford, 1981).

Kenneth O. Morgan, *Modern Wales* (Cardiff, 1995).

J. Osmond (ed.), *The National Assembly Agenda* (Cardiff, 1998).

A. B. Philip, *The Welsh Question* (Cardiff, 1975).

L. J. Williams, *Digest of Welsh Historical Statistics*, vols.I and II (Cardiff, 1985).

L. J. Williams, *Digest of Welsh Historical Statistics, 1974–1996* (Cardiff, 1998).

Volumes of the *Wales Year Book* are very useful to consult.

8. Education, Cultural Activities and the Media

Education

The Period 1945–1979

THE Butler Education Act of 1944 had required local education authorities to submit development plans for their areas, but not one was forthcoming in the allotted twelve-month period. By 1947, three authorities had still not submitted full development plans. Cardiff's plan conformed to the tripartite pattern, as did Merthyr's submission. Glamorgan County Council and Swansea County Borough Council produced plans which provoked some sharp reactions from the Welsh Department and the Ministry of Education. Glamorgan proposed a common curriculum up to the School Certificate stage, with no eleven-plus examination. All its secondary schools were to be territorial schools, taking all pupils in the local catchment area, and retaining about twenty-three of the designated grammar schools. The plan was effectively a blueprint for multilateral comprehensive education, with differentiation only appearing from the age of fifteen. Although Glamorgan submitted its plan to the Welsh Department in June 1947, final approval was not granted until December 1956. The department and the ministry firmly resisted Glamorgan's proposals and adopted a consistent line of attack: comprehensive schools were to be allowed in large conurbations on an experimental basis; experiments were only to be allowed in areas of working-class housing development, such as Kenfig or the Sandfields, near Port Talbot; existing grammar schools were to remain; and the ministry insisted that expanding school population in middle-class areas should be accommodated in segregated schools. Swansea County Borough's plan was as radical as any produced in England or Wales. It advocated the replacement of existing provision and grammar schools with multilateral schools for pupils aged eleven to eighteen, though L. J. Drew, the director of education, studiously distanced himself from the provocative proposal. The Welsh Department was prepared to consider an experiment of one such school for boys, and one for girls to serve the new housing estates. The ministry employed familiar tactics and sent no official reply to Swansea's plan for nearly three years. When the ministry did request a revised plan, Swansea deployed similar dilatory tactics until 1953. Eventually, the Conservative minister of education, David Eccles, insisted in 1955 that Swansea's grammar schools should remain; but two bilateral schools were allowed, one at Penlan (1956) and the other at Mynyddbach (1957). After eleven years of confrontation and delay, Swansea's development plan was finally approved in 1957.

The pressures on rural areas in Wales were different, and often far more intractable: problems of geographical distance; sparse, scattered populations; and relatively poor resources multiplied the difficulties facing the local education authorities. In addition, a higher percentage of the relevant age group had always attended the grammar schools in rural Wales. The dissemination of population in many areas of mid-, west and north Wales ensured that the task of trying to assemble pupils aged eleven and over into one educational centre would be formidable. In 1950, 22.5 per cent of Welsh secondary pupils were still educated in all-age, unreorganized schools. Even as late as 1961, there were 5,107 secondary pupils in all-age, unreorganized schools. Pembrokeshire education authority had to contend with a population of 91,000 in 1951, and relatively few towns. It encountered many of the familiar problems of rural Wales, and the additional complication of a linguistic divide between English-speaking southern parts, and the Welsh-speaking northern zone. The policy of tripartitism, with grammar, secondary and technical schools, seemed completely impractical in a rural county such as Pembrokeshire. The towns presented fewer problems: Haverfordwest retained its boys' and girls' grammar schools; Milford Haven became a grammar-technical school; while Pembroke and Pembroke Dock were to have a grammar-technical school and a secondary modern school. In the countryside, it was well-nigh impossible to implement the tripartite system, and the redoubtable director ensured that the authority's plan was implemented.

In Anglesey, the least complicated reorganization in Wales proved to be the most radical. Anglesey was the first authority in England and Wales to go totally multilateral. Throughout all the other Welsh counties, the Welsh Department stipulated that bilateral grammar and secondary modern schools would be the accepted model. The all-age elementary schools were to be abolished, and effective primary schools were to be introduced within the authorities. During the period of school reorganization, civil servants at the Welsh Department and the Ministry of Education had assumed that a tripartite paradigm was embedded in the 1944 Education Act. Throughout their discussions with the Welsh counties, senior mandarins had always promulgated Norwood-like notions of children possessing either grammar-school aptitudes or a secondary-modern ability. In trying to find solutions to the multifarious issues raised by local authorities, central government had to reconcile three important factors: first, the constraints of population density in rural Wales; secondly, the requirements of secondary education for all as laid down by the Butler Act; and finally, a private consensus among civil servants and ministers that demarcation between different types of secondary provision was essential. Local authorities were also political bodies and custodians of a particular heritage. While in rural Wales the county councils tended to be Liberal or Independent and somewhat cautious in their approach to educational policies, in industrial Wales the hegemonic Labour party inclined towards more radical and egalitarian models of reorganization. In devising their development plans, education authorities were influenced by many forces: the political ideas of the dominant parties; the inheritance of previous educational policies; the expectations of the electors in post-war Wales; the impact of local characteristics, such as topography, distribution of population, the availability and quality of buildings and resources in existing educational provision; the financial constraints and economic hardship of the immediate post-war period; and the pressure of additional government policies, such as the raising of the school-leaving age in 1947.

Despite the fact that many county councils waged protracted battles against senior civil servants, the period 1945–65 witnessed the establishment and consolidation of the tripartite system in most of Wales. In 1947, there were 147 grammar schools, twenty-four technical schools and 127 secondary modern schools in Wales. Welsh grammar schools continued to admit a far higher proportion of pupils than their English counterparts, but this often involved a relative neglect of the secondary modern sector. By 1949, about one-third of pupils aged thirteen and over were in grammar schools, one-third in secondary modern schools and one-third in all-age schools. By 1961, there were 88,172 pupils in secondary modern schools, 58,324 in grammar schools and 19,053 in comprehensive schools. After 1944, the distinctive administrative structure of Welsh education disintegrated as the tripartite system of secondary education became as firmly rooted in Wales as in England. A number of significant factors shaped the development of secondary education in the twenty years after 1945: first, central government had relentlessly imposed the tripartite system on Wales, with the result that there were only fifteen comprehensive schools in England and Wales in 1955; secondly, demographic changes, and especially a spiralling birth rate in the years from 1945 to 1965, had strongly influenced the pattern of educational change; thirdly, an increasing tendency for pupils to stay longer in school resulted in the growth of fifth- and sixth-form numbers; fourthly, there seemed to be no peculiarly Welsh priorities in the school system after the Second World War, apart from the growing momentum of the Welsh-language education movement; fifth, growing economic prosperity led to educational expansion from the mid-fifties onwards, with an endemic mood of optimism and reform in educational circles; sixth, the accumulation of statistical data and blueprints from government agencies and other allied institutions emphasized issues such as social deprivation, community background and inequality of opportunity. The Crowther Report of 1959 advocated a twenty-year programme of reform. The 1963 Newsome Report, *Half Our Future*, pressed for raising of the school-leaving age to sixteen, while the Gittins and Plowden Reports of 1967 promoted the expansion of nursery and primary education. One final factor which undermined the distinctive character of Welsh secondary education after 1944 was the enforcement of an examination system which clearly demarcated the grammar schools from the secondary-modern sector. In 1946, the Ministry of Education reconstituted the Secondary Schools Examination Council. This fortified central government's control of education and produced an examinations system of 'O' and 'A' levels, which sharply separated the grammar from the secondary-modern schools.

The social implications of the tripartite system are soon apparent if the career destinations of pupils are examined for the period. In 1947, only one pupil who left the secondary-modern and all-age schools went to universities, compared with 826 from grammar schools. While 4,317 secondary-modern pupils went into home employment, agriculture, mining and manufacturing, only 1,295 grammar-school pupils proceeded along these routes. Clerical and professional posts attracted 2,277 grammar-school pupils, and only 722 from the secondary-modern schools. Schools were apparently fulfilling their traditional social function of providing personnel for the blue-collar and black-coat jobs. They were also attracting higher proportions of pupils to stay on beyond the statutory leaving age. In 1953, the figure of 34.4 per cent for Wales was higher than for any region of England, and had increased to 42.9 per cent by 1961.

From the 1960s onwards, Welsh education was shaped by a combination of significant developments: first, there was the introduction of the Certificate of Secondary Education (CSE) in 1963; new initiatives in curriculum development and the style of examinations were inaugurated by the Schools Council after 1965; the comprehensivization of schools followed the Department of Education and Science's (DES) circular 10/65 in 1965; there was ROSLA (raising the school-leaving age) in 1971; the impact of rapid growth in school population up to the early 1980s, and rapid decline thereafter; and the growing commitment to teaching Welsh and to subject areas through the medium of Welsh.

Following the appearance of Crosland's historic DES circular 10/65, the movement to reorganize schooling along comprehensive lines was inexorable. Although Wales already possessed a fair share of comprehensive schools in 1964, with thirty-six of the 195 British schools in existence, by 1969 46.3 per cent of Welsh pupils were enrolled in comprehensive schools. In 1979, 96 per cent of Welsh pupils attended comprehensive schools, and only one solitary Welsh grammar school remained in Whitland. Wales had suddenly become a land of large schools. In 1977–8, 184 of the 244 secondary schools were 11–18 all-through comprehensive schools, and 14 per cent of those had more than 1,500 pupils, compared with 5 per cent in England. Despite Margaret Thatcher's reversal of Crosland's Circular by her Circular 10/70, comprehensive schools had attracted support for a variety of reasons: Labour governments of the 1960s were determined to implement a policy similar to that which they had endorsed since before the war; an increase in the school population promoted the belief that additional resources were likely to be available in larger schools; a tendency for pupils to remain in school beyond the compulsory school-leaving age had further boosted pupil numbers; there was a desire to foster equality of opportunity at all levels; the comprehensive schools seemed to offer a wider range of subjects; and there surfaced a widespread belief in the values of mixed-ability classes.

Pressure mounted in the late 1950s for an examination to be devised to test the abilities of the majority of secondary-school pupils. Following the deliberations of the Beloe Committee, the Certificate of Secondary Education (CSE) was established in 1965. In the ensuing years the numbers of candidates sitting CSE examinations increased rapidly:

Table 8.1 CSE examination, 1965–1974

	1965	1970	1974
Candidates	5230	13926	26700
Subjects	31	50	141

The demise of the eleven-plus examination, the stimulus of comprehensivization and the raising of the school-leaving age to sixteen brought fresh opportunities for curriculum development between 1967 and 1979. The Schools Council, which was established in 1964, generated initiatives in curriculum research and examinations. It encouraged greater teacher participation in syllabus construction and examination assessment, and promoted research on the feasibility of a common examination at sixteen-plus.

In October 1976, Lord Callaghan delivered the Ruskin College speech in which he drew attention to several important issues in contemporary education: first, the concern over

Table 8.2 Spread of comprehensive education: % of thirteen-year-old age group attending school (by type)

School	1961	1965	1969	1973	1977	1981	1985
Modern	60.0	54.3	33.7	9.4	6.4	1.8	0.7
Grammar	25.3	25.3	18.1	4.2	3.6	1.1	0.4
Technical	0.9	0.4	0.2	–	–	–	–
Comprehensive	10.1	15.1	46.3	85.7	89.9	97.0	98.9
Other	0.3	3.3	1.6	0.6	–	–	–

methods and aims of informal instruction; secondly, he advocated a strong case for a core curriculum of basic knowledge; third, there was the question of monitoring the use of resources and national standards of performance; the role of the inspectorate with regard to national standards was raised; the need to improve relations between industry and education was identified; and the problems of the examinations system were spotlighted.

The speech triggered a 'great debate' within the context of the 1970s. The wholesale change to comprehensive education and the liberation of primary schools from the straitjacket of the eleven-plus had spawned multifarious discussions in academic cloisters and in the labyrinthine splendours of Whitehall. An ideological debate over the curriculum, and especially primary-school subjects, had raged since the 1960s. The passionate advocates of a child-centred education were pitted against the more conservative custodians of cultural transmission. The appearance of the so-called 'Black Papers', a collection of papers on educational principles and policies, intensified the reactionary backlash, while the Plowden Report of 1967 heralded a shift to a more child-centred orthodoxy.

The Black Paper of 1975 and the Ruskin College speech raised similar issues and represented an emerging consensus among the political parties. By the mid-1970s it was clear that the ambitious programmes of the previous decade had failed to eradicate widespread educational problems. There were accusations of illiteracy and innumeracy among young employees; and large, unwieldy comprehensive systems, which had been ill-conceived and poorly planned, had often produced unmanageable neighbourhood schools. Teaching styles, syllabuses, literacy levels, and standards of attainment became the objects of intense scrutiny. After the 1970s, there developed a new momentum for a reassertion of central control in education. Ironically, the centripetal tendency was accompanied by a greater devolution of power to the Welsh Office, when, for the first time, Welsh education from nursery to university standard was entrusted to the Welsh Office.

Developments since 1980
The incoming Conservative government of 1979 was firmly convinced that standards in public services could only be improved by the imposition of free-market principles. Bolstered by large majorities, governments of the eighties moved swiftly to dismantle public monopolies, to encourage competition and to promote accountability to the consumers. Conservative administrations embarked on legislative proposals designed to reshape the educational system that had survived since 1944. They identified four principal concerns in the educational system: first, that unacceptable differences existed between schools in the content and quality of learning; secondly, that the curriculum was too overcrowded, with a distorted emphasis on the social aims of education; it was argued that too few young people were committed to a mastery of industrial, vocational and economic skills; and finally, that there were too many differences in teaching approaches.

In the 1980 Education Act measures were introduced to reduce the influence of local education authorities and to ensure that parents and teachers would be represented on the governing bodies of schools and colleges. The eighties unfolded as a decade of legislation, with widespread changes to the system of education. The white paper *Better Schools*, which was published in March 1985, declared that two aims were to be inviolate: standards were to be raised at all levels of ability; and acceptable returns were to be secured from educational investment. The government expressed its intention to examine the school curriculum, the examination system, school government and the professional competence of practitioners. The 1986 Education Act intensified the pressure on LEAs by fundamentally restructuring the balance of representation on governing bodies. The Acts of 1980 and 1986 were, however, merely a prelude to the sweeping changes inaugurated by the 1988 Education Reform Act. The latter confirmed central government's intention to impose a national curriculum and to assess the performance of pupils at the ages of seven, eleven, fourteen and sixteen.

The national curriculum provoked controversy from the outset. It prescribed core and foundation subject areas across the five-to-sixteen age range, and stipulated time allocations and programmes of study for the specified subjects. A common curriculum for all was established, prescribed in detail by central government, which teachers were merely required to deliver. A great new debate burst forth over the control and content of the curriculum, as subject areas like history, English and even physical education stimulated controversy and debate throughout the educational arena. Thousands of articles, letters and editorials sprang up in quality and tabloid press between the establishment in January 1990 of the National Curriculum Working Group for History and the publication of the revised Statutory Order for History in 1995. At the heart of the debate over history in the national curriculum were the issues of national and cultural identity, state formation, patriotism and nationalism in late twentieth-century England and Wales. Scholars of the period have argued that the great debate about history in the curriculum was as much concerned with the future, as with the present and past. It was essentially an outpouring of anxiety concerning 'the elusive and displaced notion of Englishness'. Many on the political and cultural right were endeavouring to stem the intellectual flow towards relativism and postmodernism. Exponents of the New Right ideology frantically injected contradictory strategies into educational policy in the 1980s and 1990s: choice and control, neo-liberal market individualism and neo-conservative tenets of authority, discipline, hierarchy and strong national government clashed and collided in a welter of ideas.

Perhaps one of the most remarkable features of the period was the proliferation of a consensus which identified education and training as key elements in securing a successful and competitive economy. International bodies such as the Organization for Economic Co-operation and Development (OECD), the European Union and national governments considered the creation of a well-educated and skilled workforce as an essential step towards the achievement of a productive high-technology economy. In

Britain, studies by the National Institute for Economic and Social Research argued forcefully that inferior economic performance was largely the result of a failure of the education and training system to produce workers with adequate standards of general education and technical competence. A vast catalogue of evidence presented a powerful impression of a two-track system of education and training in the UK. International studies of educational achievement in different school subject areas focused on the British distribution of pupil scores: high performances were recorded among the top 10 per cent of pupils; with a much wider distribution of lower-level performances among other pupils. Early studies had tended to confirm that Wales represented an extreme version of the British two-track education and training system. At the end of the 1970s research had highlighted the paradox that Welsh schools produced high proportions of school-leavers with commendable academic qualifications, and very high proportions with no formal qualifications. The Welsh school system, with its academic ethos, had traditionally filtered resources to an élite of academically able pupils, and starved the majority of necessary provision.

Evidence produced in 1995 seemed to reaffirm the depressing picture of a two-track system in Wales. There was still a higher proportion of young people leaving Welsh schools with no qualifications than in the rest of the UK. The advantage previously enjoyed by the most able Welsh pupils also appeared to have vanished, as Wales now lagged behind the other regions of the UK.

Table 8.3 Distribution of school-leavers in Wales and in the UK by examination results, 1991/2

Qualifications	UK	WALES
A Levels		
2 or more	24.9	21.3
At least 1	29.8	25.4
GCSE grades A–C		
5 or more	15.2	13.6
1–4	24.5	22.8
No grades/passes	6.3	12.4

The figures indicated that there was lower attainment in Wales across the examination spectrum. The number of pupils leaving with no grades or passes was almost double that for the UK as a whole. There were also substantial regional variations within Wales, with the former county of Mid Glamorgan exhibiting a concentration of under-qualifications. Nearly one-fifth of all school leavers in the county, the most heavily populated in Wales, achieved no school qualifications whatsoever. It was noteworthy that the more heavily industrialized counties tended to display the highest levels of unqualified school-leavers. More encouraging recent trends have revealed that higher proportions of young people are remaining in education after the minimum school-leaving age, and that the growth in the proportions achieving school qualifications has been consistent across all the counties of Wales. Since 1990, the performance of candidates in the GCSE examinations has also improved markedly.

Table 8.4 GCSE performance of candidates taking WJEC examinations

Year	% attaining grade A	% attaining grade C or above
1990	8.7	43.5
1992	10.3	46.7
1994	11.8	50.7
1996	12.6	53.8

Welsh-language Education

The Welsh Department and the Welsh Office have supported Welsh-language education at primary and secondary levels since the end of the Second World War. In 1953, the Welsh Joint Education Committee adopted a Welsh Books Scheme, whereby LEAs were given £107,000 between 1954 and 1959 to provide Welsh books in schools. Welsh Office policy was that Welsh and English should be taught to all children in Wales and Monmouthshire; and the first bilingual secondary school, Ysgol Glan Clwyd in Flintshire, was officially opened in 1956.

The development of bilingual education occurred as a result of a number of factors: in many ways it was a reaction to industrialization and urbanization; the impact of immigration and emigration patterns was influential in the process; the growth of mass communications and the mass media fuelled the debate; the decline of organized religion and religious attendance significantly affected the Welsh language and promoted debates concerning Welsh-medium teaching; the decline of the language and the powerful effect of census statistics engendered a passionate concern for Welsh-language education; the growth of political consciousness in the post-war period was a crucial factor in the process; utilitarian concerns surfaced as Welsh-language skills were perceived to enhance employment opportunities; there was a widespread commitment to preserve a variety of Welsh cultural forms as a bulwark against the relentless dissemination of English-language and Anglophone culture; Welsh-medium schools were also often seen as a replacement for the old grammar schools; and many parents were far more concerned about their children's future employment prospects than anything else – this latter factor often explains English-speaking parents sending their children to Welsh-medium schools. As the proportion of Welsh-speakers in the population declined remorselessly from 28.9 in 1951 to 19.0 in 1981, the number of designated Welsh secondary schools mushroomed from one in 1956 to nineteen in 1990. The number of pupils in these schools grew from 2,017 in 1970 to 12,475 in 1990. In the years 1975–80, 95.5 per cent of schools in Clwyd, 91.7 per cent in Powys, and 95.5 per cent in Gwynedd were teaching Welsh as both a first and second language.

The growth in the demand for schools providing teaching through the medium of Welsh has been a remarkable feature of modern Welsh education. Despite official support, it is unlikely that bilingual secondary schools would have succeeded without the enthusiasm and dedication of groups of parents and teachers. The growth of *Ysgolion Cymraeg* in south Wales was largely attributable to parental endeavour. Rhieni Dros Addysg Gymraeg (Parents in Support of Welsh Education) was one effective pressure group. Non-Welsh-speaking parents also goaded LEAs into providing bilingual schools. As many as 90 per cent of children in the designated schools often came from homes where both parents were unable to speak Welsh. It was observed that schools in the Welsh heartland rarely made Welsh-medium provision in their curricula. Notable subject exceptions were Welsh history and religious education. Her Majesty's Inspectors of Schools added their support to the burgeoning Welsh-language education momentum from the advent of bilingual primary schools in Aberystwyth and Llanelli to the recent compulsory publication of their inspection reports. Curricular support for teachers followed through the activities of the Schools Council for Wales, the Welsh Joint Education Committee and the more recent curriculum, examinations and assessment agencies. The university colleges at Aberystwyth and Bangor responded positively to the challenge to provide initial teacher education and in-service programmes for secondary-school teachers. Aberystwyth's contributions were manifold, ranging form the Welsh Textbooks Project, to the publication of *Cyfres Mathemateg Cambria*. The education departments and various research centres at Bangor and Aberystwyth have continued to produce material of an outstanding quality in support of Welsh-medium education. The Welsh nursery-school movement, Mudiad Ysgolion Meithrin, grew from around fifty playgroups in 1971 to 645 playgroups and 407 mother-and-child groups in 1995. There were fourteen designated Welsh primary schools in 1951, with 397 pupils, and sixty-nine such schools with 12,475 pupils in 1989.

Statistics of Education and Training in Wales reveals a steady continuous growth in Welsh-medium provision through the 1990s.

Table 8.5 Maintained primary schools teaching through the medium of Welsh

	1990/1	*1992/3*	*1993/4*	*1994/5*
Schools having classes where Welsh is the sole or main medium of instruction	445	457	460	465
% of schools	25.9	26.9	27.1	27.5
Schools where no Welsh is taught	244	118	54	27
% of schools	14.2	7.0	3.2	1.6

Table 8.6 Maintained secondary schools teaching Welsh

	1980/1	1990/1	1992/3	1993/4	1994/5
Number of schools where no Welsh is taught	35	22	17	8	3
% of schools	14.7	9.5	7.4	3.5	1.3

Government aid through the Welsh Office sponsored additional Welsh-medium teaching resources, and the Welsh Joint Education Committee responded with an increased number of Welsh-medium examinations.

Table 8.7 Subject entries through the medium of Welsh in WJEC exams (summer)

	1991	1993	1994	1995	1996
A Level					
Subjects	21	24	23	25	25
Entries	1015	1125	1226	1300	1343
% of all A level entries	3.7	3.9	4.3	4.8	5.2
GCSE					
Subjects	49	50	45	44	49
Entries	9347	12008	13909	15990	16549
% of all GCSE entries	3.7	4.8	5.4	5.5	5.7

Table 8.8 GCSE examination entries: Welsh (summer)

	1991	1993	1994	1995	1996
Welsh 1st language	2827	2665	2827	3627	3851
Welsh 2nd language	6155	5903	6393	8208	7859

There is little doubt that the inclusion of Welsh as a core or foundation subject in the national curriculum has boosted its prospects in contemporary society. Colin Baker and others have reminded us, however, of the danger of placing undue emphasis on formal bilingual education as the salvation of the language and heritage of Wales: many school-leavers may opt for universities and careers outside the Principality; the market value of Welsh may oscillate in an unfavourable direction; and there is the possibility that Welsh will become entrenched as the language of the school, while English remains dominant in everyday speech.

In the years since the passage of the 1988 Education Act, many differences have appeared in government policies as applied to England and Wales to suggest that a distinctive Welsh education policy has emerged: there were Welsh forms of the national curriculum in subject areas such as history, geography and music; the Curriculum Council for Wales often prepared recommendations and proposals for ministers; separate Further and Higher Education Funding Councils were established in Wales; a separate Curriculum and Assessment Authority and a Teacher Training Agency for Wales were set up; there were no City Technology Colleges in Wales; by 1995, only sixteen schools had 'opted-out' – eleven secondary and five primary; there was the vast expansion of Welsh-medium primary and secondary schools; and the growing experience that bilingual schools produced superior academic results – in 1992, for example, 50 per cent of their pupils achieved five GCSE subjects at grades A to C, compared with 33 per cent for the whole of Wales, and 38 per cent in England. While there has been undeniable progress in providing an education system which attempts to reflect various aspects of Welsh society, developments in the Thatcher and Major periods have reinforced the parameters within which the educational institutions are expected to function. The Welsh Office usually reacted to educational policies imposed from central government, and Wales has relied upon sympathetic ministers and officials rather than on recognized institutional independence. Despite the existence of separate funding councils in Wales, there is no evidence that these act independently of government instructions. Assessment and examinations councils are merely instruments of central policy-making agencies. There is, however, a Welsh education infrastructure and a different statutory curriculum, with its emphasis on Y Cwricwlwm Cymreig. Wales already has the potential to create a distinctive and more appropriate educational policy. It remains to be seen whether the National Assembly will grasp the nettle and expand this devolved infrastructure still further.

Higher Education in Wales since 1945

With the return of those who had served in the war, the number of students in the University of Wales increased to 4,071 in 1946–7. The presence of many mature, experienced war veterans among the student body made it increasingly difficult for colleges to maintain the pre-war rules and regulations. By 1949–50, the number of students had risen to 5,284, and, although numbers fell in the early fifties as the peak of the post-war increase had been reached, from 1955 admissions again began to climb. The student population had reached 5,445 by 1957–8, and in 1960–1 the total had grown to 6,159, 63 per cent of whom were from Wales, 31 per cent from other parts of the UK and 6 per cent had come from overseas. Numbers continued to grow steadily throughout the period 1946–64, and by 1963–4 there were 8,279 students registered in the university. Staff numbers increased in response to the expansion of the student body, and new campuses sprang up at Penglais, Aberystwyth and Hendrefoelan at Swansea.

As the proportion of non-Welsh students spiralled upwards, concerns were expressed at the apparent erosion of Welshness in the university. In the early 1950s, the idea of a Welsh-medium college was mooted. Notwithstanding these misgivings, the university continued to support Welsh ventures. The University Press Board increased its annual production of books from twenty in 1945–6 to forty in 1962–3. From 1955 to 1963, of the 130 books published by the Press Board, forty-seven were in Welsh, sixty-seven in English and sixteen in both languages. A number of new journals were founded, such as the *Welsh History Review*, edited by Professor Glanmor Williams and Dr Kenneth O. Morgan, and *Y Gwyddonydd*, edited by Dr Glyn O. Phillips.

Throughout the 1960s there was a rapid expansion of student numbers. St David's College, Lampeter, was eventually accepted into the fold by its charter of 1971, after a resolute and determined campaign by its indefatigable principal, J. R. Lloyd Thomas. With the growth in numbers, the proportion of students from Wales in the university fell to around 50 per cent by 1964. This process had attracted large numbers of academic staff who were of non-Welsh origin. The rapid Anglicization of the colleges produced numerous impassioned debates in the university and its governing bodies concerning Welsh-language courses and the whole ethos of Welshness within the federal institution. The sixties also witnessed the rise of the left, the strengthening of Welsh nationalism and the emergence of youth cultures. The cumulative effect of these forces eventually produced a challenge to the federal structure itself. In June 1960, Caerphilly Urban District Council had passed a resolution in favour of four separate universities for Wales. Of the 163 local authorities in Wales, only forty supported Caerphilly's defederalist position. A university commission set up to consider the defederation crisis produced two reports: the majority report, signed by fourteen members, boldly favoured four unitary institutions; the other report, signed by twelve members, opted for retaining the federation. At an eventual meeting of the University Court in April 1964, a vast majority of members backed the minority report. The federal university had been saved.

Extension and expansion proceeded steadily throughout the 1960s. The total of 11,026 students in the university in 1965–6 had climbed to 13,945 by 1969–70. The Welsh College of Advanced Technology was incorporated into the university in 1967, and St David's College, Lampeter, in May 1971. In 1972–3, there were 15,500 students in the university, with Cardiff's share having augmented to 3,579. A mood of optimism permeated the constituent colleges, and confident new building projects were launched on most campuses. At Aberystwyth, a new sports complex opened in May 1964, followed by a Faculty of Law and a new Llandinam building in 1965. At Cardiff, the Sherman Theatre was completed in 1970–1, a mathematics block in 1971–2 and the students' union in 1973. Swansea expanded with alacrity in the 1960s and early 1970s, when a modern library extension was erected in 1963, and extended in 1965; a new students' union was constructed in 1965; a towering applied science building appeared by 1973; a third campus hall was opened in 1968; and in 1970, a new arts building was completed to accommodate the arts departments. In north Wales, Bangor constructed a new hall of residence in 1964; three more halls between 1965 and 1968; a new students' union in 1968; further halls of residence in 1972 and 1973; and Theatr Gwynedd opened its doors in 1974.

As the university flourished, enlarged student bodies flexed their muscles and protested over a number of matters, including student participation, course construction and loftier ideological issues. There were peculiarly Welsh manifestations of student protest in the sixties and early seventies over the language, nationalistic ideals and the lack of Welsh-language teaching in the university. A number of factors had fuelled this debate: first, there was the falling proportion of Welsh students – by 1964–5, students from Wales, at 47 per cent of the total, were in a minority in the university; secondly, the debate concerning the university as a national institution, which lasted from 1960 to 1964, had ignited nationalist passions; Saunders Lewis's historic radio broadcast in 1962 led to the formation of Cymdeithas yr Iaith Gymraeg (the Welsh Language Society); and the spread of nationalism and nationalist propaganda generated a mood of defiance and determination among Welsh enthusiasts. There were increasing demands for Welsh-language teaching, and in 1966 the university established a committee to consider the matter. By 1968, appointments were made at Aberystwyth and Bangor to teach through the medium of Welsh, translation facilities were made available in the University Court, and Welsh-language hostels were eventually opened in 1968.

The year 1974, however, heralded a period of retrenchment and consolidation in the university, as the oil crisis of 1973 and spiralling inflation forced governments to impose financial restraints on the public sector. Expansion was curtailed, with undergraduate numbers rising from 13,741 in 1975–6 to only 14,641 in 1976–7, and, as late as 1979–80, they had only risen to a comparatively modest 19,694. The advent of the Thatcher era in 1979 ushered in a period of tighter central control of higher education, and by 1981 interventionist policies were compelling the colleges to consider rationalization of subjects and possible mergers. Economic restraints produced deficits at the National School of Medicine in 1975–6, and at Cardiff in the 1980s. Independent auditors confirmed that Cardiff's financial difficulties were running out of control, as the cumulative deficit mounted to £5 million in 1986–7, and its bank overdraft reached £5.3 million. By July 1987, the University Grants Committee was pushing Cardiff and the University of Wales Institute of Science and Technology in the direction of a merger. In September 1988, the new University of Wales, Cardiff, had appeared, with a new principal and the former Conservative minister, Lord Crickhowell, as its first president.

The Thatcher years had battered and bruised universities throughout the kingdom. Wales's university sought refuge within the federal structure, and the Daniel Report seemed to reinforce federation with its system of new officials. In the early 1990s, as colleges were encouraged to expand their student intakes, the old centrifugal forces re-emerged when the principals of Swansea and Cardiff argued that the university's function was as a degree-awarding body. The Rosser Committe, appointed in 1992, examined the administration and operation of the university. In July 1993, it presented a detailed survey of the University of Wales and its institutes of higher education. In many ways, the Rosser Committee fortified the centrifugal cause and supported the argument that the role of the university was to award degrees, maintain standards, provide a global university perspective, promote intercollegiate discussions and serve as a forum for strategic academic decisions. By 1993–4, the new spurt of expansion had increased student numbers in the University of Wales.

Table 8.9 Student numbers in the University of Wales, 1993/4

| College | *Place of usual residence* | | | |
	Wales	*Rest of UK*	*Abroad*	*Total*
Aberystwyth	1454	3251	540	5245
Bangor	1685 ·	2767	483	4935
Cardiff	3788	6302	1975	12065
Swansea	2699	4101	1049	7849
St David's College	286	1010	82	1378
Welsh National School of Medicine	714	509	177	1400
Total	10626	17940	4306	32872
%	32	55	13	100

At the time of its centenary celebrations in 1993–4, Bangor Normal College had been incorporated within the University of Wales, Bangor, while Gwent College of Higher Education had become part of the university as University of Wales, College of Newport. Expansion has continued steadily: student numbers have mushroomed; courses have diversified increasingly; new faculties and centres of excellence have been established; and the university has modularized its academic subjects. Departments and colleges have been actively encouraged to attract new sources of income from multifarious organizations, and wide-ranging research projects have burst forth in ever-growing displays of originality.

Cultural Activities

Welsh-language Literature and Drama

In the immediate post-war period the old luminaries of Welsh poetry departed. T. Gwynne Jones died in 1949, and R. Williams Parry followed in the early fifties. T. H. Parry-Williams survived into the 1970s and remained prolific and active in eisteddfod circles. Poetry in the 1940s was largely dominated by three important figures. 'Gwenallt', representing a new phase of commitment, produced nationalistic and sociopolitical verse. He believed that the proletariat had been exploited and deluded, and that only a Christian nationalism could restore the workers to their rightful inheritance. Saunders Lewis published at least three poems during the decade and endeavoured to promote modernism in poetic circles. The third of this triumvirate of poets was the Christian pacifist and left-wing Christian socialist, Waldo Williams. As a deeply humane and compassionate nationalist, he produced some remarkable insights and a sense of universal mystery in his poetic output. By the end of the 1940s a different note was struck by two new voices on the scene. Euros Bowen, an Anglican clergyman, who began publishing poetry in 1947 when he was in his forties, was a literary craftsman who celebrated those visible elements which had the power to symbolize an invisible world. Bobi Jones, the other controversial poet to emerge at this time, was born in an English-speaking home in Cardiff, and later converted to Christianity in the 1950s. His poetry reflected an Evangelical and fundamentalist approach of rare intensity. Certainly, the achievements of Bobi Jones, Euros Bowen and Waldo Williams augured well for the new springs of verse that were to emerge from the 1960s onwards.

Since 1969, Welsh-language poetry has largely concerned itself with sociopolitical themes, such as the politics of Welsh nationalism, gender politics, the preservation of Welsh culture, and international issues. Several factors have accounted for the upsurge of these concerns: Saunders Lewis's celebrated radio broadcast and the founding of the Welsh Language Society in 1962; the investiture of the Prince of Wales in 1969; and the depressing failure of the Welsh devolution referendum in 1979. The investiture produced a poetry of protest in the ensuing years. Gerallt Lloyd Owen's *Cerddi'r Cywilydd* (Poems of the Shame) epitomized the pervading sense of shame that sprang from the feeling that Wales had yet again rendered herself subservient to an English prince. Following the debacle of the 1979 referendum results, powerful and sensitive verse emerged from the pen of T. James Jones and others who bemoaned the lost opportunity of political liberation.

The 1950s marked a watershed in the history of Welsh-language literature. After the foundation of Yr Academi Gymreig in 1959, the Welsh Books Council in 1961 and the Welsh Arts Council in 1967, Welsh novels and children's books proliferated. Islwyn Ffowc Elis's *Cysgod y Cryman*, published in 1953, was the harbinger of a new direction in the writing of novels and paved the way for an exciting period of experimentation. Rhydwen Williams's trilogy on the Rhondda, *Cwm Hiraeth*, appeared from 1969 to 1973, Marion Eames produced a series of polished historical novels, and Aled Islwyn published seven novels between 1977 and 1994, some of which explored the anguished relationship between a female and a male student. In more recent times, Angharad Tomos and Robin Llywelyn have extended the horizons of literature even further and abandoned the old parochialism. Robat Gruffydd has explored the shadowy side of public life with his novels, *Y Llosgi* in 1986 and *Crac Cymraeg* in 1997. Throughout the 1980s, the Welsh Books Council has administered a grant of about £400,000 per annum from the Welsh Office and £180,000 from the Welsh Arts Council, which has provided support for the publication of books and periodicals, for editing and processing manuscripts. During 1988–9, 488 titles were published in the Welsh language and 200 children's books. The Arts Council tended to support periodicals such as Yr Academi Gymreig's Welsh-language quarterly, *Taliesin*, and the long-standing philosophical and critical publication, *Y Traethodydd*.

From the early 1950s, Welsh drama began to emerge from its realistic mode with the rise of the verse-drama movement. Saunders Lewis turned to verse drama in the late 1940s and

1950s, with *Blodeuwedd* in 1948 and *Siwan* in 1956. Like T. S. Eliot in the English theatre, he deployed myth and history as the foundation of his plays. *Blodeuwedd* heralded a search for a symbolic discourse which would expand the range of theatre language. The period between 1950 and 1975, with Saunders Lewis, John Gwilym Jones and W. S. Jones in the vanguard, experienced a renaissance in Welsh-language drama. In 1966, Gwenlyn Parry's play *Saer Doliau*, which was produced at the Aberafon Eisteddfod, seemed to represent a new theatre language. The mood of the 1960s was generally expansionist as university colleges established theatres: Theatr y Werin at Aberystwyth in 1972; the Sherman Theatre at Cardiff in 1971; and Theatr Gwynedd at Bangor in 1974. In 1965, Cwmni Theatr Cymru, under its director, Wilbert Lloyd Roberts, began to employ professional actors. The first Welsh-medium Theatre in Education company was formed at Aberystwyth in 1979. After 1981, Theatr Crwban provided Welsh-language theatre in Dyfed schools for children of all ages.

As Welsh theatre expanded and grew more professional, two developments challenged its *raison d'être*. First, the growth of Welsh-language television, with BBC Wales in the 1970s and S4C from November 1982, presented a serious threat to traditional stage productions. Many talented writers and actors were recruited for the expanding BBC drama department and for the Welsh-language programmes of S4C. Secondly, the theatre cooperative emerged with a legion of younger actors who believed that the élitist university campuses only provided for the tastes of educated middle-class minorities. Theatr Bara Caws challenged the alleged bastions of privilege and introduced drama directly into the small villages of the Principality. Theatr Gorllewin Morgannwg, Arad Goch and Brith Gof soon followed in the footsteps of Bara Caws. Nowadays, there appear to be few drama writers who have produced more than a handful of plays. Gareth Miles, possibly the most prolific dramatist, with seven full-length plays and six adaptations, is a political writer who often assailed Thatcherism as a vacuous and conflicting creed. Siôn Eirian's work is largely concerned with society, while Gareth Ioan's *Tŷ Ni* concentrates on English immigration into rural Wales.

At a slightly different literary level, it is important to recognize the contributions of academic works which have sought to explore Welsh traditions and to preserve different aspects of our cultural heritage. The renaissance in Welsh history since the early 1950s can be attributed to the work of such eminent pioneers as Professor David Williams, professor of Welsh history at Aberystwyth from 1945 to 1967, and to the doyen of Welsh historians, Professor Glanmor Williams, professor of history at Swansea from 1957 to 1982. In 1960, Professor Glanmor Williams founded and edited a new academic journal, *Welsh History Review*, which continues to flourish in the university. He established a centre of excellence for research into Welsh history and launched several prestigious projects, including the south Wales coalfield history survey. Meanwhile, at Aberystwyth, a Centre for Advanced Welsh and Celtic Studies has been established to explore the history of the language and literature and other aspects of the nation's heritage. A journal such as *Cof Cenedl* has provided an opportunity for the study of history through the medium of Welsh. The publication of various county histories, such as the Glamorgan, Pembroke and Cardigan series, has enriched the study of Welsh history, enhanced the nation's understanding of its past, and provided the academic fraternity and laity alike with glittering repositories of historical knowledge.

Welsh Literature and Drama in English

For a few years after 1945, the English-language poetic forms of the 1930s and 1940s were still buoyant. Dylan Thomas, Glyn Jones, Vernon Watkins and Idris Davies were still active and publishing important work. Idris Davies's *Tonypandy* in 1945, and Dylan Thomas's *Deaths and Entrances* in 1946, were lively examples of this Anglo-Welsh tradition. By 1955–6, the scene had changed and many of the actors had stepped quietly off the stage. Idris Davies died in Rhymney in 1953, and Dylan Thomas collapsed in New York in the same year. Davies Aberpennar changed to Welsh-medium writing and became known as a major poet, Pennar Davies. After the Second World War there occurred a general slump in the writing of English-language poetry. Even the literary magazines collapsed, with the *Welsh Review* disappearing in 1948, and *Wales* in 1949. A number of factors probably contributed to this air of despondency: the demise of Dylan Thomas left a huge vacuum in the movement; depression, poverty and the exhausting effects of war had made an indelible impact; the collapse of chapel culture was a contributory factor; and the gradual disappearance of the familiar industrial landscape undermined the confidence of some writers.

The generation of writers which came to inspire the 1950s and 1960s was less popular, more scholarly, and aware of the exploitation that English-speaking Wales had suffered at the hands of some of its predecessors. They were determined to engage with the history of Wales, its language and culture, with some embracing a nationalist fervour that bordered on the political. One of these writers was R. S. Thomas, whose *The Stones of the Field* (1946) was one of the very few volumes in English to be published in Wales in the fifty years before 1968. In 1946, Emyr Humphreys published his first novel, *The Little Kingdom*, which tended to reflect the author's personal stance as a nationalist. In 1949, a new literary quarterly appeared, *Dock Leaves*, published at Pembroke Dock and edited by Raymond Garlick. It provided an outlet for authors who chose to write in English, and existed for several years before transforming itself into the *Anglo-Welsh Review* in 1958. Garlick, though an Englishman, was deeply committed to the cause of Wales and set about reversing the attitudes of Dylan Thomas's generation. He sought to heal the breach between Welsh and Anglo-Welsh writers which had clouded the Anglo-Welsh tradition since Caradoc Evans's early 'treacheries'. Early contributors to *Dock Leaves* included such promising Welsh-language poets as Waldo Williams and Pennar Davies.

In the early sixties the publication pattern remained largely unchanged. The writers who were known in the metropolitan world continued to publish books like Dannie Abse's *Selected Poems* (1963) or Vernon Watkins's *Affinities* (1962), and the rising star, R. S. Thomas's *The Bread of Truth* (1963). But the tide of Dylanism was ebbing quickly and, with the death of Vernon Watkins in Seattle in 1967, the last of Dylan Thomas's peers had passed from the scene. A new source of energy emanated from a younger generation of writers. In 1965, the first issue of *Poetry Wales*, edited by Meic Stephens, appeared in Merthyr Tydfil, with poems contributed by Roland Mathias, John Ormond and John Tripp. *Anglo-Welsh Review* was also revived in the 1960s and edited by Roland Mathias. The emergence of the Welsh Arts Council in the sixties, with financial support for writers, was a crucial step in the development of Welsh literature in English. When Meic Stephens was appointed assistant director in 1968 he had £18,000 at his disposal for sponsoring literature. In August 1970, the Welsh Arts Council supported the publication of the bi-monthly magazine *Planet*, edited by Ned Thomas. This provided another critical forum for Anglo-Welsh authors and for the discussions of cultural, political and social issues relating to contemporary Wales.

After 1967, the English-language poet of outstanding quality was R. S. Thomas, an Anglican priest devoted to the countryside and to the defence of the language and culture of Wales. In the seventies and eighties he continued with *H'm* (1972), *Frequencies* (1978), *Between Here and Now* (1981) and *Later Poems* (1983). The emphasis of his poetry has ranged across such themes as the depopulated countryside, the mechanization of farming, the break-up of rural communities, a despairing nationalism, and the quest for the absent God. Raymond Garlick, who returned to the poetic scene after a sojourn teaching in the Netherlands, produced *A Sense of Europe* in 1968 and *A Sense of Time* in 1972, the latter concerned with the trials of young nationalists. His colleague Jon Dressel, an American who hailed from Missouri, engaged with the issue of devolution, which he believed to be the cardinal Anglo-Welsh question of the post-war period. Other productive poets of the 1970s and 1980s, such as Gillian Clarke, have struck a distinctly feminist note and evoked the spirit of the Welsh countryside.

While poetry thrived in this period, fiction held its own. There were individual novels of quality like *Border Country* and *The Fight for Manod* by Raymond Williams, and Emyr Humphreys continued to extend the range of his works. Drama was withering, apart from the creative efforts of Gwyn Thomas and Dannie Abse on stage, and the contributions of Alun Richards, Ewart Alexander and Elaine Morgan to the modern screen. Gwyn Thomas wrote a series of Valleys plays rooted firmly in the British socialist drama of the period, six of which were performed between 1960 and 1979. Perhaps only Alun Richards and Ewart Alexander achieved any real success on the stage, as dramatists turned increasingly to the media for financial security.

The sixties also saw the establishment of the Welsh Theatre Company, which was supported by Clifford Evans, Emyr

Humphreys and Richard Burton. Throughout the seventies there
were moves to establish smaller, specialist companies with strong
communal links. The Cardiff Open Air Theatre began in 1970,
and the Open Cast Theatre followed in Swansea. There was also
the Welsh National Youth Theatre and Theatre in Education.
Flint Theatre in Education was formed in the early seventies, and
similar groups were established to serve South Glamorgan in
1976 and Gwent in 1977. By 1988, there were eight companies
in existence, funded by a combination of LEAs, the Welsh Office,
the Welsh Arts Council and regional grants. Welsh investment in
theatres has continued largely unabated since the 1970s: the
large-scale complex of Theatr Clwyd opened in Mold in 1976;
Milford Haven gained the Torch Theatre in 1977; Swansea's
Grand Theatre was beautifully refurbished in 1990; and Theatr
Brycheiniog opened in 1997.

In Wales, the issue of identity has been inseparable from that
of language. Those who see Welsh literature in English as distinct
from English literature usually argue that its writers have been
shaped by Welsh culture, history, landscape and language. A few
Welsh writers in English have Welsh as their mother tongue,
while others have made valiant efforts to learn the language.
Contemporary writers and critics often reject the term 'Anglo-
Welsh' because of its implications of a divided national allegiance
and an acceptance of colonial linkage to England. These contemporary exponents of the genre prefer the nomenclature
'Welsh writer in English' to 'Anglo-Welsh writer'. Modern Welsh
literature in English sprang out of a distinct politico-social
environment of the 1920s and 1930s, when the coal-producing
Valleys of south Wales were crucified by depression, poverty and
unemployment, out of which the first coterie of English-language
writers like Idris Davies, Glyn Jones, Lewis Jones, Jack Jones and
Gwyn Thomas emerged. The second generation, which sprang
up in the 1960s, was led by a group of committed nationalists,
including Meic Stephens and Harri Webb. More recent writers
such as Gillian Clarke or Tony Conran have integrated elements
of Welsh culture, mythology and literary tradition into their
works. John Davies, a non-Welsh-speaker, engages with identity
in his poems, while Tony Curtis studiously avoids such issues.
R. S. Thomas, an outspoken nationalist who has learned Welsh,
feels unable to write poetry in any language but his first, English.

His life and work embody the politically charged issues of cultural and linguistic identity in Wales. Since 1946 this gifted craftsman has published twenty-four volumes of poetry on Welsh political and cultural themes and on wide-ranging contemporary matters.

The Visual Arts in Wales

In the immediate post-war years, the quality of art in Wales was unremarkable, and the indigenous artists neither formed a school nor made any lasting contributions to contemporary European art. The one artist who commanded international attention, Ceri Richards, had returned to the London scene. Graham Sutherland never lost his fascination with Pembrokeshire and established a gallery at Picton Castle in 1976. The most prominent Welsh artists of the period were Kyffin Williams, Alfred Janes and Brenda Chamberlain, who preferred to isolate themselves from current international ideas, choosing more detached and individualist styles of presentation. Deliberately ignoring modern theories of art, Kyffin Williams's paintings suggest a sense of retreat and escape. The Welsh landscape has attracted other distinguished painters apart from Kyffin Williams. Josef Herman fled from Poland and eventually settled in the mining village of Ystradgynlais, at the head of the Swansea valley, from 1943 onwards. For Herman the industrial landscape symbolized the dignity of labour and man's struggle for survival. While Herman and the Expressionist painters were absorbed by the working people and their relationship to their environment, the '56 Group' appeared in 1956 in protest against what they characterized as the official, sentimentalized painting of the period. Later renamed '56 Group Wales', the twenty members, including Arthur Giardelli, Robert Hunter and Heinz Koppel, espoused no collective ideas or common aesthetic doctrines. These artists had no pretensions to be seen as a movement or as a school of art; but they were among the first to give expression to the new ideas that were circulating through the galleries and workshops of Europe.

From the mid-1960s several factors coalesced to stimulate the development of visual arts in Wales: the Welsh Arts Council became increasingly autonomous; commercial art galleries sprang up in many places, with the Howard Roberts Gallery in Cardiff and the Dillwyn Gallery in Swansea promoting the most original contemporary work; and there was the reorganization of art schools following the publication in 1960 of the Coldstream Report. Thereafter, arts schools at Newport and Cardiff emerged as centres of excellence and practised a variety of styles, regularly inviting established artists such as David Hockney as teaching fellows. The National Museum of Wales has become the most important gallery in Wales, and the National Library has also amassed significant collections. Finally, the University of Wales became more involved in promoting art and encouraging regular exhibitions in its own newly established galleries. The University College at Bangor founded its own gallery, Oriel Bangor, in 1963. University College, Cardiff, converted the central hall of its main college building into an exhibition area, and in 1973 the Sherman Gallery was opened. At Swansea, the Taliesin Art complex was constructed on the main campus, with a gallery, theatre and college bookshop. Public patronage in the seventies and early eighties supported a number of galleries. At Cardiff, six galleries assumed the role of presenting contemporary art, and all are public galleries. Cardiff Council's own gallery, Oriel, was opened in 1974. The Photographic Gallery was sponsored by the Welsh Arts Council, and the Chapter Arts Centre by the local authorities and the Arts Council.

Some of the significant post-war developments in architectural designs graced the new towns. Cwmbran, begun in the 1950s, and Newtown, Montgomeryshire, launched in the 1960s, display work of a high environmental quality. Cwmbran incorporated old industrial villages and a series of newly built residential neighbourhoods with shopping and social facilities. Several award-winning housing projects, such as the Albert Edward Prince of Wales Home at Porthcawl, or the Trinity Court housing at Rhyl, have attracted favourable comments from reputable critics. The university colleges commissioned development plans and adopted suitable projects for their expanding campuses in the sixties and seventies. In later years, the conservation movement attracted widespread support as older and vernacular buildings became the focus of architectural attention. Many redundant buildings were skilfully transformed, as churches became offices, farm buildings transmogrified into museums, or warehouses converted into hotels. The process of urban growth has often been quite spectacular. The Lower Swansea Valley

Project and the redevelopment of the South Dock into Swansea Maritime Village are two of the most successful ventures of urban renewal in Europe. Waterside development along the coastline of Wales has produced many attractive marina sites. Other schemes like the Rhondda Heritage Park and the Ebbw Vale Garden festival represent challenging new opportunities for the future.

Music
The organization of the Youth Orchestra of Wales in 1945, the establishment of the Welsh National Opera Company in 1946, the foundation of the Llangollen International Musical Eisteddfod and the BBC Welsh Orchestra in 1947 represented exciting new developments in Welsh musical life in the immediate post-war years. The Guild for the Promotion of Welsh Music was founded in 1954, and the BBC in Wales sponsored compositions and commissioned new works. Meanwhile, the Welsh Arts Council took an active role in supporting all kinds of musical performances. By 1968–9 the Welsh National Opera made its first English tour to Birmingham, Liverpool and Stratford. In 1973, the WNO finally became international and performed at the Lausanne festival in Switzerland. In 1979, the giant oil company Amoco signed a lucrative sponsorship deal with the WNO, guaranteeing a minimum of £250,000 to finance its future programme. By the early 1970s, the WNO had its own professional chorus and orchestra with an extensive repertoire, including Mozart, Rossini, Beethoven, Verdi, Wagner and Puccini, as well as Britten's *Billy Budd* and Tippett's *The Midsummer Marriage*, productions of which were widely acclaimed in the mid-1970s, as was its 1980s production of *Falstaff* in Milan and New York. The achievements of the impressive Welsh National Opera are now legendary, despite the fact that Wales still lacks a purpose-built opera house. Ironically, Wales's most accomplished singers, like Gwyneth Jones, Margaret Price, Helen Watts, Anne Evans, Sir Geraint Evans, Stuart Burrows, Bryn Terfel and Gwynne Howell, have been regularly invited to perform on the greatest operatic stages of the world, but cannot do so in an opera house in Wales.

Since the opening of St David's Hall in 1983, the BBC Welsh Symphony Orchestra (renamed BBC National Orchestra of Wales

in the 1990s) has secured an official 'home' in the capital city. With
the additional financial support of S4C, it has come to enjoy a
reputation as the most televised orchestra in Britain. The BBC
National Orchestra of Wales has played to international audiences
in Vienna, Amsterdam, Berlin and Leningrad. The National
Youth Orchestra of Wales has also travelled widely and acted as
an accomplished ambassador for Welsh music. In recent years, it
has been skilfully supported by the National Youth Brass Band and
the National Youth Choir of Wales. In the eighties the Welsh
Chamber Orchestra and Music Theatre Wales were established in
south Wales, and Opera Gogledd Cymru (North Wales Opera)
and the North Wales Philharmonia appeared in the north.

Musical festivals have flourished in all parts of Wales. The
Royal National Eisteddfod, the Llangollen International Eisteddfod and a mosaic of local eisteddfodau have enthusiastically
encouraged the amateur tradition. Professional festivals prospered in Swansea, Llandaff, Cardiff, Fishguard, Aberystwyth, the
Vale of Glamorgan, the Gower, St Asaph, and in Beaumaris
since 1986. There was also the crusading work of the university
music departments at Aberystwyth, Cardiff and Bangor. With
the rationalization of university departments Aberystwyth closed,
less than a century and a quarter after its foundation, while the
departments at Bangor and Cardiff were enlarged and modernized during the 1970s by Professors William Mathias and Alun
Hoddinott.

Of the first generation of twentieth-century Welsh composers,
Grace Williams, Arwel Hughes and David Wynne were all well
established before 1945. Daniel Jones's early reputation was
established in London in the late 1940s and early 1950s. Arwel
Hughes and Mansel Thomas played a pivotal role as musical
administrators in the BBC at a time when they could establish its
orchestra and the foundation of musical patronage. Most of the
Welsh composers born before 1940 were either wholly educated,
or completed their education, outside Wales. The two Welsh
'second-generation' composers, Alun Hoddinott and William
Mathias, whose talents were immediately recognized, have given
Welsh music an international profile. Hoddinott's first five symphonies and Mathias's two were given their initial performances
by prestigious British orchestras. Both composers hailed from
south Wales and, after university education in Wales, they

studied in London before returning to the land of their birth. In 1967, Hoddinott became head of the music department at Cardiff, while Mathias was appointed to the chair at Bangor in 1970. In 1967 and 1972 they founded respectively the Cardiff Festival of Twentieth-Century Music and the North Wales Music Festival, and were acknowledged as the pre-eminent Welsh composers of the period.

The Press and Media

By the 1960s, five major newspaper groups dominated the Welsh press, as the concentration of ownership produced a shift away from the weekly to the daily newspapers. The Thomson papers were in the lead: the *South Wales Echo*, an evening paper, had a circulation of 151,000 in 1961; the *Western Mail*, a morning paper, had sales of 104,198 in the same year. Welsh-language newspapers were not as successful. *Sulyn*, the first Welsh-language Sunday newspaper, was launched on 12 October 1982 and survived for only fourteen issues. The most remarkable development of the 1980s was the growth of monthly and community newspapers, especially the Welsh *papurau bro*. By 1990, there were fifty-three titles with an estimated combined circulation of about 70,000. The diversity of ownership, which was lost in the newspaper press, has been maintained in the magazines and other periodicals, of which there were forty-four separate titles in the Welsh language alone in 1990.

Recent years have seen a dramatic concentration of ownership. In November 1995, the *Western Mail* and *Echo* were taken over by Trinity International, the largest owner of regional newspapers in the UK, which already owned the *Daily Post, Wales on Sunday* and twenty-six other titles in Wales. The history of the press in Wales resembled that of the UK as a whole, with a loss of local ownership, declining circulations and the demise of a radical tradition. In the period 1981–94 circulations of regional morning newspapers fell by around 10 per cent, and of evening provincials by 20 per cent. No Welsh title has much significance compared with the circulation of the London-based newspapers; overall only 13 per cent of newspapers sold in Wales are produced there. The *Sun* has the highest level of household penetration in Wales with 22.5 per cent of the market, while the

Western Mail and *Daily Post* each have 6 per cent. Circulation of the evening titles is largely confined to the urban centres: the Cardiff *South Wales Echo* sells around 80,000 copies; and the Swansea *South Wales Evening Post* about 69,000 copies.

Against a backdrop of severe cuts in public spending, it is hardly surprising that public support for Welsh-language publications has been trimmed. The two main sources of funding are the government's publishing grant scheme of about £600,000 per annum, administered on behalf of the Welsh Office by the Welsh Books Council; and a Welsh Arts Council grant of £300,000 to support literary magazines. Between them, the Books Council and the Arts Council provide grants to support the publication of around 200 Welsh-language books and eighteen Welsh-language magazines every year. The support for Welsh-language publishing appears to have been highly effective. Since the various support schemes were introduced in the fifties and sixties, the number of new Welsh-language books published each year has more than quadrupled from a hundred in 1950 to over 450 by the early 1990s. Similarly, over sixty Welsh-language magazines and newspapers appeared regularly in the mid-1990s.

Since the establishment of a 'regional' radio station in Cardiff in 1923, and of the BBC in Wales in 1924, broadcasting has grown steadily. In the late 1970s the BBC split the Home Service in Wales into two stations, Radio Wales in 1978 and Radio Cymru in 1979. Independent radio stations emerged in the 1970s: Swansea Sound began in 1974, Cardiff Broadcasting Company was established in 1980, Gwent Broadcasting in 1983 and Marcher Sound began its operations from Wrexham in 1983. With the resumption of BBC television in 1946 and its extension to areas outside London and the south-east, a whole new dimension of communications was launched. ITV started in 1955, and the first consortium was established a year later to serve south Wales and West of England. TWW opened in 1958 and broadcast from the Pontcanna Studios in Cardiff. In 1967, it lost its franchise to Harlech Television, which attracted polished and ebullient broadcasters like John Morgan and Wynford Vaughan Thomas.

Until the establishment of BBC Wales in 1964, television output in Wales was largely similar to England's. Since 1964, BBC Wales has grown consistently to become the largest broadcasting organization outside London. In the late 1990s, however, the output of BBC Wales is different from its UK counterpart for only about 10.5 hours a week. The equivalent figure for HTV is eleven hours a week of Welsh regional output. The most significant step forward in Welsh broadcasting was the establishment of Sianel Pedwar Cymru (S4C) in 1982. Both Radio Cymru and S4C have defined Wales as a distinct political constituency, and provide Welsh-speakers with a Welsh perspective on national and international affairs. Overall, Welsh television broadcasts around eighty-eight hours a week of programmes specifically made for Wales, but only 25 per cent of these are in the English language. There are in fact only twenty-four hours of television every week for English-speakers in Wales, who constitute four-fifths of the population. Meanwhile, S4C attracts on average 70,000 Welsh-speakers in the evening, and a total of 82 per cent of Welsh-speakers watch the channel at some point in the week. It received a budget allocation of £63 million in 1995, £17 million worth of programmes from the BBC and ninety-seven hours of free programming from Channel 4, making it one of the most subsidized television channels in the world.

New incursions have appeared in more recent years. Cable and satellite television have spread into Wales since the early nineties. In Wales, satellite ownership was near the UK average of 21 per cent in 1995. The Internet, with its on-line service of news and publishing, has rapidly disseminated through the political, commercial and educational sectors. BBC Wales, HTV and S4C have launched sites, while the Welsh-language publication *Y Cymro* displays most of its journalistic content on Thursdays. New media technology promises to transform the parameters of Welsh broadcasting. The arrival of digital technology in hyperbolic language will help to create a multiple-channel and digitally-driven universe for the new century.

The National Assembly will need to ponder a vast array of issues and to formulate policies as it seeks to grapple with the contemporary media industry: first, the greater diversity of programming available diminishes the capability of national broadcasting organizations, such as the BBC, HTV and S4C, to address the whole nation; the growth of cross-media ownership and the concentration of media control, largely as a result of the deregulation process initiated by the 1996 Broadcasting Act, may result in the appearance of large external media corporations; thirdly, huge questions emanate from the globalizing and homogenizing tendencies of the modern media. National identities, and even a fragile and burgeoning European identity, may well be influenced by unleashed commercial and global forces. In this context, the National Assembly will need well-defined cultural and media policies to bolster public account-ability and to protect the native film and television sectors.

SUGGESTED READING

D. Cole (ed.), *The New Wales* (Cardiff, 1990).

T. Conran, *Frontiers in Anglo-Welsh Poetry* (Cardiff, 1997).

D. Johnston (ed.), *A Guide to Welsh Literature, c. 1900–1996* (Cardiff, 1998).

Gareth Elwyn Jones, *Which Nation's Schools* (Cardiff, 1990).

Gareth Elwyn Jones (ed.), *Education, Culture and Society* (Cardiff, 1991).

Gareth Elwyn Jones, *The Education of a Nation* (Cardiff, 1997).

R. Mathias, *Anglo-Welsh Literature* (Cardiff, 1987).

Kenneth O. Morgan, *Rebirth of a Nation: Wales 1880–1980* (Oxford, 1981).

Prys Morgan, *The University of Wales 1939–1993* (Cardiff, 1997).

E. Rowan, *Art in Wales: An Illustrated History 1850–1980* (Cardiff, 1985).

M. Stephens (ed.), *The Arts in Wales* (Cardiff, 1979).

L. J. Williams, *Digest of Welsh Historical Statistics, 1974–1996* (Cardiff, 1998).

Conclusion

THROUGHOUT this century those powerful forces which initially shaped modern Wales have declined dramatically. Agriculture, the old staple industries, organized religion and the Liberal Party have been undermined and marginalized in the new Wales. At the beginning of this century it seemed as if these forces would have a lasting effect on the fortunes of the new age. Coal mining was thriving, immigrants were pouring into the Rhondda Valleys, and Nonconformity was a dominant influence in the religious and political life of communities.

As we approach the new millennium Welsh agriculture is in a perpetual state of crisis. The numbers employed in farming, the total number of holdings, and farm incomes have fallen steadily since the Second World War, while increasing costs of production have aggravated the position still further. The new Welsh Assembly was established at a critical time for the rural economy, as it faced an immediate economic crisis and a longer-term process of marginalization. Rural areas are affected by a conglomeration of factors which threaten all advanced countries: globalization, increased competition and the restructuring of enterprises present enormous challenges, as does the maintenance of a 'free-market' ideology; the move to internationalize the terms of trade and to remove economic and other protective barriers is a factor of considerable importance; the uneven spread of new technologies; demographic changes, leading to the ageing of the farming community; increasing personal mobility, including commuting, migration and tourism; and a search for new forms of regulation and government, with an emphasis on private and public 'entrepreneurship', are forcing the industry to reconsider its contribution to the Welsh economy.

The collapse or rationalization of the old heavy industries has been one of the central themes of the century. Old King Coal was finally toppled from his throne, and now only two deep mines remain in Wales, employing about 2,000 men in deep and drift mines. In 1971 coal mining and metal manufacture accounted for 14 per cent of the workforce, whereas by 1997 these two industries barely accounted for 2.7 per cent of all employees. The dominant interpretation of Welsh economic life in recent years has portrayed a radical transformation from a dependence on a declining, Victorian industrial base into a vibrant, technological enterprise economy. A recent report from the Institute of Welsh Affairs, *Wales 2010* (IWA, 1996) extolled the virtues of the manufacturing sector in an ebullient fashion: 'Praise the Lord we are a manufacturing nation.'

While it cannot be denied that the restructuring of the economy has resulted in significant improvements and changed the face of industrial Wales in many important ways, this trans-formation has been unspectacular and not as promising as the prevailing and propagandist interpretation suggests. Manu-facturing makes a higher contribution to regional GDP in the north of England, the West Midlands, the East Midlands and the North West than it does in Wales. Internationalization has not increased the share of British and European economic activity taking place in Wales; and there are serious questions concerning employment and joblessness, especially in the old industrial Valleys and in south-west Wales. The SME (Small and Medium Enterprises) sector is championed by political and industrial figures as the key source of future employment in Wales; yet, as recent experience has shown, this can be a particularly volatile and unpredictable sector. Between 1991 and 1995 more than 5,000 very small businesses were founded, but a far larger number disappeared. In the period 1979–92 the increase in employment in small manufacturing businesses (those employing under a hundred) was only about one-fifth of the increase in the preceding thirteen-year period, and half the jobs created in the 1980s disappeared during the recession of the 1990s. The emphasis on inward foreign investment can also be misleading for, although Wales has performed well in attracting investment from abroad, the foreign sector accounts for less than 8 per cent of total employment in Wales, and much of this is heavily concentrated in the south-east and north-east corridors. There is a growing body of evidence to show that, within mainland

Britain, Wales is now the least successful of all regions: Wales has the unenviable distinction of containing three out of the six districts with the worst unemployment figures in Britain, with Merthyr Tydfil registering a record level of 33.4 per cent; it is also the region most dependent on social security benefits, which account for 20 per cent of personal incomes, a figure almost double the proportion of south-east England.

On the threshold of the new millennium, it seems as if the end of the distinctively Welsh expressions of Christianity may be looming on the horizon. There is no Evan Roberts in sight to rekindle the flame of religious enthusiasm, and no charismatic or prophetic leader to inspire the land of William Morgan and William Williams, Pantycelyn, or to reawaken the Welsh from their spiritual slumbers. Indeed, academic theologians seriously question the hypothesis that Wales is still a Christian country, when all the evidence suggests that Welsh society has entered a post-Christian phase. At Christmas 1994, for example, the combined total attendance in the Church in Wales and the Roman Catholic Church, numerically the leading churches in Wales, was no more than 200,000, a figure well short of 10 per cent of the total population of Wales. It would seem as if the Christmas message has become a matter of indifference to the vast majority of the Welsh population. The chronicle of religion, certainly in the post-war period, has been one of unremitting decline: total membership figures have continued to fall; church buildings have closed or fallen into a state of disrepair; financial resources have dwindled; ordination figures have plummeted; and the churches seem bewildered and confused in the secular and pluralist society. The picture, however, is not entirely bleak and there are some signs of hope that a Christian witness will survive, or even revive, in Wales. Three religious traditions, the Church in Wales, the Roman Catholic Church and the new churches of the conservative Evangelical movement, seem to grow stronger. Even as institutional churches decline in popularity, there are other arenas of growth: there is a widespread awareness of the 'spiritual' dimension of human experience and a significant expansion of a network of small groups of Christians; the number of students pursuing courses in religious studies has expanded considerably over the last few decades; departments of theology and religious studies at colleges and universities have flourished, with a range of new and challenging courses; there seems to be a greater commitment on the part of church members to explore new forms of worship and to participate in interfaith discussions – Cytûn is a particularly good example of an all-Wales forum for the discussion of inter-church matters; and ecological concerns and the struggle for social justice have risen to prominence in church discussions. The churches may be marginalized, but this may also be a crucial factor in their re-formation and reorientation.

As the chapels declined and the influence of Nonconformist Christianity collapsed, so the language of Wales was weakened. The two domains in which Welsh had remained secure during the nineteenth and the early decades of the twentieth century were the chapel and the home (*y capel a'r aelwyd*). The Sunday School and the use of the Welsh Bible were critical factors in the preservation of the language during the nineteenth century. Social changes, such as the instability of marriage, the frequency of 'mixed marriages', enhanced mobility, and the impact of telecommunications and the mass media, have combined to undermine the effectiveness of the home as a custodian of the language. As the chapels, Sunday Schools and the family have declined in importance as progenitors of the language, other sources have appeared to promote a Welsh-language renaissance. Aitchison and Carter have drawn our attention to an 'impressive and extensive infrastructure' which is now in position, based on developments in education, a formal Welsh Language Act, and the strength of the language in publishing and the media, which should ensure the regeneration of the language. Welsh-medium education, Welsh-medium nursery schools and the sheer determination of parents have been factors of special importance in the campaign to preserve the language and culture of Wales.

During the 1990s the percentage of the total population speaking Welsh fell by only 0.4 percentage points, and the actual number of Welsh-speakers by only 1.4 per cent, as compared with the decade 1961–71, when the percentage of the total population speaking Welsh fell by 5.2 percentage points and the decrease in the actual number of Welsh-speakers was 17.3 per cent. It does seem as if it is now possible to predict a real increase in the numbers of speakers in the last decade of the twentieth century.

Also, during the last years of the final decade of the century, the Welsh have witnessed a form of devolution of power from Westminster to a new National Assembly in Cardiff. Although the vote in favour of an elected assembly was narrow, and its powers are very limited, it would be inappropriate to take a negative view of devolution in Wales. For the first time in their history, the Welsh have voted for devolution of power, and there is an elected assembly established in the capital city.

Devolution in Wales is an important part of a new concept of politics, and it presents a challenging prospect for the future. The reform of government will enable an all-Wales viewpoint to be taken at the point of decision-making for the first time in modern history. Secondly, the Assembly, with a range of talented and vigorous politicians, will undoubtedly relish the prospect of responsibility. Rhodri Morgan, Dafydd Wigley and other enthusiastic members of the Assembly will want to challenge and question primary legislation and, above all, to act forcefully in support of Wales. Thirdly, the National Assembly will inevitably seek to forge a new and dynamic relationship with the European Union. A Europeanized devolved Wales, with a more flexible and contemporary range of relationships between national, regional and local communities, is an enticing prospect for the future.

Select Bibliography

1. GENERAL WORKS

David Cole (ed.), *The New Wales* (Cardiff, 1990).

John Davies, *A History of Wales* (London, 1993).

Trevor Herbert and Gareth Elwyn Jones (eds.), *Wales 1880–1914* (Cardiff, 1988).

Trevor Herbert and Gareth Elwyn Jones (eds.), *Wales Between the Wars* (Cardiff, 1988).

Trevor Herbert and Gareth Elwyn Jones (eds.), *Post-War Wales* (Cardiff, 1995).

David W. Howell (ed.), *Pembrokeshire County History*, vol.IV (Haverfordwest, 1993).

Geraint H. Jenkins and Ieuan Gwynedd Jones, *Cardiganshire County History*, vol.III (Cardiff, 1998).

Philip Jenkins, *A History of Modern Wales 1536–1990* (London, 1992).

Richard Jenkins and Arwel Edwards (eds.), *One Step Forward* (Llandysul, 1990).

Arthur H. John and Glanmor Williams (eds.), *Glamorgan County History*, vol.V (Cardiff, 1980).

R. Brinley Jones, *Anatomy of Wales* (Cardiff, 1972).

Gareth Elwyn Jones, *Modern Wales: A Concise History* (Cambridge, 1994).

Kenneth O. Morgan, *Rebirth of a Nation: Wales 1880–1980* (Oxford, 1981).

Kenneth O. Morgan, *Modern Wales: Politics, Places and People* (Cardiff, 1995).

Prys Morgan (ed.), *Glamorgan County History*, vol.VI (Cardiff, 1988).

David Williams and Ieuan Gwynedd Jones, *A History of Modern Wales* (London, 1977).

Gwyn A. Williams, *When Was Wales?* (London, 1985).

John Williams, *Digest of Welsh Historical Statistics*, vols.I and II (to 1974) (Cardiff, 1985).

John Williams, *Digest of Welsh Historical Statistics 1974–1996* (Cardiff, 1998).

2. THE ECONOMY

Colin Baber and L. J. Williams (eds.), *Modern South Wales: Essays in Economic History* (Cardiff, 1986).

W. G. V. Balchin (ed.), *Swansea and its Region* (Swansea, 1971).

K. D. George and Lynn Mainwaring (eds.), *The Welsh Economy* (Cardiff, 1988).

Graham Humphreys, *Industrial Britain: South Wales* (Newton Abbot, 1972).

Jean Lindsay, *A History of the North Wales Slate Industry* (London, 1974).

E. Nevin et al., *Structure of the Welsh Economy* (Cardiff, 1966).

Graham L. Rees, *Survey of the Welsh Economy* (London, 1973).

Brinley Thomas (ed.), *The Welsh Economy* (Cardiff, 1962).

Dennis Thomas and Dot Jones, *Welsh Economy and Society post-1945: A Database of Statistical and Documentary Material* (Cardiff, 1996).

Readers should also consult, *Contemporary Wales: An Annual Review of Economic and Social Research*, vols. I (1987)–XI (1998).

3. ORGANIZED RELIGION AND SOCIAL HISTORY

John Aitchison and Harold Carter, *A Geography of the Welsh Language 1961–1991* (Cardiff, 1994).

Paul Badham (ed.), *Religion, State and Society in Modern Britain* (Lampeter, 1989).

P. H. Ballard and D. Huw Jones (eds.), *The Land and People* (Cardiff, 1979).

D. Beddoe, *Back to Home and Duty: Women between the Wars 1918–1939* (London, 1989).

T. Brennan et al. (eds.), *Social Change in South-West Wales* (London, 1954).

D. P. Davies, *Against the Tide: Christianity in Wales on the Threshold of the New Millennium* (Llandysul, 1995).

Russell Davies, *Secret Sins* (Cardiff, 1996).

Ian Hume and W. T. R. Pryce (eds.), *The Welsh and their Country* (Llandysul, 1986).

Angela V. John (ed.), *Our Mothers' Land: Chapters in Welsh Women's History 1830–1939* (Cardiff, 1991).

Bob Morris Jones and Paul Singh Ghuman (eds.), *Bilingualism, Education and Identity* (Cardiff, 1995).

David J. V. Jones, *Crime and Policing in the Twentieth Century* (Cardiff, 1996).

R. Pope, *Building Jerusalem* (Cardiff, 1998).

D. T. W. Price, *History of the Church in Wales in the Twentieth Century* (Penarth, 1990).

Gareth Rees and Teresa Rees (eds.), *Poverty and Social Inequality in Wales* (London, 1980).
David Smith and Gareth Williams, *Fields of Praise* (Cardiff, 1980).
Carol White and Sian Rhiannon Williams (eds.), *Struggle or Starve: Women's Lives in the South Wales Valleys between the Two World Wars* (Cardiff, 1998).
Gareth Williams, *1905 and All That* (Llandysul, 1991).
Glanmor Williams, *The Welsh and their Religion* (Cardiff, 1991).
Glyn Williams (ed.), *Social and Cultural Change in Contemporary Wales* (London, 1978).
Glyn Williams (ed.), *Crisis of Economy and Ideology: Essays on Welsh Society (1840–1980)* (Bangor, 1983).

4. POLITICS

K. D. Brown (ed.), *The First Labour Party 1906–1914* (London, 1985).
Charlotte A. Davies, *Welsh Nationalism in the Twentieth Century* (New York, 1989).
D. Hywel Davies, *The Welsh Nationalist Party 1925–1945* (Cardiff, 1983).
David Foulkes et al. (eds.), *The Welsh Veto* (Cardiff, 1983).
Hywel Francis and David Smith, *The Fed: A History of the South Wales Miners in the Twentieth Century* (London, 1980).
M. Francis (ed.), *The Conservatives and British Society, 1880–1990* (Cardiff, 1996).
D. Griffiths, *Thatcherism and Territorial Politics: A Welsh Case Study* (Aldershot, 1996).
Deian R. Hopkin (ed.), *Class, Community and the Labour Movement: Wales and Canada, 1850–1930* (Llafur/CCHL, 1989).
R. Merfyn Jones, *The North Wales Quarrymen, 1874–1922* (Cardiff, 1981).
Peter Lynch, *Minority Nationalism and European Integration* (Cardiff, 1996).
Kenneth O. Morgan, *Wales in British Politics 1868–1922* (Cardiff, 1991).
John Osmond (ed.), *The National Question Again* (Llandysul, 1985).
John Osmond, *The National Assembly Agenda* (Cardiff, 1998).
A. Butt Philip, *The Welsh Question: Nationalism in Welsh Politics 1945–70* (Cardiff, 1975).
David A. Pretty, *The Rural Revolt that Failed: Farm Workers' Trade Unions in Wales 1889–1950* (Cardiff, 1989).
David Smith (ed.), *A People and a Proletariat: Wales 1780–1980* (London, 1980).
Bridget Taylor and Katarina Thomson (eds.), *Scotland and Wales: Nations Again?* (Cardiff, 1999).
Chris Williams, *Democratic Rhondda 1885–1951* (Cardiff, 1996).
Chris Williams, *Capitalism, Community and Conflict: The South Wales Coalfield, 1898–1947* (Cardiff, 1998).

5. EDUCATION

W. Gareth Evans (ed.), *Perspectives on a Century of Secondary Education in Wales, 1889–1989* (Aberystwyth, 1990).

Geraint H. Jenkins, *University of Wales: An Illustrated History – 1893–1993* (Cardiff, 1993).

Gareth Elwyn Jones, *Controls and Conflicts in Welsh Secondary Education 1889–1944* (Cardiff, 1982).

Gareth Elwyn Jones, *Which Nation's Schools* (Cardiff, 1990).

Gareth Elwyn Jones (ed.), *Education, Culture and Society* (Cardiff, 1991).

Gareth Elwyn Jones, *The Education of a Nation* (Cardiff, 1997).

D. Gerwyn Lewis, *The University and the Colleges of Education in Wales, 1925–1978* (Cardiff, 1980).

Richard Lewis, *Leaders and Teachers: Adult Education and the Challenge of Labour in South Wales, 1906–1940* (Cardiff, 1993).

Prys Morgan, *The University of Wales, 1939–1993* (Cardiff, 1997).

Catrin Stevens, *Meithrin: Hanes Mudiad Ysgolion Meithrin, 1971–1996* (Llandysul, 1996).

J. Gwynn Williams, *The University of Wales, 1893–1939* (Cardiff, 1997).

6. CULTURAL ACTIVITIES

David Ian Allsobrook, *Music for Wales: Walford Davies and the National Council of Music, 1918–41* (Cardiff, 1992).

David Berry, *Wales and Cinema: The First Hundred Years* (Cardiff, 1994).

Tony Conran, *Frontiers in Anglo-Welsh Poetry* (Cardiff, 1997).

T. Curtis (ed.), *Wales: The Imagined Nation* (Bridgend, 1986).

John Davies, *Broadcasting and the BBC in Wales* (Cardiff, 1994).

R. Fawkes, *Welsh National Opera* (London, 1986).

Dafydd Johnston (ed.), *A Guide to Welsh Literature c. 1900–1996* (Cardiff, 1998).

Aled Jones, *Press, Politics and Society* (Cardiff, 1993).

R. Gerallt Jones (ed.), *Poetry of Wales 1930–1970* (Llandysul, 1974).

R. Mathias, *Anglo-Welsh Literature* (Bridgend, 1987).

Thomas Parry, *A History of Welsh Literature* (translated 1955) (Oxford, 1955).

E. Rowan, *Art in Wales 1850–1980* (Cardiff, 1985).

Meic Stephens (ed.), *The Arts in Wales 1950–1975* (Cardiff, 1979).

Meic Stephens (ed.), *The New Companion to the Literature of Wales* (Cardiff, 1998).

Anna-Marie Taylor (ed.), *Staging Theatre: Welsh Theatre 1979–1997* (Cardiff, 1997).

M. Wynn Thomas, *Internal Difference: Twentieth-Century Writing in Wales* (Cardiff, 1992).

7. JOURNALS, PERIODICALS AND ANNUAL REVIEWS

1. County Publications and Transactions

Anglesey Antiquarian Society.
Brycheiniog.
Caernarvonshire Historical Society.
The Carmarthenshire Antiquary.
Ceredigion.
Denbighshire Historical Society.
Flintshire Historical Society.
Merioneth Historical and Record Society.
Merthyr Historian.
Monmouthshire Antiquary.
Montgomeryshire Collections.
Morgannwg (Journal Glamorgan History).
Radnorshire Society.

2. Historical Journals, Annual Reviews and Literary Publications

Contemporary Wales: An Annual Review of Economic and Social Research (1987–).
Cof Cenedl (Welsh-medium) (1986–).
Historical Society of the Church in Wales.
Llafur (Journal of the Welsh Labour History (1972–).
National Library of Wales Journal.
Planet: The Welsh Internationalist.
Transactions of the Honourable Society of Cymmrodorion.
The Wales Year Book (1993–) HTV Publication.
Welsh History Review (1960–).*

*The *Welsh History Review* contains useful references to articles published on Welsh history, and guides to unpublished theses.

Index